THE BIBLE AND LITERATURE

THEOLOGY IN DIALOGUE SERIES

Russell A. Butkus, Anne Clifford, Carol J. Dempsey, Series Editors

The Theology in Dialogue Series expresses a vision for the possibilities of theology in conversation with other academic disciplines. The series stems from two primary sources. The first is historical. To some degree Christian theology has always been in dialogue with the major elements of its social context, drawing on insights and methods from diverse knowledge traditions in order to address pressing and timely issues. The second source is the contemporary world. Given the complexity of contemporary life, its questions and struggles, books in the Theology in Dialogue Series reflect the perspective that creative dialogue and strategic collaboration between theology and other disciplines are necessary in seeking effective solutions to contemporary problems.

Yes, resolving problems is important, but our hope is that creative dialogue will result in more than problem solving, that it will make the positive contributions needed in an increasingly complex world. The overarching aim of the series is to demonstrate the creativity of theology in dialogue with various academic disciplines and, in doing so, to broaden the appeal of theology while enriching the pursuit of intellectual inquiry.

Previously published in the series

Reading the Bible, Transforming Conflict
Carol J. Dempsey and Elayne J. Shapiro

Environmental Science and Theology in Dialogue
Russell A. Butkus and Steven A. Kolmes

THE BIBLE AND LITERATURE

ELIZABETH MICHAEL BOYLE
AND CAROL J. DEMPSEY

Maryknoll, New York 10545

Founded in 1970, Orbis Books endeavors to publish works that enlighten the mind, nourish the spirit, and challenge the conscience. The publishing arm of the Maryknoll Fathers and Brothers, Orbis seeks to explore the global dimensions of the Christian faith and mission, to invite dialogue with diverse cultures and religious traditions, and to serve the cause of reconciliation and peace. The books published reflect the views of their authors and do not represent the official position of the Maryknoll Society. To learn more about Maryknoll and Orbis Books, please visit our website at www.maryknollsociety.org.

Published by Orbis Books, Maryknoll, New York 10545–0302.
Manufactured in the United States of America.

Library of Congress Cataloging-in-Publication Data
Boyle, Elizabeth Michael, 1927-
The Bible and literature / Elizabeth Michael Boyle and Carol J. Dempsey.
pages cm. — (Theology in dialogue ; #3)
Includes bibliographical references and index.
ISBN 978-1-62698-127-0 (pbk.)
1. Bible and literature. 2. Bible as literature. I. Title.
PN56.B5B69 2015
809'.93522—dc23
2014044338

To all of our students—aged seven to seventy—
whose questions keep us seeking throughout a lifetime

and to this volume's marvelous poets and storytellers—
ancient and new—on whose shoulders we stand
with deep respect and gratitude
for their creative and inspired works
that have made this work possible.

CONTENTS

ACKNOWLEDGMENTS

Writing and bringing a book to birth is no easy task. The creative process takes time, dedication, and the gracious assistance of many "midwives." We would like to acknowledge those who have helped us bring this new volume to fruition. We are especially grateful for the gift of time to do what we love to do—to write—even in the midst of full teaching loads, family and community responsibilities, and the mundane tasks and chores of everyday life. Thank you to our Caldwell University and University of Portland library colleagues whose help with research has been invaluable. We are also indebted to our wonderful students throughout the years whose questions and insights pertaining to the Bible and contemporary literature have kept us engaged in the search for truth together and whose sense of wonder has always kept the classroom dialogue fresh and intriguing. Elizabeth Michael is especially grateful to the leadership of our Dominican congregation for having given her a sacred space in which to write, and to her former student and now "colleague" and friend, Carol Dempsey, for her long, long drive to make something good happen in that sacred space. Likewise, Carol is grateful to Elizabeth Michael for her great patience in waiting for this manuscript to take shape after many years of planning and writing, individually and in conversation with each other.

To all of our colleagues at Orbis Books who worked so carefully with us at each stage of this project, we say "thank you," with a special thanks to Sue Perry for helping us start this project before she retired. We would be remiss if we did not offer deep appreciation and gratitude to Jim Keane, our editor, who has been with us every step of the way. Jim's unflagging good humor and wonderful spirit, his marvelous expertise and consistent words of encouragement, his willingness to entertain conversation throughout the entire project, and his flexibility with ideas and deadlines has not only helped us with our endeavors but also made the work on this project a sheer joy. And finally, we are grateful to you, our readers, for pondering with us the various texts within each chapter as we listen together to the joys and struggles of the human condition lived under promise and peril but never without hope. The gift of the poet, the gift of the storyteller is to help us to see not only what is but also what can be. Through their works, they keep hope, imagination, and inspiration alive within us all as we journey together from light into Light, one step at a time.

INTRODUCTION

Everyone loves a good story, and both consciously and unconsciously, every family, every religion, every national culture and subculture, is shaped by its stories. The stories we hear as a child often influence our personal self-image and sometimes influence our choices. Parents, teachers, various leaders, and others use stories to establish societal expectations, mold public and private consciences, and embody national identity. Some of these shared stories are based in history; others pre-date history and were transmitted orally from generation to generation for centuries before they entered written literature. Communities incorporate their favorite stories into prose and poetry, into film and song, into slogans and prayers, into religious and national rituals. Psychologically, the act of repeating the story of "how it all began" seems to release into assembled groups something of the energy and hope that launched a people's common origins or the shared courage that assured its survival through historic disasters. So too, the act of repeating the story of a religious or national hero seems to transmit that person's values to a new generation. From the beginning of human speech to the present day, ritual storytelling has founded and grounded every human tribe and nation and every family in it.

The more stories a people share, the more cohesive its culture becomes. Although recent immigrants from Africa, Asia, and the Americas have enriched the culture of the United States with many new stories, one book of compelling narratives and wondrous poetry still surpasses all others in the number of Americans it influences. Written by many authors in many centuries, this book serves as a continuing reference point and as a perennial source of artistic inspiration. We call this book simply "the Bible."

Many reasons exist for the wide and enduring appeal of the Bible. First, throughout the world, many faith communities revere its words as sacred texts. Jews, Christians, and Muslims all trace their beginnings to one ancestral patriarch, Abraham, whose story is told in the Bible. Many Jews and Christians read the Bible daily; many listen to its stories and poems in church or synagogue once a week. In a 2008 NPR interview, Rabbi Sharon Brous, who founded a vibrant young Jewish congregation in downtown Los Angeles, explained why the biblical texts continue to appeal even though they are repeated, word for word, every liturgical year: "The words are the same, but you are different. That's why they become more and more meaningful. Hearing them, you feel called to be different."[1] Devout Jews, Christians, and Muslims at all levels of scholarship would agree.

For much of the twentieth century, the Bible was read aloud in American public schools as part of a morning ritual, which also included the Pledge of Allegiance. Although almost all public schools have discontinued this practice and religious pluralism now prevails in America's classrooms, many public figures still continue to invoke characters and events from the Bible. In courts of law, those making testimonies are asked to place their right hand on the Bible and then take an oath. If a person refuses, that person is counted as a conscientious objector. At U.S. presidential inaugurations, presidents being sworn into office are also asked to place their right hand on the Bible and then take the oath of office. Professional speechwriters know that orators inspire special confidence and establish strong connections to an audience's deepest hopes and fears when they cite biblical texts. Speeches by historical heroes like Dr. Martin Luther King Jr. derive much of their power from allusions to the Bible. More recently, Barack Obama, America's first African-American president, appealed to an audience of young voters by inviting them to leave the "Moses Generation" and join "the Joshua Generation." He expected them to recognize that while Moses had led his people out of slavery, Joshua was the one who marched with them into the Promised Land, according to the biblical text.[2]

Because of its strong emotional appeal, the Bible can be and has been abused to enshrine some false ideologies. One good example would be what scholars call "the myth of redemptive violence," that is, a willingness to use military might to resolve political conflicts "in the name of God." Using the name of God in selected biblical quotations to justify an addiction to war has been rightly labeled "nothing short of idolatry and blasphemy."[3] Such violence also presupposes a literalist and fundamentalist understanding of the biblical text, especially in relation to the books of the major and minor prophets, where the biblical writer often portrays God as a "warrior God."[4] This "warrior God" is Lord of creation, Lord of history, and Lord of hosts, the "commander-in-chief" of all the heavenly and earthly militia. Such a view of God lacks an understanding of the biblical text, whose content and portrayal of the Divine reflects the culture, history, and theology of its day.

Because both artists and "con artists" recognize the power of sacred stories, the modern communications industry deliberately recycles familiar biblical, fictional, and historical characters in screenplays, television series, and political campaigns. Advertising agencies recruit creative teams of artists and writers who know how to capitalize on the appeal of the most popular images. With figures from mythology and history like Venus, Icarus, and Abe Lincoln, for example, advertising has constructed an effective shorthand for commercial selling points like beauty, daring, and honesty. In the same way, commercial artists do not hesitate to use familiar biblical characters like Moses, the Good Samaritan, and Mary Magdalene to sell films and other cultural artifacts.

Even today, the Bible outsells all other books. Plot-driven novels that enjoy a few weeks as bestsellers and go on to become Hollywood blockbusters rarely survive in the conversation of the next generation of readers. Biblical narratives, by contrast, do not diminish in appeal once the reader learns "how it all turns out." In fact, the most distinguishing feature of a biblical narrative is that it is written so that the real drama begins when the final curtain descends and the community recognizes itself as the protagonist. Although the youngest story in the Bible is nearly two thousand years old, novelists, poets, and playwrights writing during our lifetime continue to make these stories new. Their authors assume that a contemporary reader will recognize allusions to biblical characters and scenarios and be challenged and enriched by their universal human significance.

For all these reasons, no one, regardless of religious conviction or lack of it, can remain ignorant of at least the most familiar Bible stories and still be considered an educated adult. Hence, courses in biblical literature abound at virtually all schools of higher education, even those with no religious affiliation. This text, however, is distinct from other books of its kind that are used in these courses. Unlike traditional texts, which trace a history of biblical influence on British-American literature, this multicultural volume explores forms, genres, and themes of just a few biblical texts which have influenced the many twentieth and twenty-first-century authors who keep the Bible alive in countries from Sweden to Saudi Arabia.

The dialogue that occurs between the biblical stories and poems and the contemporary multicultural literature included in this text is one of commonality and difference. In other words, sometimes the biblical text has inspired a contemporary writer to create a poem or story that reflects the main points, themes, and the theology of the biblical story or poem. Other times, contemporary writers have used various biblical texts and poems as springboards to create new stories and poems that move the ideas or themes of a biblical text in new directions, ones that sometimes challenge or shed a different light on a specific theological point. Sometimes the biblical stories and poems are juxtaposed against the multicultural contemporary stories and poems, adding new perspectives to both the biblical text and the contemporary piece of literature.

In literary works of the twentieth and twenty-first centuries, biblical allusions take many forms. Some references are overt and easily understood. For example, writers like Shusaku Endo will create a character who maintains a spiritual relationship with Jesus or some other biblical hero. Other authors' allusions are more subtle, but even then, the author counts on both believers and agnostics to recognize the old story as a universal context for a new situation. Short fiction artist Robert Coover, for example, never explicitly refers to scripture. Obviously, he counts on readers of his startling fusion of two familiar biblical narratives to recognize these tales from scripture and to appreciate the cleverness of his irreverent revisions. A reader with no knowledge of the Bible would miss the most important themes of the modern stories chosen for this course—and of many others.

Content Overview

In Part One, the reader will learn how knowledge of literary genres helps to recognize a biblical author's intention. With this understanding, an informed reader avoids the merely literal interpretation of each story, which can lead the uninformed to miss its "point." Interdisciplinary commentary in this section explains and exemplifies the genres of myth, archetypal myth, parable, dramatic and lyric poetry, first with biblical selections, and then with works by masters of twentieth and twenty-first-century literature. Specifically, Part One explicates selections from Genesis, Job, Isaiah, Psalms, and the Gospels of Matthew and Luke in conjunction with two novels, a short story, two plays, and a selection of African-American lyrics.

Chapter 1 opens with a demonstration of the role of genre in understanding scripture by defining and clarifying the term "myth" as it is used respectfully by biblical and literary scholars. Analyses of Genesis 1–3 and of Par Lagerkvist's *The Sybil* focus on the values and challenges of both narratives as symbolic expressions of humanity's quest for an authentic experience of God.

Chapter 2 introduces the Jungian concept of the mythic archetypes and illustrates one of them: the hero who dies for his or her people. This archetype presented in the poetry of Isaiah, namely in Isaiah 52:13–53:12, comes to life in the passion of Jesus as depicted by the synoptic Gospel writers, and in the historical novel *Silence* by Shusaku Endo. Endo's novel dramatizes the power of Jung's "archetype of archetypes" to shape the life choices and self-image of a committed Christian.

One Old Testament story that has been the topic of Hollywood movies and children's books alike is the story of Noah and the Flood in Genesis 6–8. The New Testament story of the "Parable of the Two Sons"

(Lk. 15:11–30), otherwise known as "The Prodigal Son," is a story that teaches the ageless lesson of forgiveness and right relationship. Robert Coover's short story "The Brother" employs the story of Noah and the Prodigal Son to elucidate those specific strategies of the parable which subvert conventional moral values. Chapter 3 explores the genre of the parable, the story of Noah and the Flood in Genesis 6–8, the parable of the Two Sons in Luke 15:11–30, and Coover's short story to discover what these three stories have to teach readers today.

Perhaps one of the best loved dramatic poems of all time is the drama of Job, who despite all loss, pain, and judgment on the part of his family and friends remains faithful to his God. Job's experience of suffering, in the face of a God who remains silent until the end of the drama, captures the human experience of the struggle and search for God in the midst of crisis. Chapter 4 focuses on the Book of Job, *J.B.* by Archibald MacLeish, and *The Trial of God* by Elie Wiesel. These two modern theatrical versions of the Book of Job explore the crisis in faith provoked by the Holocaust.

Chapter 5 first synthesizes the Exodus account of Egyptian oppression of the Hebrew people (Exod. 1:8–22) and then explores two biblical psalms of lament—Psalm 22:1–21 and Psalm 44, whose style and spirituality find a home in the lament of African slaves in the lyrics of spirituals which adopted the Hebrew experience as their own.

Part Two focuses on the themes of spiritual quest, romantic love, war and peace, and liberation. Grounded in an analysis and understanding of various biblical stories and poems, each chapter of this section analyzes the imaginative adaptation of these themes that appear in three novels and a play.

Chapter 6 captures the lifelong experience of searching for an understanding of self, community, the virtuous life, and ultimately, one's understanding of and relationship with the Sacred Presence dwelling in the midst of all that exists. Two works that engage the theme of "the spiritual quest" are the Book of Jonah and the *Life of Pi* by Yann Martel. These two tales of adventure and surprise invite readers to embark on a timeless journey of discovery packed with wisdom.

Passionate, romantic love is the theme of Chapter 7, exploring the sensuous biblical poem, the Songs of Songs. The chapter also focuses on the Gospel story of the Woman Caught in Adultery (John 7:53–8:11) to set the stage for Graham Greene's *The End of the Affair*, a mystery novel which takes the reader deep into the mystery of divine love.

The Story of Cain (Gen. 4:1–16) and David (2 Sam. 8–18) are action-packed texts that describe the power and pitfalls of conflict, as in the case of Cain, and royal warfare at the time of David when Israel was still a united kingdom. These stories contrast with Christopher Fry's gentle, poetic protest drama, *A Sleep of Prisoners*. These texts in Chapter 8 remind readers that the ancient theme of conflict and war still colors the fabric of life today and can inspire an alternative vision for life on the planet.

Finally, Chapter 9 focuses on the theme of liberation, a theme underlying the biblical texts of Amos 2–3:15; 4:1–5; 5:10–13; and 8:4–14 and in the contemporary novel *The Weight of All Things* by Sandra Benitez. Benitez, a Latina novelist, condemns the socio-economic situation of El Salvador much as the Israelite prophet Amos did in his day.

We have included an Epilogue as a brief summary. The Epilogue also raises several important questions for further reflection and offers some possible new directions for further study of the Bible in relation to contemporary multicultural literature.

Chapter Design

With occasional variations, each chapter follows this design: after a brief introduction, the first section takes the reader to the *source*, where "Drinking from the Spring" explains the biblical text(s) in relation to genres and themes. Next, "Playing in the Fountain: The Literary Text" directs attention to a modern literary text that makes use of variations on biblical genres or themes. In this section, after a few relevant facts "About the Author," the study proceeds with a focus and comments on various literary elements such as genre, style, structure, and theme in relation to how these elements contribute to the appreciation of both biblical literature and contemporary literature. The section "Drawing from the Well: Theological Themes" offers critical theological reflection on the texts and draws out various theological points that the texts embody. The final sections of each chapter are geared toward integrating into one's life what has been learned in each chapter. "Wading Deeper on Your Own," poses various questions for additional reflection and discussion; "Suggestions for Writing and Journaling," offers possibilities on how to personalize the experience of the chapter by writing about it; and "Irrigating Other Fields" tries to offer suggestions about how to connect insights gleaned from a particular chapter to other fields of study.

Finally, we hope that this volume will invite you, our readers, to ponder deeply the text of life from which the many authors have drawn their inspiration to create stories and poems of wonder, surprise, and delight. Common to the biblical and literary texts is the fact that these texts are "sacred" in the broadest sense of the term. All of these texts have been inspired and have the potential to awaken the human heart, mind, and spirit as we search together for a vision of truth at the center of all life and creativity. Let us begin our wondrous journey through the intriguing world of story and poetry. . . .

Part One

An Interplay of Biblical and Literary Genres

Long before psychologists, politicians, and family counselors wrote books about the power of stories and poems to shape human behavior, the anonymous authors of biblical literature appreciated storytelling and poetic expression for its effectiveness in communicating values. The Bible as we have it today is an imaginative, fascinating, and complex text written by some of history's greatest storytellers and poets who created stories within stories and poems that evoke the fullness of human emotions, ranging from passionate love to gut-wrenching lamentation. All of the biblical stories and poems bear the marks of the cultural, social, political, and theological influences and ideologies of their writers and later editors who shaped and reshaped these texts. Their points of view were often retrospective in relation to historical events, and often they shaped the texts in relation to the communities who would be receiving, reading, and rereading these texts. Many of the Bible's stories and poems have some basis in history, but the texts themselves are not historical accounts of how things really happened in ancient Israelite and early Christian times. Given the rich literary nature of biblical literature, historical fact, then, is never a story's or poem's primary value. Therefore, contemporary biblical scholars encourage readers to consider the "genre" of a biblical text when pondering the text's content.

This first section of this book gives consideration to the literary genres of myth, parable, and dramatic poetry. By using these various genres, biblical writers tried to capture and create the dynamic relationship that existed between God, humankind, and the natural world. The biblical stories and poems attest to the faith of the ancient peoples, their struggles to be faithful to their God and God's ways, and the enduring love and presence of their God, which continues for all ages. Biblical scholars' focus on myth, especially with regard to the opening chapters of the Book of Genesis, has been useful in liberating the Bible from literalism, and scholars keep moving beyond all forms of literalism to explore the Bible's rich literary content from the perspective of literary, rhetorical, and narrative criticism. The literary study of the Bible acknowledges that the biblical text represents ancient cultures and their ancient beliefs and customs, and therefore, the important task of biblical scholars is to hold up the entire Bible for ongong critical reflection, especially in the areas of theology, ideology, genre power, social order, social location, and perspective. Thus, critical thought on the Bible, inclusive of exegesis and heremeneutics, can open up new understandings and readings of the biblical stories and poems and help pave the way for a healthy encounter with the Spirit that, for many faith communities, breathes within and through the biblical text and within and through the communities hearing and reading these texts. Hence, as works of literature, the biblical stories and poems can become a vehicle for religious experience—the sacred encounter with the Divine whose transformative Presence dwells in the midst of all.

Other genres like parable and dramatic poetry are also found in the literature of the Bible. Characters in New Testament parables are distinguished by anonymity: "A certain man had two sons," which is the opening line to the parable about the prodigal son. No one mistakes what follows for history. The characters exist only as emblems of an idea, a recommended attitude, or an instructive model of behavior. Clearly, the intent of the author is to teach an ethical, theological, or spiritual lesson. Through parables, the storyteller hopes to awaken the conscience of his or her audience to inspire change.

A story like that of Job can best be expressed as a dramatic poem. Conflict is the essence of drama; the biblical author deliberately creates an imaginary dialogue with God, infused with all the contradiction, confusion, ambivalence, anger, and sense of injustice which assail people of faith in any situation where their God seems unreasonable.

1

MYTH

Stories of Creation and Adam and Eve

Genesis 1–3

The Sybil

Par Lagerkvist

Introduction

A generic approach to the Bible inevitably involves defining and redefining myth. Few words are more misunderstood than the term "myth." The Greek word "mythos" (tale, story, legend, fable) has a rich background, but the concept itself is not without controversy. Far too often myth has been associated with something that is thought to be "untrue." Such a narrow connotation does not do justice to the deep meaning that myths are trying to convey. Myths are found in all primitive, ancient, modern, and contemporary cultures. Myths are one of the ways that have enabled people to deal with the origins of the world, their own origins, and their relationship to the Divine. Myths also help people deal with the elusive questions surrounding ideals, aspirations, death, why bad things happen to good people, and what happens when we die.

Post-Enlightenment scholars, who emphasized rationalism and objectivity, decried myth and saw it as an unscientific and primitive way of dealing with life and life's questions. In the nineteenth through the twentieth centuries, however, intellectual history moved through two phases. At first, humanist scholars set about successfully debunking the idea of myths as literal history. In the second phase, under the influence of literary critics and specialists in many fields of study, scholars began searching myths for the spiritual and psychological truths they convey. Hence, psychologists like Freud studied classical Greek and Roman mythology for models of human behavior. Later, historians cited the Holocaust as a modern historical myth because it demonstrated the power of a narrative of shared tragedy to shape the life of a community. Telling and retelling this true story of a death experience shared by six million people communicates more than the facts: it communicates the strength of its heroes to their descendants and thus calls living Jews to new strength of their own.

Also in the twentieth century, great poets and writers began to recognize and celebrate a mythical-poetic view of reality. Myth was heralded as that which was opposed neither to what is real nor to history. Thus, myth was recognized as having its own form of expression and its own validity, and because myths often address the important questions of life, myths enable people to live in the midst of mystery at its deepest core. Properly understood, then, creating myth is an intellectual activity of neither delusion nor deception.

Mythmaking is a valuable function of the human psyche, evident not only in ancient religious traditions but also in modern social and political life. For example, the term "American Myth," the belief that those who work hard can free themselves from economic and social limitations, is based on the history of the nation. The first Americans really were people of vision and character who carved out of the wilderness a nation free from a European economy based on inherited wealth. That true story has inspired all succeeding generations of Americans to believe that they are free to shape their own destinies. African-American slaves, who did not share that freedom, did not relate to the American Myth. They endured their long road to emancipation by comparing it to the biblical journey of the Jews out of Egypt into the Promised Land. Both of these are examples of myth rooted in history with the power to shape people's lives.

Biblical writers drew on many ancient myths from various cultures, especially those from Mesopotamia and Canaan, when they were writing and shaping their texts. Two popular myths that influenced the biblical creation story and the story of the flood were the *Enuma Elish* and the *Epic of Gilgamesh*, respectively. Biblical myth is often seen as being different from the stories of Israel's contemporaries because Israel's material reflects and contains a unique history and theology. Even though the Hebraic use of myth has many of the literary characteristics of its neighboring cultures' myths, Old Testament myth is different in content and purpose. Israel's myths had a focus on monotheism and portrayed the ongoing deeds of Israel's One True God who was in a special relationship with Israel, while also in a relationship with all other peoples and all creation. Thus, the biblical writers went beyond the literary forms and genres of ancient stories and infused their stories with a perception of God and descriptions of how God relates to humankind and the human condition. Such stories, then, even though they may be "myths," contain and disclose a theology.

Woven into the biblical myth is Israel's self-understanding that, unlike other gods who are often unpredictable, unreliable, and unknowable, Israel's God is revelatory. Israel's God makes known a Sacred Presence in ways that are both transcendent and immanent. Israel's God is a living presence, fully engaged with all of creation and especially with the human condition.[1] The biblical stories and poems, whether they are myths, parables, poetic dramas, or other genres, attest to this important point. This first chapter looks at Genesis 1–3 and *The Sybil* by Par Lagerkvist from the perspective of genre, specifically "myth," and explores how this genre becomes a point of intersection and connection between two distinct texts, an ancient biblical text and a contemporary literary text.

Drinking from the Spring
The Biblical Text
Genesis 1–3

The biblical creation story of Genesis 1–2 is a marvelous, imaginative, and faith-filled story of how the universe, the earth, and all that inhabits the earth began. The biblical story presents us with a picture of God the Creator who, for six days, expounded incredible energy and creativity to create and bring forth the beginings of the universe, Earth, and all that dwells on and within the earth. Did you ever stop to think, however, about how old creation might be? Science and evolutionary theology estimate that Earth is around 4.5 to 5 billion years old, that the probable age of the entire universe is between 15 and 20 billion years old, and that it began as a burst of stupendous energy when hydrogen and helium came into existence.

Did you also stop to wonder if all of this wondrous creation happened in six days? Again, science tells us that creation was an evolutionary process that happened over billions and billions of years. Somewhere around approximately 14 billion years ago, galaxies and primal stars were born; 4.5 billion years, ago the sun and solar system came into being; 4.45 billion years ago, planets were formed, and earth brought forth an atmosphere together with oceans and continents; 3.9 billion years ago, life began in the sea, and photosynthesis occurred in simple organisms; 600 million years ago, jellyfish emerged; 550 million years ago, animals with shells, such as clams and snails, appeared; 420 million years ago, the first land plants emerged from the sea; 395 million years ago, the first land insects emerged; 370 million years ago, the first trees appeared; 235 million years ago, dinosaurs appeared and flowers spread; 216 million years ago, the first mammals appeared; 150 million years ago, the first birds appeared; 2.6 million years ago, the earliest human types emerged; and 2,000 years ago, Jesus of Nazareth was born.

What an incredible portrait of the emergence of life that spanned billions and millions of years! Some scientists even tell us that more than one universe exists, that there are parallel universes, that all of life, all of creation is one big web held together by strands of vibrating energy.

Such is the thought of scientists working in the area of string theory.[2] What we do know today is that creation was a creative, mysterious, and evolutionary process that occurred over billions of years. This creative, mysterious, evolutionary process continues today as new species on our planet continue to evolve and be discovered even in the midst of horrific climate change that is causing many species to die off.[3]

Thus, creation as we know it today is a profound and beautiful mystery that did not happen in six days as depicted by the biblical creation story. Does this mean that the story is to be discounted as fiction? Certainly not. The biblical creation story, based on, yet different from other creation stories and myths of its time, is a story told from an ancient faith perspective meant to help people wonder about, be grateful for, and celebrate the origins of creation. It also introduces that Sacred Presence called "God" who, for believers, is the Source of all being, whose Spirit brought everything into existence, and whose great love sustains and nurtures all that has been created. This Sacred Presence that interacts with all of creation is Mystery itself.

In addition to wondering about creation, have you ever wondered about how transgression and the breach and breakdown of right relationship occurs in our world today? In Genesis 3, the ancient biblical writers tried to explain how sin came into the world. In order to provide an explanation, they told a story about a man and woman—Adam and Eve—who, according to the creation story, were the first people on earth. These two people enjoyed a wonderful relationship with God until a series of events occurred that caused them to suffer pain; the worst of all was the pain of the loss of an idyllic relationship with their Creator God. This mythic story contains many elements of etiology[4] and continues to influence theological thinking today.

Thus, two well-known stories that can be understood as biblical "myths" are contained in Genesis 1–3: the story of creation (Gen. 1–2) and the story about the first transgression (Gen. 3).[5] Neither the creation story nor the story of Adam and Eve in the Garden of Eden are based on historical facts, but both stories have the capacity to communicate in an imaginative way the truth about creation and about sin, the latter of which results in a breach in right relationship among human beings and human beings in relation to the Sacred Presence. The two realities of creation and sin continue to perplex us today as we ask the perennial questions: "How?" "Why?" Let us now look at Genesis 1–3, to see how myth explains the mystery of creation and how sin entered the world.

An Ever-Ancient, Ever-New Creation Narrative
Genesis 1 and 2

Perhaps one of the most familiar and popular "myths" in the Bible is the creation story found in Genesis 1 and 2, which has traditionally been divided into the Priestly version (Gen. 1:1–2:4a) and the Yahwist version (Gen. 2:4b-25) of creation. Biblical scholars, however, have recently begun to view the two versions as a whole. Bruce Birch, Walter Brueggemann, Terence Fretheim, and David Peterson argue for a newer and more unified reading of Genesis 1 and 2, one that not only recognizes the texts' inherent differences but also draws upon the texts' points of complementarity:

> Many [readers] of Genesis 1 and 2 think that these chapters consist of two creation accounts, assigning 1:1–2:4a to the Priestly writer and 2:4b–25 to the Yahwist. Differences in type of literature, structure vocabulary, style, and center of concern have been noted. Yet, while the two accounts have different origins and transmission histories, they have been brought together in a theologically sophisticated fashion to function together as the canonical picture of creation. As such, they reveal key points of complementarity: God as sole creator of a good and purposeful world; the key place of the human among the creatures on a cocreative role; the social character of the human as male-female.[6]

In keeping with this unified canonical picture of creation, Genesis 1 and 2 presents a beautifully crafted design of interrelated divine, human, and nonhuman relationships. Before anything comes into existence, God's *ruach*, God's "breath," "spirit," "wind," is active, sweeping over the face of the waters (Gen. 1:2). With this "wind," this "breath," this "spirit," the creation process begins almost magically through word (Priestly version) and through deed (Yahwist version).

On the first day, God proclaims, "Let there be light," and light comes into being and is then separated from darkness, and both are named accordingly: "Day" and "Night" (Gen. 1:3–5). These two aspects of creation are distinct from and independent of each other; yet they complement each other and function interdependently.

On the second day, a dome is created in the midst of the waters to separate one original body of water into two distinct realms (Gen. 1:6–8).

On the third day, the waters under the sky are gathered together into one place—the sea—so that the dry land could appear: the earth (Gen.

1:9). One aspect of creation gives way to another, and both comprise central habitats for life on the planet. The waters become home for the sea creatures; the birds fly above the earth across the dome of the sky (Gen. 1:20–21). Both the sea creatures and the birds receive a divine blessing, enabling them to share in God's creative process. This blessing and its related creative process is also bestowed on human beings (Gen. 1:20–22, 28).

On the fourth day, lights appear in the dome of the sky—the sun, the moon, and the stars. These lights have their respective functions during the day and the night, and they also separate the light from the darkness, and day from night (Gen. 1:14–19; cf. Gen. 1:4–5).

On subsequent days of creation, the earth brings forth vegetation (Gen. 1:9; cf. Gen. 2:9), a food source for human beings, birds, and all other earthly creatures (Gen. 1:29–30). The vegetation and its growth, however, are dependent upon two things: (1) rain, which according to the biblical writer is a phenomenon caused by God; and (2) human cultivation (Gen 2:5). Even though a stream rises up to water the face of the ground, the ground does not have the impetus to bring forth the needed vegetation (Gen. 2:6). Thus, in order to be fully "fruitful," the earth needs both God's and humankind's care. Furthermore, the earth brings forth living creatures of every kind; from the earth—out of the ground—God made cattle, creeping things, and wild animals (Gen. 1:24; cf. Gen. 2:19). Out of the dust of the ground, God also formed a human being (Gen. 2:7). Finally, part of the earth is turned into a garden that God plants (Gen. 2:8). The garden is entrusted to the human being whom God places in it "to till it and keep it" (Gen. 2:15). The emerging picture of the creation story thus far is one of interdependent relationships among the divine, human, and nonhuman worlds.

As the creation account continues to unfold, we see that the animals are intended to be helpers as partners for the human being (Gen. 2:18–19), and likewise human beings are to be helpers as partners for one another (Gen. 2:20). The fact that the first humans created are male and female indicates sexual differentiation; the description that they are to be helpers as partners indicates a sense of mutuality. The point that the woman is created from human bone suggests equality between male and female genders, an equality that the biblical writer celebrates with a vivacious exclamation on the part of the male human being:

> Then the man said,
> "This at last is bone of my bones
> and flesh of my flesh;
> this one shall be called Woman

for out of Man this one was taken"
(Gen. 2:23).[7]

Bone of bone, flesh of flesh, the man and woman become one (Gen. 2:24), metaphorically symbolized by the language of espousal: "Therefore a man leaves his father and his mother and clings to his wife, and they become one flesh" (Gen. 2:24).

These human beings are created in God's image, *imago Dei*, according to God's likeness (Gen. 2:26–27). The ancient people hearing these stories understood that to be created in the divine image meant that a person shared in God's creative process and God's work, which was to exercise dominion (Gen. 1:28). Birch, Brueggemann, Fretheim, and Petersen make the point that "God is not in heaven alone, but is engaged in a relationship of mutuality and chooses to share the creative process with others. Human beings are thus created in the image of one in a way that shares power with others, which would be congruent with the command in 1:28."[8] They argue further:

> As image of God, human beings function to mirror God to the world, to be as God would be to the nonhuman, be an extension of God's own dominion. This text democratizes an ancient Near Eastern royal use of image language; all human beings are created in the image of God. That both male and female are so created . . . means that the female images the divine as much as the male. Likeness to God pertains not only to what male and female have in common but also to what remains distinctive to them.[9]

The *imago Dei*, then, pertains to one's sense of self as well as one's role in creation.

With respect to "subdue" and "dominion" in verse 28, Birch, Brueggemann, Fretheim, and Petersen offer clarification on the often misconstrued interpretations of these two terms: "The command to have dominion (1:28), in which God delegates responsibility for the nonhuman creation in a power-sharing relationship with humans, must be understood in terms of care-giving, not exploitation (see the use of the verb *radah* in Ps. 72:8–14; Ezek. 34:1–4)." The verb *subdue*, while capable of more negative senses, here has reference to the earth and its cultivation and, more generally, to the becoming of a world that is a dynamic, not a static reality.[10] We have only to look at Psalm 104 to understand the term "dominion" in relationship to God who, as creator, provides bountifully for all creation.

The divine charge to the human being "to till and to care for" the garden follows the same vein of thought as Gen. 1:28. In their report to the 2002 General Assembly, members of the Presbyterian Church (USA) interpreted this biblical charge through an ecological lens:

> "Tilling" symbolizes everything we humans do to draw sustenance from nature. It requires individuals to form communities of cooperation and to establish systematic arrangements (economies) for satisfying their needs. Tilling includes not only agriculture but mining and manufacturing and exchanging all of which depend necessarily on taking and using the stuff of God's creation.
>
> "Keeping" the creation means tilling with care—maintaining the capacity of the creation to provide sustenance for which tilling is done. This, we have come to understand, means making sure that the world of nature may flourish, with all its intricate, interacting systems upon which life depends.[11]

In retrospect, then, the creation story shows us that animals and human beings share a common origin and participate in a wonderful relationship. Created by God from the ground, they are meant to assist one another as helpers, as partners in God's work on the planet and, in the case of the ancient agrarian world, to share in the common work of cultivating the land. The relationship of human beings with the natural world is further enhanced by the divine charge that humanity exercise dominion, a task that goes hand-in-hand with humankind's being formed in God's image, according to God's likeness. Not only do human beings live by God's breath of life (Gen. 2:7), but so does the rest of creation (Gen. 1:30). At this juncture, we see a series of distinctive yet interrelated relationships that exist between creator and creation.

In summary, Birch, Brueggemann, Fretheim, and Petersen observe:

> Both God and creatures have an important role in the creative enterprise, and their spheres of activity are interrelated. God is not present as powerful and the creatures powerless. In spite of the risks involved, God chooses the way of less than absolute control, for the sake of a relationship of integrity in which power is shared with that which is other than God. In the very act of creating, God gives to others a certain freedom and independence, and catches them up in creativity. . . . Creation is process as well as event. . . . God has established a relationship with

> human beings such that their decisions about the creation truly count—both for God and the creation.[12]

These relationships are deepened through divine wonder and freedom, and the process of "naming." God does not name either the animals or the human beings. Rather, God brings the animals to the first human being to see what that person would call them, and whatever names were given were to be the names (Gen. 2:19–20). The first human being also gives a name to the second human being (Gen. 2:23). Naming, in the ancient world, was for the purpose of establishing a relationship; it entailed neither control nor subordination.

One last element in the creation story that establishes a sense of order within creation is the element of time. According to the biblical narrative, all of creation takes place in the course of six days; God rests on the seventh. If we view the time element linearly, then the creative process leads up to and culminates in the creation of the human being. If viewed cyclically—which would be more in keeping with the ancient world's understanding of time in relation to seasons—then the human being becomes part of the whole. Sharing in the distinctiveness of each aspect of creation, humankind becomes part of the rich picture of biodiversity that the biblical creation story presents and helps to form part of the magnificent web of life to which all creation is connected, including God.

The seventh day, the day of rest—the Sabbath—is a gift not only enjoyed by God but also extended to people, livestock (Exod. 20:10), and the land (cf. Lev. 25). Like humankind and the animals, the seventh day—the day of rest—is blessed by God. Thus, God's blessing implies activity as well as "being."

Finally, each aspect of creation is "good" (Gen. 1:4, 10, 12, 18, 21, 25) and all of creation is "very good" (Gen. 1:31), not because of any utilitarian purpose but simply because it exists. Creation is intrinsically good. This point retrieved from the biblical creation account is now a "given" for many theologians developing a theology of creation, one that flows from the biblical tradition. If creation is intrinsically good, then how is one to understand evil in regard to creation? In his work, Langdon Gilkey takes up the question of creation's intrinsic goodness and the existence of evil. He states:

> [T]he Genesis account makes very clear, [that] all of creation is 'good' because it was made by a caring God. Thus there is, and there can be, nothing essentially evil, an evil, so to speak, built into things as part of their intrinsic nature, and so irremovable

> and unredeemable, a necessary aspect of temporal and worldly existence. On the contrary, each part of reality has possibilities for good—even, to Augustine's Hellinistic consternation, matter and the body, both of which, as he had to admit, God had created and, therefore, despite appearances, must be good![13]

Therefore, even though the Genesis 1 and 2 creation account is myth, the story presents us with a striking and accurate reality; namely, that creation is a series of interdependent and interrelated relationships, many of which are mutual, and all of which comprise the glorious, wondrous, and evolutionary web of life. This idyllic picture of creation in which human beings live contentedly in a garden—in Eden—does not last forever. Genesis 3 unveils the story about the first transgression and features the man and woman of Genesis 2 receiving stern consequences for the choices they make that lead to a breach in right relationship for all parties involved.

Trouble in the Garden—The First Sin
Genesis 3

One story that enjoys a rich history of interpretation is Gen. 3:1–24, the story of Adam and Eve in the garden. Like the creation story of Genesis 1 and 2, Genesis 3 is a myth that tries to explain how sin entered the world and became a part of the human condition even until now. The setting is the garden and the main characters are Adam, Eve, God, and the serpent. Commanded by God not to eat of the fruit of a certain tree, both Adam and Eve do the opposite (vv. 1–7). The serpent, a mythical figure,[14] tempts Eve, and she listens to the voice of the reptile (vv. 1–6a). She then entices her husband to taste the fruit, which he does (v. 6b).

Their deed evokes a response from God who enters into dialogue with the couple (vv. 8–13). Instead of accusing Adam and Eve outright, God asks them several questions aimed at disclosing the truth and affording the man and woman their integrity. By giving the sort of answers that they did, the two human beings indict themselves, and their sins of pride, failure to take responsibility, and disobedience become self-evident. Verses 14–19 are a description of the consequences that the serpent and Adam and Eve will have to bear. Because of the choices made, the serpent is cursed, destined to slither on its belly all its days, and will eat dust. Enmity will exist between the serpent and the woman, and between the serpent's and woman's offspring (v. 14). The woman, Eve, will suffer pain in childbirth, be under the control of her husband, and experience insatiable sexual longing for her husband while experiencing no sexual satisfaction from him (v. 16). The man, Adam, will have to toil by the sweat of his brow on account of the ground being cursed (vv. 17–19).

Following the divine chastisements enumerated in verses 14–19 is a comment by the narrator (vv. 20–21), the most important of which is verse 21: "And the Lord God made garments of skins for the man and for his wife, and clothed them."[15] At this juncture in the Genesis story, nakedness becomes associated with sin as well with as the loss of innocence. Being naked causes Adam distress. The act of God clothing the couple in order to cover their nakedness can suggest that a person's sinful state is not permanent; God will continue to work with the human condition to transform it.

Verses 22–24 continue God's response to Adam and Eve on the occasion of their transgression. The final consequence that Adam and Eve will have to endure on account of their actions is expulsion from the garden.[16] Immediately following is Genesis 4:1, which opens the next story with the man "knowing" his wife Eve, who conceives and bears Cain.

As mentioned earlier, fertility in the ancient Near East was often a sign of divine blessing. Thus, even though the two human beings sin and a breach in right relationship occurs, they still remain graced and blessed. Human beings and their God no longer enjoy the fullness of union and communion they once enjoyed before their transgression. Their relationship will remained graced, but the intimacy that they once knew and experienced with the Divine will no longer exist as it did before transgression entered into the situation.

Playing in the Fountain
The Literary Text
The Sybil

About the Author
Par Lagerkvist (1891–1974)

Although not widely read in the United States, this Scandinavian Nobel Laureate produced forty volumes of prose, poetry, and drama. A person of great complexity, Par Lagerkvist described himself as "a deeply religious atheist," yet all his most popular works in translation are novels that use characters from the New Testament to explore questions about the nature of God and the search for life's meaning without God. Hence, no writer better represents the relevance of biblical literature to the ideas and emotions that have inspired mythmaking from ancient times to the present.

In 1966, Lagerkvist gathered five of his biblically-based novels into a "pentology," published under the title: *Pilgrims*. These five novels were translated into English by Naomi Blair and published in New York by Random House: *Barabbas* (1951); *The Sybil* (1958); *The Death of Ahasuerus* (1962); *Pilgrim at Sea* (1964); and *The Holy Land* (1966). Each of the five novels takes as its theme the itinerancy of the human soul. Lagerkvist believes that everyone is a traveler who can never know more than the journey itself, who can never know even if he or she has "arrived." In this conviction, Lagerkvist expresses what has come to be known as the "postmodern sensibility," an attitude toward truth as ultimately unknowable.

Many literary critics have said that all of Lagerkvist's work is characterized by the split in him between an intellect of the late twentieth century and the heart of a faithful peasant. His sensitivity anticipates a dilemma whose intensity is still evident in our twenty-first-century conversations. Many readers will recognize as their own the voice of the child in Lagerkvist's early short story: "I had an obscure foreboding of . . . all the *unknown* which Father did not know and from which he could not protect me."[17] In his novel *Barabbas*, Lagervist seems to express his own ambiguous relationship with religion.[18] In the New Testament, specifically in the Gospel of John, Barabbas is simply referred to as the criminal who was set free when Jesus was crucified (John 18:40). Lagerkvist invents for this robber a whole lifetime in which he tries unsuccessfully to achieve belief. The novel's last line is an ironic parody of Jesus' final words from the cross. With the last breath from his own cross, Barabbas addresses his prayer to the darkness: "Into your hands I commend my spirit." As an agnostic, Barabbas denies himself the certainty of atheism and commends his searching soul to the darkness of permanent doubt.

In the third novel of the pentology, Lagerkvist seems to echo the feelings of many sincere spiritual seekers who, rejecting the contradictions and compromises of their parents' religion, still find themselves haunted with desire for some experience of transcendence:

> Beyond the gods, beyond all that falsifies and coarsens the world of holiness, . . . there must be something stupendous which is inaccessible to us. Our very failure to capture it demonstrates how inaccessible it is. Beyond all the sacred clutter, the holy thing itself must exist . . . Something so important that it were better to lose one's life than one's faith in that thing.[19]

Reflecting on Genre

Literary Myth

Like the stories of creation and Adam and Eve in Genesis 1–3, *The Sybil*, one of Lagerkvist's better known novels, is an example of a literary myth, an original narrative that is not inherited from ancient times but that imitates classical or biblical myth in content or style, or both. Lagerkvist makes his mythic intent obvious immediately by making all the characters anonymous: the old woman, the wanderer, the little servant, the one-armed lover. Lagerkvist appropriates much of the content of *The Sybil* from the civilization which gave us Greek mythology: he sets the action in the landscape of classical Greece, draws on Greek mythology for the character of the Sybil and for her parents, who practice a primitive paganism which worshipped trees, holy springs, and sacred groves. The novel's most dramatic scenes vividly describe rituals that were actually practiced in the temple and in the pit of the Pythia. *The Sybil*'s brief romance ends tragically with the drowning of her beloved, dramatizing the mythical perception of the forces of nature as servants of a jealous god. Lagerkvist also combines mysterious allusions to the incarnation with one of the most repulsive themes of classical myth: the rape of a human woman by an animal inhabited by a god. Despite all these specifics that locate the novel in first-century Greece, the author signals its mythic scope by repeatedly referring to an ageless Sybil for whom time does not exist. Above all, Lagerkvist has created a literary myth by inventing two protagonists who embody the very definition of myth as a narrative of belief with the power to control people's lives.

Like myth, Lagerkvist's novel seeks to embody in his invented story the human search for answers which go beyond the accessible moral directives implied in parables and fables. Although the situations in the story are unique, they embody contradictory experiences of God: mercy and cruelty, blessing and curse, love and terror. Moreover, the questions the fictional situations raise are the universal quotidian questions asked by all thoughtful people in every nation and generation. For example, no religion has ever satisfactorily "explained" the problem of evil. Every day's newscast dramatizes how bad things happen to good people and vicious people seem to prosper. How does a loving God permit this injustice? Lagerkvist raises this question, but does not answer it.

In *The Sybil*, as in all novels of his pentology, Lagerkvist steadily asserts that ultimate truth is concerned not with fact, but with mystery. In this regard, Lagerkvist reflects the thought of the biblical writers of Genesis 1 and 2, whose intent was not to explain how creation happened from a factual perspective but rather to communicate to readers an element of truth embedded in the mystery of creation, namely, that creation did not come into existence on its own. For the biblical writers and the communities of faith who received the text of Genesis 1 and 2, creation began with the source of all life—God—whose Spirit brought everything into being and whose divine Presence, forever interacting with creation, is Mystery itself.

In *The Sybil*, each of Lagerkvist's fictional characters searches for truth and confronts mystery. Because his works deny the reader any final religious consolation, Lagerkvist can be accused of writing "anti-myths." Myth embodies mystery; it does not explain it.

Reflecting on Structure

When we examine the structure of *The Sybil*, we recognize the virtues that Lagerkvist admired in the artistic movement of Cubism. The Cubist artist strips away all surface detail and reduces the subject to its underlying architectural forms. As the critic Everett Ellested has pointed out, a Cubist writer creates architecturally balanced characters and situations by juxtaposing opposites.[20] *The Sybil*'s plot fulfills such an architectural structure by juxtaposing a series of opposites: two faces of God, benign and cruel; two faces of human nature, magnanimous and petty; two faces of love, possession and dispossession. A Cubist painting also balances three-dimensional shapes in a way that engages light and shadow in dialogue. Lagerkvist's style masterfully mirrors his themes of paradox and contradiction in humanity's ageless dialogue with God.

Reflecting on Literary Style

Lagerkvist aimed for a literary style that paralleled some of the effects he admired in visual art. He himself spelled this out in an essay, "Literary Art and Visual Art," published when he was only twenty-two years old.[21] Here Lagerkvist condemns art that renders a realistic representation of life in favor of methods which emphasize life's spiritual realities. In *The Sybil*'s anti-realistic style, he incorporates into narrative fiction the shock techniques exploited by expressionist painters and dramatists. Lagerkvist's literary "shock treatment" seeks to draw attention to moral atrocities that have become too familiar. By staging these situations in a way that makes them deliberately strange, exaggerated, or distorted, he achieves his desired effects. In presenting the Nobel Prize to Lagerkvist, the Swedish Academy described his unique style as "words and ideas which, in their profound and fearful tenderness, carry at the very heart of their purity a message of terror."[22]

One of Lagerkvist's stylistic decisions that derives directly from his mythic intent is his reduction of each anonymous character's physical description to a bare minimum. Mythmakers and biblical authors typically do not provide the vivid physical descriptions we expect from novelists. No eyewitness could describe Adam, Noah, or King Herod in a police lineup. Physical details make a character a real individual to the reader. In myth, the absence of a specific face, bodily build, voice, and distinctive personal demeanor makes each character representative of humanity itself. Hence the character's fate as the plot unfolds becomes of ultimate moral and spiritual consequence beyond the tale's entertainment value. Most of the time, Lagerkvist observes this convention. When he deviates from it, the effect is a compelling example of his shock tactic. Such is the case with the author's treatment of Jesus. Although Jesus appears in only one brief scene in the novel, and is not named there, Lagerkvist's focus on his face is arresting, especially since nowhere in the New Testament do we find a description of Jesus, his face, or his facial expressions. Because Christian visual art has so persistently presented Jesus' face as the face of human suffering, most readers think they know what he looks like. In *The Sybil* each time Lagerkvist has chosen to refer to this beloved person, the image is repugnant. Early in the novel, the stern expression on the face of the criminal who curses the Jew who denied him minimal compassion is shocking. In a later allusion to incarnation, however, the smile on the face of the god's idiot son, a smile indifferent to both good and evil, is more than shocking; it is deliberately scandalous. This Buddha-like smile appears again in the final novel of the pentology, like the coda to a symphony: "No one understood that insistent smile, or what it concealed. . . . And indeed, had it ever been comprehensible to human beings?"[23]

Drawing from the Well *Theological Themes*

The stories of creation, Adam and Eve in the garden, and *The Sybil* transcend time and space and deal with the enduring questions of life and life's universal dilemmas: How are we to understand the mystery of God and the mystery of how everything came into being? How are we to understand sin and the loss of right relationship in the midst of gracious divine benevolence? How are we to understand disbelief and belief in the face of restless wandering, anguish, and suffering? Both Genesis 1–3 and *The Sybil* present us with stories from which we can gain insight as we draw out the stories' rich theological themes that can help quench the incessant thirst for truth.

In reflecting on Genesis 1–3 as a whole, we see an attempt to explain how creation took place. The story, though a myth, does communicate to its readers the interrelatedness of all creation, a creation that is not only good but very good. We see a God whose word and deed is both creative and powerful, and we learn that all has been given as gift to be cared for and cherished. Within the garden is an atmosphere of right relationship with all that exists and indeed with the Divine as well. This atmosphere of right relationship, however, becomes tainted when the first human beings transgress. Despite their transgression, they remain graced and blessed by God, who metes out consequences for their wrongdoing but who also acts with compassion toward them, even though the trust in the relationship has been breached. The myths of Genesis 1–3 present us with powerful lessons that reflect the reality of life and provide us with a window into understanding the mystery of the Divine and the human condition, a theme that resounds in Lagerkvist's works, especially in *The Sybil.*

In reflecting on the works of Lagerkvist, we see that none of Lagerkvist's novels belongs to the genre of historical fiction, but one could say that *The Sibyl* is haunted by a historical consciousness, consciousness of a unique experience of the Judeo-Christian God during the most shameful historical event of the author's lifetime, the Jewish Holocaust. In the novel where the character Jesus Christ makes only a cameo appearance, Lagerkvist shapes the scene to shock complacent Christians into seeing the ugly face of Christ that some of them presented to a European Jew.[24] Later in the novel, when Lagerkvist deliberately sets up an almost blasphemous parody on the birth of Jesus, Christian readers are pushed to feel revulsion at such a depiction.

Lagerkvist's historical scope, like that of myth, always transcends any single historical period. *The Sybil*'s two leading characters represent opposite extremes of the same universal dilemma: the nameless wanderer who cannot believe and the ageless Sibyl who cannot stop believing even when her god seems to mistreat her. Possibly, through the Sibyl's anguish, the author tries to communicate the ambivalence of faithful people in every age and every religion whose suffering somehow unites them to a god who, from the perspective of those suffering, seems to have abused and abandoned them.

The novel's conclusion is intentionally unsatisfactory, for this is not the story of two individuals who have been touched by God as in the case of Adam and Eve. Rather, *The Sybil* enacts the experience of a whole culture in relation to God. On the one hand, this culture engages in a restless wandering, a refusal to let God into daily life; on the other hand, because of the suffering of humanity, history forces an encounter with that incomprehensible God.

The most mysterious plots in myth involve divine and human interaction. In classical mythology, this interaction is often shocking. For example, a lustful god in the form of a swan rapes Leda, the human beauty; an avenging god condemns the hero Prometheus to be consumed by a ravenous bird over and over again. Like classical mythology, but unlike the biblical story of Adam and Eve, *The Sybil* presents its share of shocking divine and human interaction. Writing for a sophisticated modern audience, however, Lagerkvist is careful to suggest a "natural" explanation for "supernatural" events like the lover's "accidental" death, the Pythia's pregnancy and its startling outcome. When reading *The Sybil*, be prepared to be shocked into rethinking Judeo-Christian concepts and behavior. When reading Genesis 1–3, be prepared to meet divine creativity and benevolence, but also a divinity who casts judgment upon humanity and a curse upon the human and nonhuman worlds alike. Such judgment seems deserved, on the one hand, and, on the other hand, undeserved.

Thematically, *The Sybil* can be summarized as a startling version of the mythic conflict between the gods of classical polytheism: Apollo, the god of light, and Dionysus, the god of chaos. Some version of these gods survives in all forms of religion. Although the novel builds a consistently critical attitude toward religious personalities, at the same time, it repeatedly describes what life is like for a person or community who denies God a place in their lives. The most outstanding characteristic of such a person is restlessness, a compulsive wandering from one disappointment to another.

To represent the restlessness of a godless culture, Lagerkvist makes his first protagonist a nameless version of the legendary figure known as "The Wandering Jew." In *The Sibyl*, the man's encounter with the divine is aborted by sheer thoughtlessness. Unaccustomed to attaching divine significance to anything, he treats Jesus, a criminal on his way to execution, as simply "none of my business." The first evidence of this ordinary man's fatal mistake is sexual sterility. In many myths, a person or community who disobeys the gods is cursed with sterility. Although some biblical stories portray this situation to be the case, in actuality, such suffering is not caused by the Divine, and in fact the relationship between suffering and transgression is influenced by the deuteronomic theology of retribution (see Deut. 28). This theology that the ancients devised to explain sin and suffering is a theological construct and not the actual lived experience of the Divine, whose ways are not punitive. The lesson learned from the fate of the characters in both Genesis 3 and in *The Sybil*, however, does contain a grain of truth: consequences exist for those who act unjustly. In the story of Adam and Eve, God does not curse Eve with sterility, but God does curse her both with pain in childbearing and with a lack of satisfaction in her sexual relations with Adam. Furthermore, an observable historical phenomenon is the reality that a spiritually dysfunctional society eventually "dries up," ceasing to be creative and productive.

According to Lagerkvist's insightful novel, however, secularists are not the only ones who marginalize God. In its characters and episodes, the novel presents a comprehensive contrast between characters who are examples of "pure" religion and others who represent the different distortions of religion which effectively keep God at a distance. Perhaps in memory of his own grandparents, Lagerkvist's first favorable version of religion is communion with nature in the pure paganism of the Sybil's parents, an experience that we then see corrupted in the organized paganism of the temple where religion degenerates into everything from "big business" to hatred of the world to hysteria. Around the temple we see assembled typical religious predators, like pragmatists, who seek religion as a career for either money or power, or vultures who feed on gossip about the priests.

In radiant contrast to the above stereotypes of religious fraud, Lagerkvist offers us two embodiments of authentic spirituality: the mystic and the humble servant. Despite his antipathy to organized religion, Lagerkvist's mystical theology is quite orthodox. Like virtually all of the mystics of the Christian tradition, the Sibyl's first direct experience of her god as indescribable peace is soon replaced by the dark ecstasy of apparent abandonment.

In the Sibyl's darkest hour, Lagerkvist transforms the "minor" character of the little servant into the vehicle for the author's boldest religious idea. The "divine," he believes, is a dimension of the human expressed whenever a person performs an act of pure compassion, a gift that the character God extends. This truly spiritual servant does not judge either the Sibyl or her assailants. He simply acts to save humanity from its own propensity for violence. Through the agency of this little nobody, the Pythia is brought into the sanctuary at the right moment and enjoys the most mysterious beauty in the novel.

Thus, from Genesis 1–3 and the story of *The Sybil*, we gain a glimpse into the mystery and a vision of the Divine, and through these stories, these myths, we are invited to dwell in Mystery, beauty, and wonder.

Wading Deeper on Your Own

Questions for Reflection and Discussion

1. What seem to be the author's assumptions: About the reader? About the world?
2. What do you remember most from this novel? What makes it memorable—the action, the characters, the style?
3. What unanswered question or paradox of your own experience does the myth explore, reverse, protest, reinvent?
4. What questions does the work raise about the nature of God? About nature itself including human nature?
5. What experience of God do you think the author is trying to communicate through the Sybil's son?
6. What experience of God are the biblical authors trying to convey through Genesis 1 and 2, and Genesis 3?
7. What new questions did the novel provoke in you?

Suggestions for Writing and Journaling

You may use published readings to enhance your own thoughts, provided you document your sources.

1. Lagerkvist's fiction is dominated by a paradox he has observed in the world around him: institutional religion is inadequate to satisfy the human need for God. Yet, the human need for "the holy" survives the inadequacies of religion. Write an essay commenting on this paradox with observations from your own experience of religion in the world in which you live and of your own experience of "the holy."
2. In the fatal romance between the Sybil and the one-armed man, Lagerkvist seems to protest the body and soul dualism of which religion has been accused. Write an essay correcting this distortion with a clarification of authentic Christian sexuality.
3. If you were to rewrite the creation story today, what would that story be? Write it from a contemporary perspective, ever mindful of the scientific knowledge we now possess that pertains to the cosmos, creation, and evolution.
4. Write a sequel to the story of Adam and Eve in Genesis 3. What is life like for them now that they are no longer in the garden? How are they now relating to God?

Irrigating Other Fields

The texts presented in this chapter will be of maximum benefit to you if you try to integrate what you have learned in this chapter and future chapters with material that you have read or studied, for example, the influence of myth-making in "secular" fields like history, politics, psychology, art, and science.

2
ARCHETYPAL AND HISTORICAL MYTH

The Suffering Servant

Isaiah 52:13–53:12; Matthew 26–27;
Mark 14–15; Luke 22:47–23:56

Silence

Shusaku Endo

Introduction

Contemporary biblical scholars who have studied the literary genres represented in the Bible observe that biblical characters and plot lines are closely related to what the twentieth-century psychologist Carl Jung called "archetypes," images and narrative patterns embedded deep in human consciousness. According to Jung:

> All the most powerful ideas in history go back to the archetypes. This is particularly true of religious ideas, but the central concepts of science, philosophy, and ethics are no exception. . . . For it is the function of consciousness not only to recognize and assimilate the external world through the . . . senses but to translate into visible reality the world within us.[1]

Jung popularized the term "archetype" to denote "a primordial image," the "psychic residue" of repeated patterns of experience in the lives of ancient peoples that survives in the "collective unconscious" of the human race. On the basis of his study of thousands of myths and dreams, Jung theorized that everyone is born with a collective memory, a databank of visual images that recur in the dreams, rituals, and literature of each new generation. This memory transcends time and space; hence archetypal images and narratives are familiar to people from all ages and on different continents and evoke a profound emotional response. Regardless of whether the literary critic accepts Jung's theory of how these images came to be in an author's mind, literary criticism routinely employs the term "archetype" to designate recurrent character types and narrative patterns in works of poetry, prose, and drama. "Archetype" should not be confused with the derogatory referent "stereotype."

An archetype refers to a recurring image or pattern representing universal elements of human experience. Archetypes take the form of a universal pattern in image or symbol, that is a mountaintop, a plot motif (such as a crime and punishment), and a character type (such as a jealous sibling). One archetype that has influenced contemporary literature is the suffering servant of Isaiah that later Gospel writers came to associate with Jesus. Whether or not Jesus himself identified with the suffering servant is speculative, but one thing is certain: his life experience, especially his passion and death, bear remarkable similarities to Isaiah's suffering servant image, and thus, through their passion narratives, the synoptic Gospel writers bring the archetype of the suffering servant to bear in the life of Jesus. The association of the suffering servant archetype with Jesus situates Jesus in the prophetic tradition and brings the prophetic tradition to deeper fulfillment through his life.

Among the archetypes that appear in the Bible are several variations that define the relationship of the hero to his people: the Hero as Savior, the Outcast as Hero, and the Suffering Servant. The lives of these heroes follow narrative patterns that recur in both the Hebrew and Christian scriptures: the Journey of the Hero, the Testing of the Hero, and the archetype of all archetypes, the Birth-Death and Resurrection of the Hero.

Drinking from the Spring
The Biblical Text
Isaiah 52:13–53:12

Perhaps one of the best known groups of poems and most frequently used texts for the Advent and Lenten liturgical seasons and readings are the servant songs from Isaiah.[2] The most familiar one of all is Isaiah 52:13–53:12, often called "The Song of the Suffering Servant." Among scholars, no consensus exists with respect to the identity of the servant, nor is the picture of the servant a homogeneous one throughout the songs.

The word, *'ebed*, "servant," is used extensively throughout the Hebrew Bible to refer to people who are at the service of another person, as in the cases of those who assist Pharaoh or a king such as David or Hezekiah. Oftentimes the servant has a relationship with the Divine, as in the case of Abraham, Isaac, and Jacob—the patriarchs—who were called "God's servants." The same holds true for Moses, the prophets, Job, and Israel (Jacob)—names representative of the Israelite community. This "servant" may refer to actual historical persons or a historical community. The "servant" could also be a literary construct.

In Isaiah 1–39, 40–55, and 56–66, the "servant" embraces all of the three aforementioned images. For example, in Isaiah 20:4, the servant is Isaiah, the one who walked naked and barefoot for three years as a sign against Egypt and Ethiopia. In Isaiah 22:20, the servant is Eliakim, son of Hilkiah. In Isaiah 41:8, 9; 43:10; 44:1–2, 21–26; 45:4; and 48:20, the servant is Israel (Jacob), and whether or not the reference is to an individual or the Israelite community is an issue of lively debate. In Isaiah 42:1–4, 18–19; 49:1–6; and 52:13–53:12, the servant is unnamed. This anonymity adds greater obscurity to the question of the servant's identification.

The servant songs as a whole present a picture of leadership, and one that speaks of a new vision and accompanying challenges, difficulties, and sometimes pain that is part of becoming the new leader and part of a new vision. They also offer a portrait of the fullness of life for all creation made possible through the effective exercise of justice and righteousness. Finally, the servant songs are an invitation to prophetic leadership, to become not only a leader who serves but a leader who is a "light." Having situated Isaiah 52:10–53:12 in the context of the Isaian servant songs, let us now take a closer look at the Suffering Servant Song.

"Surely He Has Born Our Infirmities . . ."

The Suffering Servant Song can be divided into four parts: (1) Isaiah 52:13–15, a divine speech; (2) Isaiah 53:1–6, a report; (3) Isaiah 53:7–11a, a divine reflection; and (4) Isaiah 53:11b–12, a divine speech. In each part, the character of God is the main speaker who communicates through the poet-prophet to teach a lesson by way of example (52:13–15; 53:11b–12) and reflection (53:1–11a). The lesson assures the righteous and sinners alike and all who are enduring the suffering of exile that there is hope, that God's vision is for all to be saved, and that both hope and salvation include a concern for social order.

Isaiah 52:13–15

The passage opens with a portrait of God's servant as described by God, who speaks through the poet. In verse 13, one hears that the servant will prosper and be exalted. The tone changes in verse 14, where the servant is presented as one who is both disfigured and repulsive. In verse 15, the tone shifts again. The servant who once astonished many by his terrible appearance will now startle nations and cause kings to shut their mouths in awe and respect.[3] Although the passage offers hope to a beleaguered exile community and sets the stage for what follows, this portion of the song reveals that the servant will prosper, but through humiliation.

Isaiah 53:1–6

The speaker of these verses is most likely an anonymous group ("we") that quotes a report about someone whom society has deemed repulsive who turns out to be God's servant (Isa. 52:13; 53:11). The report opens with two rhetorical questions (v. 1) that continue the awe-struck tone of

Isaiah 52:15. Although the identity of the "we" is obscure, it is possible that they are a group of Israelites living in exile, some of whom are the servant's opponents. Verses 2–6 describe the suffering of the repulsive one. Verse 2 describes the ordinary appearance of the servant before his suffering; verse 3 describes his pain as one despised, rejected by others, acquainted with infirmity, and held of no account. In verses 4–5, the speakers come to realize in retrospect why the servant has been suffering so severely. The suffering servant was not suffering because of his sins or because of divine chastisement, but because he was identifying with the sickness and pain of his people and the oppression that such infirmities bring. Verse 6 is a confession, using a simile to present the speakers acknowledging their waywardness and the suffering it has caused to the servant.

Isaiah 53:7–11a

These verses are a divine reflection. Here the poet portrays God as the speaker who recounts the suffering of the servant—the figure in the report heard earlier (Isa. 53:1–6). Images from the agrarian world—lamb, sheep—capture the innocence of the servant who remained silent in the midst of such undeserved suffering (v. 7). The poet then features God reflecting on God's own deeds to assure listeners that God had allowed such suffering as a means of restoration. In verses 10b–11a, God describes the rewards of the pain endured by the servant who did not deserve to suffer.

Isaiah 53:11b–12

In what is cast as a divine speech, the poet now has God continue the teaching about the servant which was begun in Isaiah 52:13 and 15. The servant is called "the righteous one"; the dishonorable one becomes the honorable one (cf. Isa. 49:7). One could argue that the Suffering Servant in Isaiah 52:13–53:12 is not a historical person but rather a literary construct meant to serve as a model of hope for the righteous ones of the exiled community of Second Isaiah (the second presumed author in Isaiah, who may have been a prophet who lived with the Jewish exiles during their captivity in Babylon). In this figure the community can see themselves, and for later readers of the text, the suffering servant continues to be a source of understanding and hope for those who choose to live out the divine vocation of a prophet.[4] Finally, the archetype of the suffering servant comes to life in the synoptic Gospel writers' portrayal of Jesus in the passion narratives.

Matthew 27; Mark 14–15; Luke 22:47–23:56

The life of Jesus as portrayed by the synoptic Gospel writers was a life centered in God, focused on the reign of God, and demonstrative of

God's great unconditional love for all people, all creation. Through their Gospel narratives, Matthew, Mark, and Luke each invite us into the life, ministry, and mission of Jesus as he journeys throughout Galilee and surrounding regions, preaching the good news of God's promise and gift of salvation, healing the sick, teaching the crowds about the cost of discipleship and the law of love, opening the eyes of the blind, challenging the religious and political leaders of his day, casting out demons, forgiving sins, and liberating people from whatever was binding them. Because of the work he was doing and because he was shaking up the status quo, the people of Jesus' day either welcomed him into their homes, their hearts, and their lives, or they sought ways to hurl him off the cliff (Lk. 4:29) in response to what he was teaching and preaching. Jesus' journey reaches its high point when he sets his face toward Jerusalem and walks the final road to his passion and death. Jesus' whole life, and indeed his final hours, shows us what it means to be like Isaiah's Suffering Servant, and is an archetype for all time.

The passion narrative as recorded by the synoptic Gospel writers can be outlined as follows:

The Plot to Kill Jesus (Matt. 26:1–5; Mk. 14:1–2; Lk. 22:1–2)
The Anointing at Bethany (Matt. 26:6–13; Mk. 14:3–9)
Judas' Agreement to Betray Jesus (Matt. 26:14–16; Mk. 14:10–11; Lk. 22:3–6)
Passover Celebration (Matt. 26:17–25; Mk. 14:12–21; Lk. 22:7–13)
Institution of the Last Supper (Matt. 26:26–30; Mk. 14:22–25; Lk. 22:14–23)
Dispute about Greatness (Lk. 22:24–30)
Peter's Denial Foretold (Matt. 26:32–35; Mk. 14:26–31)
Jesus' Prayer in the Garden (Matt. 26:36–46; Mk. 14:32–42; Lk. 22:39–46)
Betrayal and Arrest of Jesus (Matt. 26:47–56; Mk. 14:43–52; Lk. 22:47–53)
Jesus' Appearance before the High Priest (Matt. 26:57–68; Mk. 14:53–67; Lk. 22:66–71)
Peter's Denial of Jesus (Matt. 26:69–75; Mk. 14:66–72; Lk. 22:54–62)
Purse, Bag, and Sword (Lk. 22:35–38)
Jesus' Appearance before Pilate (Matt. 27:1–2; Mk. 15:1–5; Lk. 23:1–5)
Jesus' Appearance before Herod (Lk. 23:6–12)
Judas' Suicide (Matt. 27:3–10)

Interrogation of Jesus (Matt. 27:11–14)
Crowd's Choice: Barabbas or Jesus (Matt. 27:15–23; Mk. 15:6–15; Lk. 23:13–25)
Passion of Jesus (Matt. 27:24–31; Mk. 15:16–20; Lk. 22:63–65)
Crucifixion of Jesus (Matt. 27:32–44; Mk. 15:21–32; Lk. 23:26–43)
Death of Jesus (Matt. 27:45–56; Mk. 15:33–41; Lk. 23:44–49)
Burial of Jesus (Matt. 27:57–61; Mk. 15:42–47; Lk. 23:50–56)
Tomb Secured (Matt. 27:62–66)

For the most part, the Gospels of Matthew, Mark, and Luke all contain similar material that describes the passion of Jesus with the exception of a few additions or omissions that are unique to one or more of the Gospels.[5] The discussion that follows is a narrative reading of the story about the Passion with an eye toward how Jesus embraces the archetype of the Suffering Servant described in Isaiah 52:13–53:12. The three Gospel accounts are considered collectively and not individually.

The Passion Narrative opens with the plot to kill Jesus. In Matthew's Gospel, Jesus has foreknowledge of his impending death (Matt. 26:2). All three Gospels show that Jesus' death was premeditated by the religious leaders of Jesus' day (Matt. 26:3–4; Mk. 1; Lk. 22:2) Even though Jesus acknowledges that he knows he is about to be crucified, he tries neither to defend himself nor to verbalize any complaint against God or anyone else concerning his impending, conspired, planned death.

Both Matthew's and Mark's Gospels feature the story about the anointing at Bethany (Matt. 26:6–13; Mk. 14:3). With graciousness, Jesus receives the pouring of the woman's ointment on his body, which Jesus sees in Matthew's Gospel as a gesture that is done to prepare his body for burial. In the story, Jesus' attitude is one of openness and receptivity to the gift the woman offers him. Even though the anointing foreshadows Jesus' own burial, Jesus offers no resistance. He simply receives the gift of anointing as he continues to allow the events of his passion to unfold.

All three Gospels contain the story of Judas' agreement to betray Jesus (Matt. 26:14–31; Mk. 14:10–11; Lk. 22:3–6). Insidious is the fact that Judas, as the Gospel stories portray him, was supposedly a trusted friend of Jesus and one of the Twelve, who becomes Jesus' betrayer for a mere thirty pieces of silver.

The story of the Passover takes place in Matthew (26:17–25); Mark (14:12–21); and Luke (22:7–13). Matthew and Mark provide the details regarding the Passover meal while Luke presents only Jesus' instructions to his disciples concerning the preparations for the Passover. In Matthew's and Mark's version of the story, we see that Jesus is somewhat matter-of-fact in revealing to the disciples with him that he is going to be betrayed by one of his own among them. Jesus' statement causes distress among his disciples, but Jesus expresses no personal emotion. He continues to allow the events to unfold, events about which he appears to have intuitive knowledge and understanding from all that he has done in relation to his mission and ministry thus far.

What follows the story of the Passover is the story of what has come to be known as the Institution of the Lord's Supper (Matt. 26:26–30; Mk. 14:22–25; Lk. 22:14–23). Using symbols, Jesus explains what is about to happen to him very soon. The bread broken will be his body crucified; the wine poured out will be his blood spilled out during the flogging and the crucifixion itself. When Jesus invites his disciples to partake in the bread and the wine, he is inviting them to share in his death. For Jesus and for some of the disciples, this experience will be the result of the divine mission and ministry whose focus on justice for all may demand the highest price—the cost of one's life. In Matthew 26:28, the phrase "the blood of the covenant" refers to Exodus 24:8, where Moses seals the old covenant by sprinkling the Israelites with blood. The phrase "for many" suggests atonement, which in turn can be heard as an allusion to the atoning suffering of the Suffering Servant mentioned in Isaiah 53:12. The atoning value of Jesus' death is for the forgiveness of sins. The meal that Jesus shares with his disciples anticipates the eschatological banquet that will be spread out for all in the reign of God.

Even though Jesus' words are foreboding during this part of the meal, he once again expresses no emotion, unlike his disciples, who begin to question which one of them would do such a deed as betray Jesus (Lk. 22:23). Luke then has the disciples arguing among themselves as to who would be regarded as the greatest among them (Lk. 22:24–30). Jesus immediately squelches their debate by informing them that because they have stood by him in his trials, they will be given a kingdom, will have a place at Jesus' table at the eschatological banquet, and will sit on thrones in the reign of God, gifts that Jesus himself will confer on them (Lk. 22:28–30). Here we see that in Jesus' final hours of life, his focus is not on himself and what he is about to experience. He continues his ministry by focusing on others, providing them with words of comfort and promise.

All three synoptic Gospels record a story concerning Peter's denial (Matt. 26:31; Mk. 14:26–31; Lk. 22:31–34). Here Jesus tells Peter that he anticipates Peter denying knowing him when the events leading up to

Jesus' crucifixion begin to heat up. Peter states that he would never deny Jesus, but Jesus continues to tell him otherwise. Again, the exchange between Jesus and Peter is candid, but never once does Jesus either express any personal emotion about his impending death or upbraid Peter for what Peter is about to do very soon. Jesus simply allows the events to unfold. We are now given to wonder what Jesus must have felt in his heart, knowing that one of his own is about to betray him and another will deny him.

Luke follows the prediction of Peter's denial with another short text related to a purse, a bag, and a sword (Lk. 22:35–38). In this passage, Jesus gives his disciples a directive. Verse 37 is significant because it is a direct allusion to Isaiah's Suffering Servant Song (see Isa. 53:12). It seems, then, that Luke understands Jesus to be one like the suffering servant. Perhaps the actual Jesus, like the character Jesus in Luke's story, may have even understood this about himself, since he had the texts of the prophets available to him. Clearly Luke sees Jesus as fulfilling the archetype of the Suffering Servant, thereby bringing the prophetic texts to a deeper fulfillment.

Perhaps the most poignant story in the entire synoptic passion narratives is when Jesus prays in the Garden of Gethsemane on the Mount of Olives. For the first time, we see and hear the anguish of Jesus. We meet the face of one like the Suffering Servant. Luke conveys Jesus' anguish: "In his anguish he prayed more earnestly, and his sweat became like great drops of blood falling down on the ground" (Lk. 22:44). How Jesus would have loved for God to take away the cup that he is about to drink—the cup of death, but Jesus knows that he has to be faithful to his mission and ministry, he has to continue to move forward out of great love for his God and all God's people, and so after he utters his heartfelt words to his God, he gathers himself and he moves forward, heading toward Jerusalem and his own crucifixion. Surprisingly, God's voice is silent in the midst of all of Jesus' experiences thus far, and most noticeably in Jesus' prayer to God in the garden. The only divine response given is an angel who comes to strengthen Jesus (Lk. 22:43). The disciples, in Jesus' toughest hour before his death, are all sleeping. The burden of Jesus' impending death into which the disciples have been clued is borne by Jesus alone.

The next set of events brings the passion and death of Jesus closer to being realized. A large crowd with Judas arrives in the garden and there, Judas betrays Jesus just as Jesus had foretold earlier. One of his trusted disciples has now turned against him (Matt. 26:47–56; Mk. 14:43–52; Lk. 22:47–53). In another episode, a second trusted disciple—Peter—also turns against Jesus: he denies him just as Jesus had foretold earlier as well (Matt. 26:69–75).

Leading up to the story of Jesus' crucifixion is the story of Judas' suicide (Matt. 27:3–10) and then a series of stories that describe Jesus being interrogated by Pilate, the high priest, all the chief priests, the elders, the scribes, and, in the case of Luke's story, by Herod. In each of the various accounts, we encounter Jesus answering the questions posed to him in a way that show him to be confident, strong, self-controlled, and knowledgeable. He knows who he is; he knows what he has to do; he knows what is going to be done to him. He is straightforward in answering the religious leaders, despite some of their false testimonies, and he is even clever in some of his responses to his interrogators. Jesus stands his ground, allowing the events of his foreboding death to continue to unfold as he continues to move forward. The synoptic Gospel writers next record how Jesus is handed over to be crucified, how the Roman soldiers mock him, and finally, how he is sentenced to death by the people who demand the release of Barabbas instead of Jesus. Jesus stands before the condemning crowd and utters no word of condemnation in return, no word of judgment, no word of scorn. He simply allows himself to be handed over for crucifixion (Matt. 27:26; Mk. 15:15; Lk. 23:25).

All three synoptic Gospel writers present the story of Jesus' crucifixion (Matt. 27:32–44; Mk. 15:21–32; Lk. 23:26–43). Two thieves, one on either side of him, are crucified with him. Jesus is stripped of his clothes that are divided among his crucifiers, who cast lots for them. He is mocked and scorned, given hyssop to drink, and in the midst of this horrendous ordeal, Luke depicts Jesus making a plea to his God on behalf of all the people: "Father, forgive them; for they do not know what they are doing" (Lk. 16:34). In the midst of his horrible suffering, we hear and see Jesus still focused on others and caring for them until he reaches his bleakest moment when he is about to die. Only then do we hear these words from Mark: "'Eloi, Eloi, lema sabachthani?' which means 'My God, my God, why have you forsaken me?'" (Mk. 15:34). Finally, we hear the deep suffering of Jesus, to whom God offers no response. In the midst of such excruciating pain that grips Jesus' total person, God remains silent. Then in the final moment, Luke gives us a picture of Jesus who, in a loud voice, lets go in the face of God's silence and says, "Father, into your hands I commend my spirit" (Lk. 23:46). And then the innocent man nailed to a tree, the man who spent his entire life trying to reform legalistic, exclusionary laws while trying not only to educate people in the ways of God's love but also trying to free them from whatever was binding them, expires (Matt. 27:50; Mk. 15:37; Lk. 23:44).

Following Jesus' death, he is laid in a tomb that belonged to a righteous man named Joseph (Lk. 23:50–56), a respected member of the council (Mk. 15:42) who was wealthy (Matt. 27:57). The story of Jesus' passion and death closes with the body of Jesus laid in a tomb owned by someone other than Jesus or his family. Matthew tells us that on Pilate's orders, a guard of soldiers was sent to the tomb to make it as secure as possible, which meant that it was sealed with a stone (Matt. 28:62–66). Not until three days later when the Resurrection event takes place do we hear the voice of God, who acts on Jesus' behalf by raising him from the dead, whereby Jesus becomes the Word of God par excellence, the Word of everlasting life and eternal, compassionate, dynamic presence (Matt. 28:1–10; Mk. 16:1–11; Lk. 24:1–12).

In viewing Isaiah's Suffering Servant Song (52:13–53:12) in relation to the synoptic Gospel writers' accounts of Jesus' passion and death, we see how images of the Isaiah text find an echo in the Gospel narratives of Jesus' last days on earth. Jesus is the one who eventually is lifted up on high (cf. Isa. 52:13). He is the one whose appearance was marred during his passion that entailed being flogged, during his crowning with thorns, and of course during his crucifixion (cf. Isa. 52:14–15). Jesus was the one who appeared to be an ordinary person who wore no regal robes like David and who astonished many by his teachings (Lk. 4:16–30; cf. Isa. 53:1–2). He was despised and rejected by others, even from among his own disciples (cf. Isa. 53:3). He was the one wounded for the transgressions of others—he was an innocent man condemned and put to death by other human beings—who pleaded with God to forgive the people of this transgression and others because they did not know what they were doing (cf. Isa. 53:4–6).

His appearance before the Sanhedrin and other officials creates the impression of the lamb led to slaughter, and as noted in the text and this narrative study, he never once opened his mouth in complaint or condemnation (cf. Isa. 53:7). By a perversion of justice, he indeed was led away and cut off from the land of the living the minute the crowds shouted for the release of Barabbas instead of Jesus (cf. Isa. 53:8), and he was laid to rest in a borrowed tomb among the rich (cf. Isa. 53:9). Through Jesus' death, many are made righteous, for he has borne the iniquities of the unjust (cf. Isa. 53:11). He poured himself out to death, bore the sin of many, and made intercession for his transgressors (cf. Isa. 53:12). Thus, for the synoptic Gospel writers, Jesus embodies the archetype of the Suffering Servant, with one exception: according to Isaiah, it was the will of the Lord to crush the servant with pain (cf. Isa. 53:10). In the case of Jesus, he was crushed with pain as a consequence of the mission and ministry to which he gave his life—and that, ironically, cost him his life. God's will for Jesus was that Jesus live, and hence we have the mystery of the Resurrection, recorded by all four evangelists.

This focus on Isaiah's Suffering Servant Song and the synoptic writers' portrait of the passion and death of Jesus sets the stage for the discussion of Shusaku Endo's novel which now follows.

Playing in the Fountain
The Literary Text
Silence

Although many authors follow archetypes unconsciously, in Shusaku Endo's novel *Silence*, the protagonist deliberately patterns his entire life on Jesus Christ, whom he understands to be a "suffering servant."

About the Author
Shusaku Endo (1923–1996)

Born in Tokyo, Shusaku Endo began life surrounded by people of the Buddhist and Shinto religions. When he was only eleven years old, his mother converted to Roman Catholicism and a year later persuaded her son to be baptized. Endo did not feel at home in this religion chosen for him because, in a country where Christians comprised only 1 percent of the population, Catholics were regarded as outsiders. His schoolmates mistrusted him in much the same way that some American children in the twenty-first century mistrust their Muslim classmates. As a young Japanese adult, Endo likened his Catholicism to an arranged marriage. "He could not live with this arranged wife; he could not live without her. Meanwhile, she kept on loving him, and to his surprise, eventually he grew to love her in return."[6]

After World War II, Endo went to France to study the Catholic novelists he admired, but he endured racial prejudice, even from fellow Catholics. Returning to Japan, he discovered a museum in Nagasaki devoted to the Christian martyrs of the seventeenth century. Ironically, after almost two hundred years of fidelity to a minority and sometimes persecuted religion, the last remnants of a Catholic population had been destroyed by the atom bomb. In this museum, for the first time, the author saw a bronze, a wooden painting of Christ used by Japanese persecutors to persecute Christians (who would be told to deface it with their footprints). Endo became fascinated by these fellow "outsiders," and because of his own ambivalence toward religion, felt an instant kinship, not with those who had died heroically for their faith, but with those who had denied it. He determined to tell their story. Instinctively, Endo planned to model his protagonist on the archetype of "the outcast as hero."

In preparation for his literary task, Endo journeyed to Palestine to research the life of Jesus. There, as he joined pilgrims following the Way of the Cross, this Japanese Catholic who had never felt God's presence in a cathedral came face-to-face with a bedraggled and rejected Jesus Christ. The suffering servant presented by the prophet Isaiah offered to him the true face of Christianity. Endo became a genuine convert to Catholicism, and from then on the fictional narrative of a seventeenth-century Christian began to merge with his own spiritual biography.

Writing about "losers" and outsiders, Endo became one of Japan's most successful authors. At the same time, he enjoyed a career as a popular comedian and the star of his own television show. Although nominated often for the Nobel Prize, Endo was denied that ultimate honor by countrymen, especially Catholics, who misunderstood *Silence* and lobbied successfully to defeat his nomination.

Reflecting on Genre

Archetypal and Historical Myth

Silence is a masterful melding of religious myth and historical fact. Faithfully recorded in the letters and journals of European missionaries, in the oral histories of Japan's "hidden Christians," and in the documentation for the canonization of 188 Japanese martyrs as recently as November 24, 2008, the chronicle of Christianity in Japan attests that the most shocking details in this novel were not invented by the author.[7]

As the translator's prologue tells us, Saint Francis Xavier introduced the Japanese to Jesus Christ in 1549, and for over sixty years the number of Christians in that land grew. At the beginning of the seventeenth century, however, the shoguns expelled the Jesuits and launched an era of ruthless persecution. The repulsive methods of torture described in *Silence* were actually widespread. Many Christians died slow deaths hanging upside down over a pit of excrement. Ironically, the Shinto faith itself died a sudden death in Japan in 1945 when the startled people heard their emperor announce on the radio that he was not their god.

Father Cristovao Ferreira, the Portuguese missionary who mysteriously betrayed the faith, is a figure taken straight from the Jesuit annals of Japan. The novelist does not invent his mysterious apostasy. He does give a fictitious name to a priestly detective to track down the spiritual criminal and identify the motive for his crime. And here Endo's search for the truth merges with the psychological process of personal myth and the historical process of distorting it. Myths go through a historical process that resembles a photocopying machine with enlarging and reducing capabilities. The transformation of the "original myth" is usually a reduction into the image of the self or the culture.

The novel *Silence* is an appropriate text for our study of this process because it actually embodies the two opposite definitions of myth:

1. A story—either historically or symbolically true—involving the relations between God and humanity; a narrative having the power to control people's lives.
2. The same story that becomes essentially false when people believe it literally to the point that it controls them.

Father Sebastian Rodrigues is an outstanding example of both forms of myth: Jesus' story powerfully inspires a good person's behavior and leads him to living truth. On the one hand, Rodrigues' imitation of Christ is conscious and pervasive. He models his every move on the gospel narrative of Jesus Christ that he knows "by heart." He speaks to Jesus in prayer and hears Jesus respond. On the other hand, however, the cult of martyrdom for its own sake is in itself a false myth, a desire for heroism that eventually devolves into an image of God as a monster who demands and enjoys human sacrifice. Endo's novel embodies the insight that to relinquish martyrdom can be a greater sacrifice than to embrace it. In fact, Christian teaching, recognizing the subtle pride that can seduce an otherwise holy person, warns that a Christian must never actively seek martyrdom.[8]

Endo, a superb psychological novelist, renders in meticulous detail all the psychic anguish of a genuinely holy priest who sees this truth and acts on it, and then suffers from uncertainty about the purity of his motives. T. S. Eliot, another Christian writer, probed the same struggle in his play about the English martyr Thomas à Becket: "The last temptation is the greatest treason: to do the right thing for the wrong reason."[9]

Reflecting on Structure and Style

In this novel, the author's structure and style are inseparable. Endo divides his novel into ten chapters, with a Prologue and an Appendix. These chapters are subdivided into two distinct literary styles. First, in the Prologue and Chapters 7–9, he uses the prosaic, journalistic, third-person style of the historical narrative; second, in Chapters 2–5, he adopts the intimate, first-person style of letters and diaries. The style of the historical account is vivid, believable, and forceful. Chapter 10 and the Appendix—though they account for the discovery of the missionary's diaries—are anticlimactic and unnecessary. Although perhaps the author desired to provide a complete historical record, these addenda create the impression that, like an industrious graduate student, Endo wants credit for every word of his voluminous research. Unfortunately, from a literary perspective, the final pages simply undermine a great novel's dramatic conclusion.

The style of Rodrigues' letters, on the other hand, and even more of his diary entries, is poetic, evocative of his sensitive personality, and richly symbolic. Endo, for example, repeatedly draws attention to God's silence by contrasting it with sounds in nature: the roar of the sea, the chirping of birds, the rasping and droning of insects. Yet, with all the sensory detail that Rodrigues adds to the journalistic account, we can call his style economical, for the letters do double service as Endo's principal instrument of characterization.

Drawing from the Well
Theological Themes

Endo did not create the plots and subplots in his novel. Externally, he neither enhanced nor distorted the historical facts. Japanese history itself features all the main character types in *Silence*: heroic martyrs and compassionate apostates, as well as "Judases" who sold these heroes to their executioners. Endo's achievement is to use this local history creatively to explore several themes of universal significance. Although many themes dictate the structure of the novel, two significant themes are the plot of the two faces and the true face of Christianity.

As a Japanese writer, Endo had a unique appreciation for the significance of "face" with which he structures his narrative, around two parallel plot lines: the public ceremony of the trampling on the sacred face, and Rodrigues' prayerful communion with the face of Jesus. Although "face" is not mentioned in Isaiah's poem of the suffering servant specifically, the impression of "face" created by the poem's vivid descriptions is significant because this impression bears the suffering of the servant and, implicitly, the suffering of God and the people.

To appreciate how forcing a Christian to step on the face of Jesus could be more painful than physical torture, we need to place the *fumie* ceremony in its anthropological context. Concern for "face" is prominent in what anthropologists label "high-context cultures." Such cultures regard any act to be a "loss of face" which humiliates a person or a group. High-context cultures value the common good above individuality. In these societies (China, Japan, Korea, Egypt, Iran), sensitivity to honor and shame renders humiliation worse than death.

In this system of classification, America and other Western nations would be considered "low-context societies" because, in general, personal rights and the act of being true to oneself are valued more than the common good. Although the missionaries in *Silence* were European (low-context), they also belonged to the high-context society of Catholicism, in which protecting the honor of the group took priority over individual needs. This is evident in their motivation. "Their plan was to . . . atone for the apostasy of Ferreira which had so wounded the honor of the Church."[10]

Even today, both religious and political martyrs regard apostasy as a betrayal of something greater than themselves. Endo uses the recurring test of the *fumie* as an opportunity to dramatize the difference between true and false heroism and the impossibility of judging the invisible human motivation that distinguishes them. At the same time, he also uses the "face" theme to symbolize the way every culture creates a god in its own image. Ferreira explains that the god the Japanese worship has been transformed into someone who meets their standards.[11] Endo's insight about Japan is something he himself does not understand as a universal phenomenon. In fact, history shows that true Christianity is often muted beyond recognition when some Christians make God over into a superstar because they are embarrassed by values that make them outsiders.

Endo's most creative use of history in *Silence* is his appropriation of the concept of "face" in the recurrence of the captive missionary's obsession with the face of Jesus Christ. "I feel great love for that face," he says early in the novel, "like a man fascinated by the face of his beloved."[12] He repeats similar sentiments throughout the novel.[13] Through his private, personal communion with Jesus, whom Rodrigues understands as "the suffering servant," Rodrigues comes to see the true face of God. A person who has never read the New Testament could recreate the entire passion of Jesus from the pages of *Silence*. For someone familiar with the Gospels, this familiarity could prove redundant or tiresome. Endo's first audience, however, is non-Christian Japan. In his conversations with the Holy Face, Sebastian Rodrigues misses the fact that he, too, has been making God over into someone who answers his needs, and here the theme of the face segues into a parallel and even more universal theme, the silence of God, which is also an important theme in Isaiah 52:13–53:12 and the synoptic passion narratives.

Sebastian Rodrigues, like everyone else, needs a God who is not silent in the face of human suffering. "Behind the depressing silence of the sea, the silence of God . . . the feeling that while men raise their voices in anguish, God remains with folded arms, silent."[14] Artists of twentieth-century fiction, drama, and film, like Ingmar Bergman, Samuel Beckett, and Elie Wiesel, are obsessed with this theme. Unlike his contemporary authors, Endo's protagonist also needs to believe that his life is a faithful imitation of the face of Christ. He needs to rediscover a Christ who also experienced the silence of God as we have seen in the synoptic accounts of Jesus' passion and death. God's silence penetrates the consciousness of Sebastian Rodrigues repeatedly, but especially at moments when he turns from himself toward others.[15] Not until the final chapter does Rodrigues discover that he himself is God's eloquent answer, much like the suffering servant of Isaiah and the Jesus of the Gospels.

Wading Deeper on Your Own

Questions for Reflection and Discussion

1. Compare and contrast Isaiah's portrait of the suffering servant with Endo's portrait of this archetype. What lessons do both images teach us?
2. What are the similarities between the portrait of Isaiah's suffering servant and the synoptic Gospel writers' portrait of Jesus during his passion?
3. In *Silence*, why does Endo say: "The priest looks down at the face which he now meets for the first time since coming to this country"?
4. How do the final lines of the book involve the reader in the central question of the novel?
5. Which of Rodrigues' many questions do you find most relevant today?
6. In the conversation between Rodrigues and Inoue, Endo explores *xenophobia*—the fear and loathing of foreigners. During the years since this book was written, massive migrations from Africa, Asia, and Latin America have created multicultural societies in Europe and the United States. Is there still evidence of xenophobia in your community? In your life?

Suggestions for Writing and Journaling

1. "Christ did not die for the good and beautiful; the hard thing is to die for the miserable and corrupt." Using this statement from the novel as your theme, write an essay commenting on Christian life today. Be specific.
2. Choose a passage from one of Rodrigues' letters or diaries that you believe reveals both his strengths and weaknesses. Tell why you would or would not want to have him for a friend.
3. Choose one or more passages in Chapters 7–9 of *Silence* where you detect that the author has committed the crime of which

bad journalists are accused, that is, mixing his own opinions and feeling into the objective facts. Comment on how this adds to or detracts from the novel.

4. Looking at the archetype of the suffering servant in the Isaiah text and the passion narratives of the synoptic Gospels, write a description of the life of someone who embodies this archetype today.
5. What do these various texts explored in this chapter teach us about suffering today? Write your reflections.

Irrigating Other Fields

Those readers interested in the fields of history, political science, and psychology will find it enriching to apply insights from this chapter by making a list of the Jungian archetypes and considering each of the historical and political figures they encounter in light of them. Art majors will find it interesting to trace the influence of archetypal theory in the creation of "heroic" public art and sculpture—for example, in the nation's capitol.

3

PARABLE

Noah and the Flood

Genesis 6:5–8:22

The Parable of the Two Sons

Luke 15:11–32

"The Brother"

Robert Coover

Introduction

Before delving into this chapter, readers should carefully read the literary selection, "The Brother." This first experience of a twentieth-century parody of a biblical parable is important for three reasons:

1. The parable is a genre of the oral tradition.
2. This particular twentieth-century parody is written in an oral style that demands to be performed by a reader with excellent breath control.
3. Its impact depends upon the device of delaying recognition of the biblical narrative to which it alludes until it dawns slowly upon a live audience.

This chapter focuses on two familiar biblical narratives, one from the Hebrew Scriptures and one from the New Testament: the story of Noah and the Flood (Gen. 6:5–8:22) and the Parable of Two Sons (Lk. 15:11–32). Following the analysis of these two texts, focus shifts to the modern short story, "The Brother" by Robert Coover, to see how an author uses the stories of Noah and the Prodigal Son to challenge our commonplace definitions of righteousness.

Drinking from the Spring

The Biblical Text: Noah and the Flood

Genesis 6:5–8:22

A favorite story among children and adults alike is the story of Noah and a wondrous ark that houses his family members and pairs of all kinds of animals, securing them all against death from a catastrophic flood that God sends as a chastisement upon humankind because they have acted wickedly (see Gen. 3–6:4). Children's books have featured the story of Noah, banners have been made of Noah and the Ark, babies' rooms have Noah and the Ark décor, and TV movies have been made of the story.

The biblical flood story is a mythic narrative, the storyline of which bears the influences of other flood stories found in the ancient Near Eastern world and its literature. For example, the biblical flood story has some similarities to the flood narrative in the Babylonian Epic of Gilgamesh XI, the Sumerian flood narrative, and the flood narratives of Apollodorus and Ovid, among others, especially in the region of Mesopotamia.[1] While no one knows the precise author of the biblical flood story, the presumed sources have traditionally been called the Yahwist and the Priestly writer. Whether or not these so-named authors actually exist remains a debate among Pentateuch scholars.

On one level, the biblical flood story tries to explain the reason why great floods happen. Even though the story of Noah and the Flood is not a typical parable per se, the story can be read through the lens of the parable insofar as the narrative teaches an invaluable lesson about the importance of the virtue of righteousness. Because of Noah's righteousness, many human beings and nonhuman lives are saved from death. Finally, throughout the story, the biblical writers use the literary technique anthropomorphism which is the art of ascribing human qualities to God.

The Flood Story can be divided into five units:

6:5–8	Divine Motive for the Great Flood
6:9–22	Preparations for the Great Flood
7:1–24	The Great Flood
8:1–19	The Flood Subsides
8:20–22	A Divine Promise to Noah

Divine Motive for the Great Flood

Genesis 6:5–8

The story of Noah and the Flood opens with a statement as to why such a catastrophic disaster is about to befall the earth and all its inhabitants:

> The LORD saw that the wickedness of humankind was great in the earth, and that every inclination of the thoughts of their hearts was only evil continually. And the Lord was sorry that he had made humankind on the earth, and it grieved him to his heart. So the Lord said, "I will blot out from the earth the human beings I have created—people together with animals and creeping things and birds of the air, for I am sorry that I have made them." (6:5–7)

The people have become wicked because their hearts are inclined toward evil continually. In the ancient world, the "heart" was the central organ of intelligence. As the seat of intelligence, the heart understands, remembers, and considers things carefully. In biblical times, the heart was also used figuratively to refer to a person's inner life. The Hebrew word for "heart" is *leb*, and it appears in the Hebrew Scriptures approximately eight hundred times. The heart is also the center of one's relationship with God: it communicates with God, trusts in God, receives God's word, and helps one to follow God's ways.

Unfortunately, the people's hearts in the time of Noah were not in line with the heart and spirit of God and God's ways, which caused God great grief and paved the way for a great flood, a disaster that the ancient people interpreted as a form of divine chastisement. The story has a turning point, however, in Genesis 6:8: "But Noah found favor in the sight of the LORD."

Preparations for the Great Flood

Genesis 6:9–22

This next section opens with a brief genealogy of Noah's descendants and a further statement about Noah. Noah's sons are Shem, Ham, and Japheth. Noah, for his part, is "a righteous man, blameless in his generation" and he "walked with God" (Gen. 6:9–10). For the biblical people, righteousness was associated with justice and integrity. Those who were considered righteous had a relationship with God and walked in God's ways. The righteous ones were concerned for and safeguarded the common good. Noah's righteousness is about to serve him well.

In vv. 11–22, the biblical writers reiterate the corruptness of Earth, especially as it is seen in God's eyes, and now God communicates to Noah what the divine intention is in order to deal with such corruption (vv. 11, 12). God gives Noah specific instructions on how to build the ark (vv. 13–17), and informs him of the divine intention to establish a covenant with Noah (v. 18); God then tells him who is to board the ark (vv. 19–21). Noah does all that God commands him to do (v. 22).

The Great Flood

Genesis 7:1–24

The Great Flood takes place in Genesis 7:1–24. Here we hear a second version of God's command in Genesis 7:1–4, and again, we are told that Noah does exactly as God commands him to do (Gen. 7:5–9). After a week of building and preparing, Noah is ready for the rains to come and flood the earth. The windows of the heavens open up and pour water upon the earth for forty days and forty nights. All told, the waters swell on the Earth for 150 days, and only Noah and those in the ark with him survive (Gen. 7:11–24).

The Flood Subsides
Genesis 8:1–19

After devastating the entire Earth, the Great Flood recedes. The recession of the waters begins when, according to the story, God "remembers" Noah and all the animals and all that is with him in the ark (v. 1). In the ancient biblical world, to be remembered by God is to be favored by God. God makes a wind[2] blow over the earth and the waters subside; the fountains of the deep and the windows of the heavens are closed. Gradually, the waters abate in the course of time, and after Noah sends out a raven and then a dove, the dove returns to him with a freshly plucked olive branch in its beak, a signal that the face of the ground is finally drying and soon dries completely (vv. 6–14). God then commands Noah to have everyone leave the ark, and so all the families of the earth begin their trek out of the ark to resettle on dry land once again (vv. 18–19).

A Divine Promise to Noah
Genesis 8:20–22

The Flood Story ends with Noah offering a thanksgiving sacrifice to God that not only appeals to God's senses but also evokes a promise from God:

> I will never again curse the ground because of humankind, for the inclination of the human heart is evil from youth; nor will I ever again destroy every living creature as I have done.
>
> As long as the earth endures,
> seedtime and harvest, cold and heat,
> summer and winter, day and night,
> shall not cease.

The next part of the text features God entering into covenant with Noah and all creation, thus solidifying for all time the divine promise made with all life (see Gen. 9:1ff.).[3]

Noah and the Flood, as presented by the ancient biblical writers, is an imaginative story that showcases the human condition and God's frustration and love for all that has been created, while teaching the lesson that sin has consequences and righteousness has rewards. A similar theme is picked up in the story of the Parable of the Two Sons in Luke 15:11–32.

The Biblical Text: The Parable of the Two Sons
Luke 15:11–32

Only found in the Gospel of Luke, the Parable of the Two Sons (often referred to as The Parable of the Prodigal Son and His Brother) is one of Luke's most famous, and one that is often used by teachers and preachers to teach a lesson about righteousness and reconciliation. This parable is part of a series of three about finding something that has been lost. The other two in the trilogy are the Parable of the Lost Sheep (Lk. 15:1–7) and the Parable of the Lost Coin (Lk. 15:8–10). The latter of these two parables is also only found in the Gospel of Luke. Together these three parables teach lessons about righteousness and reconciliation. In the context of Luke's Gospel, they respond to those who question Jesus' table companions (Lk. 15:1–2) and serve as an invitation to the Pharisees and legal experts to join in the celebration at the table with the lost ones who have been restored. Both the Pharisees and legal experts had formerly expressed indignation at such a celebration, but now they are being given a second chance to respond positively.

The parable in Luke 15 can be divided into four units:

vv. 11–12: Division of Property
vv. 13–20a: Plight of the Younger Son
vv. 20b–24: Encounter between Father and Younger Son
vv. 25–32: Exchange between the Father and Older Son

This Lukan parable is a celebration of love extended to those family members who have fallen by the wayside and are welcomed back into the family. Through this parable, Luke has Jesus making an indirect statement about his own ministry, namely, that he has come to seek out and bring back the lost, especially sinners.

Division of Property
Luke 15:11–12

Luke opens his narrative with Jesus telling the Pharisees and the tax collectors a parable. The characters in the parable are a father and his older and younger sons. The younger son's request sets the action of the parable in motion: "Father, give me the share of the property that will belong to me" (v. 12). The father obliges the younger son, and the story unfolds as follows.

Plight of the Younger Son
Luke 15:13–20a

Having received his portion of the property, the younger son sets out for a distant country and squanders his portion in dissolute living. He finds himself in need when a famine strikes the land. In order to survive, he hires himself out and experiences hard times in the fields where he is working. He finds that people are not generous in their treatment toward him, and he begins to reflect on how gracious his father has been to his hired hands. Such reflection initiates a change of heart on the part of this younger son, to the point that he decides to return home with the plan that he will confess his sin to his father and offer to be considered one of his father's hired hands instead of his son.

Thus far, we see that the younger son has had an experience of pain and suffering that is the direct result of his own poor choices and decisions. This pain and suffering, however, lead him to be remorseful and to take responsibility for himself and his actions. His sin is that he has broken trust with his father, a sin for which he plans to atone. So the younger son then sets out to go back to his father.

Encounter between Father and Younger Son

Luke 15:20b–24

What follows next in the parable is an example of great compassionate love. The father sees his son at a distance, runs to him, puts his arms around him, and kisses him. Such a welcoming greeting makes the task of confessing his sin and taking responsibility for his actions easier for the younger son. The son confesses; the father does not give a second thought to what he has said. Instead, the father dresses him in fine clothes and commences a celebration in his younger son's honor. The change in clothes is the father's way of recognizing the change of heart that his younger son has had. The father is jubilant that his "lost" son has now been "found." The younger son's choice to act righteously before his father—to confess and take responsibility for his actions—led to forgiveness and reconciliation without any formal word of forgiveness being spoken. The celebration outweighs any verbal exchange; the father restores his younger son to the family and to the family table.

Exchange between Father and Older Son

Luke 15:25–32

Such a joyous celebration for his wayward younger brother sparks a sharp reaction from the older son. Hearing about the return of his brother, and presumably knowing what his younger brother had done and now seeing the celebration happening, the older brother refuses to enter the house to join in the celebration. The father pleads with his older son to have a change of heart, to which the older son responds with even greater vehemence:

> Listen! For all these years I have been working like a slave for you, and I have never disobeyed your command; yet you have never given me even a young goat so that I might celebrate with my friends. But when this son of yours came back, who has devoured your property with prostitutes, you killed the fatted calf for him!

With compassion, the father reminds the older son that all that the father possesses belongs to the older son, and then the father tries to explain his decision regarding the younger; namely, that it was imperative to have a celebration for his younger brother who was considered "dead" but now is alive again, and what was considered "lost" is now "found." Thus, the father has acted righteously and compassionately toward both sons, but the decision to act accordingly toward his younger brother and to join in the celebration remains with the older brother. Luke does not tell us what the older brother decides to do. Luke leaves us pondering the story. And so it is with Jesus who seeks out and waits to welcome the return of the lost into the reign of God, where a place at the table has been set for a celebration, a celebration to which all are invited. The parable invites us to a new understanding of righteousness that goes beyond fidelity. This new righteousness calls us to reach out to the lost, to the one trying to find his or her way back to right relationship, to reach out to that person even before that person reaches out to us, and to welcome that person back into our lives with hospitality and compassion. Such is the welcome God extends to all; such is the welcome that Luke and Jesus challenged people to live out among themselves then and even now.[4]

Strains of the stories of Noah and the Flood and of the Parable of the Two Sons can be heard in the short story entitled "The Brother" by Robert Coover, who weaves the threads of the two biblical stories into his own story to create a new story that speaks to our own lives and hearts today.

Playing in the Fountain

The Literary Text

The Brother

About the Author

Robert Coover (1932–present)

Born in 1932 in Iowa, Robert Lowell Coover grew up in Illinois, studied at Southern Illinois University, and graduated from Indiana University with a degree in Slavonic languages. He was raised in the United Church of Christ, with which he remains loosely affiliated, although he now describes himself as "a Unitarian Universalist for whom Jesus is not an active presence."[5]

After divorce separated Coover from his church, as well as his family, the writer became spiritually "homeless." The playfulness and flippancy with which he masks a serious theme in his parodies on Scripture is evident in this lyric he composed to describe his ongoing quest for an authentic spirituality:

> I don't want no white bread Jesus
> He's too bland for me.
> I'm lookin' for a whole grain Jesus.[6]

Although the modern short story now includes a multiplicity of forms and "experiments," few of which communicate any clearly defined moral lesson, Robert Coover is one writer who has frequently written successful fiction inspired by biblical characters and stories that do communicate to the reader's conscience. Among these works, some can be usefully compared to the parable. As one of the earliest and most respected artists in an iconoclastic movement known as postmodernism, Coover offers deliberately secular versions of these familiar stories. Much postmodern art attempts to undermine the foundations of "conventional wisdom" and popular cultural values to expose their emptiness. One could argue that Jesus' parables did the same thing.

Since his first prize-winning novel, *The Origin of the Brunists* (1966), Coover has steadily published novels and literary criticism that have earned him critical acclaim as a truly original voice in American letters. Many of the literary "tricks" that twenty-first-century novelists continue to call "experimental" were introduced as early as the fifties by Robert Coover. Even readers unfamiliar with postmodernism, however, are likely to be entertained by one or more of his idiosyncratic parodies on fairy tales and other folk genres, even populist history. Coover's inventive style features some "alienation" devices.[7]

Coover's career successfully combines the profession of writer with that of university professor. Since 1981, he has been writer-in-residence at Brown University, where one student characterized his style in both professions as "sinister vaudeville."

Reflecting on Genre
The Parable

One of the goals of this text is to demonstrate how the understanding of a literary form in which a biblical text is written assists our interpretation of the Bible by liberating us from the stranglehold of an unsustainable literalism. Often the literary insight that demolishes a story as history can simultaneously strengthen faith in its deeper significance as religious truth. A close look at the biblical genre of parable exemplifies this process.

Parables have two distinct qualities: realism and symbolism. Parables portray life as we live it in the real world. They capture the mundane events of everyday life such as sowing seeds, harvesting crops, cleaning the house, extending wedding invitations, searching for lost items or animals that we cherish, baking bread, lighting lamps, and so forth. The main characters in parables are ordinary people: farmers, bakers, housekeepers, fathers, sons, wives, daughters, herders, widows, merchants, and peasants, among others. Thus, parables are concerned with concrete and tangible situations rooted in real life.

Besides being rooted in realism, parables have a symbolic quality. They function on the symbolic or allegorical level of meaning. Some of the images presented in the biblical parables already possessed well-known symbolic meanings such as the "seed" as the "word of God," the owner of a vineyard as God, and the feast as emblematic of the future eschatological banquet, among other examples.

Simply defined, a parable is a short narrative with two levels of meaning. On its first level, the fictional plot engages the reader or listener's curiosity; then, immediately below the surface, a universal moral or psychological truth challenges the reader or listener's conscience. In the fictional mirror we see more clearly a specific spiritual, theological, historical, or ethical reality of concern hidden in a commonplace situation. Often this is a reality we are inclined to ignore at our peril. Parables, then, reflect "an ancient, culturally universal method of teaching an ethical lesson applicable to everyday life, by using symbolic stories with concrete characters and actions."[8] Hence, the Hebrew term usually translated as parable means "any dark saying intended to stimulate thought."

Like myths, most of the short stories within the longer stories in the Hebrew Scriptures survive as literature even in a culture which ignores or abandons their spiritual or moral truth. At the time these stories originated, people recognized the storyteller's use of the parable as a pedagogical tool. So popular was this device in ancient times that some contemporary biblical scholars do not hesitate to interpret all biblical narratives, even those with a foundation in fact, as essentially parables. Reading the Bible centuries after its original audience, some contemporary readers are still inclined to interpret these literary works as literal history. Educated readers avoid this error by focusing on the deeper truths clothed in compelling fiction.

One element common to all parables is the fact that they adhere to the rules of storytelling. As stories, parables have a beginning, a middle, and an end, as in the case of Mark 4:2–9. Sometimes parables include brief images (Mk. 13:28), aphorisms (Mk. 7:15–17), and traditional proverbs (Lk. 4:23). Sometimes, the parable comes as a story within a story as, for example, when a respected character or prophet gives the people ethical instruction in the form of a narrative. At other times, as in the case of the legendary adventure of Jonah and the whale, a patently fictional tale is woven about a character who may have credible historical roots. The story of Nathan and David (2 Sam. 12:1–15) is a good example of a fictional embroidery on a real canvas. The anecdote involves two historical characters, King David and the prophet Nathan.

King David's greatest sin was to send a man named Uriah to certain death so that the king could legitimately possess the dead man's wife, Bathsheba. Nathan tells King David a little story about a rich man who kills a poor man's favorite lamb. David is so incensed against the rich villain that he condemns him to death. Only then does the prophet point out to the king that the wicked deed in the story is fiction, but the real crime is David's own adultery. The fact that Nathan offers an immediate explanation distinguishes how Old Testament prophets usually explained a parable from how Jesus used parables. In the Gospels, we see that Jesus prefers to deny his audience an immediate homily, thus provoking them to ponder over an interpretation for themselves or their society. Jesus' strategy is so consistent that if he deviates from it, some contemporary scholars suspect that in these rare exceptions, the Gospel authors of the early church probably invented Jesus' explanations themselves.[9]

Parables are more commonly used in the New Testament than in the Old Testament. Fully one-third of the synoptic Gospels are in the form of parables. Old Testament commentators suggest that some New Testament stories are actually a midrash on a familiar story from the Jewish tradition. *Midrash* is the Hebrew term for an explanation of a scripture, often in story form.[10] Biblical scholars are careful to warn against assigning each character and figure in a parable a single symbolic equivalent—as in allegory. Jesus does this only once (Mk. 4:1–9). According to Amos Wilder, "in its Semitic background, the category *parable* is wide enough to include both anecdote and riddle."[11] Having said that a parable might even be a riddle, however, Wilder adds this: "Although Jesus clearly intended to startle and disorient his audience, he did not intend his message to be hidden so deep that it needs to be laboriously decoded."[12] Ideally, then, each parable can be described as a "language event" designed to challenge the hearer to a conversion of values and lifestyle. Finally, parables can also instruct and console a community as in the case of the Potter and the Wheel in Jeremiah 18:1–6 and the story of the baskets of good and bad figs in Jeremiah 24:1–10. Two biblical stories that could be considered parables are Genesis 6–9, Noah and the Flood, and Luke 15:11–32, The Parable of the Two Sons. Both of these stories influenced Robert Coover in his writing of the literary short story entitled "The Brother," which could be considered a "parable."[13]

In twentieth- and twenty-first-century literature, the genre that most often imitates the biblical parable is the short story. This is so not just because it is short, but because it is so tightly constructed to support a single effect. In this respect, Coover, whose stylistic preference favors deviation from other literary traditions, has here chosen to strive for the ideal recommended by Edgar Allan Poe (1809–1849). Poe published a definition of the ideal short story that guided writers of fiction for a century. This master of short fiction identifies the following essentials in the ideal short story:

- The author constructs and combines setting, characters, episodes, and events to create a single "effect."
- He or she deliberately controls these elements by selecting imagery and vocabulary with a "tone" that contributes to the designed effect.
- This method dictates an economy, for "there should be no word written of which the tendency . . . is not to the pre-established design."[14]

Not every short story is intended to be a parable. In fact, in an age that has abandoned moral clarity, critics sometimes deride an author's clarity of moral purpose. When, however, the unified "effect" so admired by Poe is moral, ethical, philosophical, or spiritual, most literary critics analyze the work as a parable. Despite deliberate aberrations and distortions by authors in the years since World War II, Poe's ideal is evident in the literary characteristics identified in the biblical parable and in its modern counterpart.

Reflecting on Literary Style and Structure

- Biblical parables lack all the color, action, and special effects of a successful page-turner, yet millions of people read them daily in every known language. Hence, Coover's short story carefully imitates the following characteristics of the parable.

- Little or no physical description of the setting or the characters exists. With rare exceptions, the figures in a parable have neither faces, costumes, nor other distinguishing features. A police sketch artist would not be able to produce a useful likeness of either Noah or the Prodigal Son, nor would an eyewitness recognize either suspect in a "lineup." Hence, each character resembles not someone, but everyone. Coover's story deviates from this ideal somewhat because, as narrator, the brother reveals more about himself than a biblical storyteller would. Furthermore, Coover's choice of a first person point of view contributes an emotional intensity to the story of the flood that is absent from the Genesis account.

- A short story is structured in two or three movements. Each movement presents a situation that requires a personal decision (explicit or implicit). In the Parable of the Two Sons, for example, each of the three characters makes three crucial decisions. The younger son decides to leave home; to squander his inheritance; to return home. The father decides to give him the money; to forgive him; to celebrate his return. The elder son chooses to remain a faithful and undemanding son; to resent his brother's behavior and his father's generosity; to refuse to go to the party. The effect of this parable hinges on an audience's ability—or willingness—to recognize itself, not in the misbehavior of the younger son, but in the way the other two characters in the family treat him. The audience is subtly instructed to emulate the father, or at least to feel guilty if they do not. Robert Coover's short story structure contains no explicit decision making. In fact, however, the narrator is reacting throughout to decisions made by others before the story begins—decisions and consequences he is powerless to change. Nevertheless, it is a drastic choice on God's part that sets the whole plot in motion.

- Vital information is withheld or ambiguous.

- Motivations are left unexplained, questions unanswered. In Genesis, Noah is clearly motivated by obedience to a God in whose superior knowledge and wisdom he trusts. Coover's story never mentions God. He implies, however, that the author of the flood chooses to leave no one alive except a man capable of abandoning his brother's family to death by drowning. The author's intention is obviously to provoke a questioning of God's goodness, as well as Noah's. Did Noah know that one of those left behind was his brother? Aren't we all related? Considering God's action in the story of the flood can we really be expected to believe that?

- The cumulative effect is deliberately shocking. Both stories feature extremes, one of evil and the other of love. The ruthlessness and self-centeredness of Noah in Coover's story contrasts with the loving excesses of the prodigal and his father in the parable. Coover adds emotional shock by introducing a pregnant wife as a victim of the flood. In the parable, the storyteller "piles it on," appearing almost to dare the father's limits. The sinful son doesn't just waste his dad's money; he spends it on "harlots." Against all common sense, the father retaliates with equal "prodigality." He doesn't just forgive the son, he throws an extravagant party for him. In both the biblical and the modern parables, the storyteller deliberately violates conventional expectations.

A classic parable moves from the ordinary to the extraordinary. The author begins with a familiar situation and then introduces an element of surprise. Even readers unfamiliar with the Bible will recognize the story of Noah, because the ark and its passengers have entered popular culture (through, among other avenues, the toy store). The figure of Noah himself, however, becomes shockingly unfamiliar as he morphs into a villain. Literary analysts call drawing attention to a character or situation by reversing values in this way, "inversion." In the calloused behavior of Noah, Coover dramatizes his idea that a competitive economy can create a system where "good guys finish last," and the survival of the average person will eventually provoke the perversion of virtue.

Postmodern writers delight in another surprising reversal: the perversion of "literary" language itself. Coover freely acknowledges as his literary "father" the Nobel laureate Samuel Beckett, whose novels feature the unpunctuated run-on sentences of the narrative technique known as "stream of consciousness."[15] The voice in "The Brother" clearly represents the outpouring of an angry, distraught person's mind. Another name for stream of consciousness is "interior monologue." Since there is no one else alive to hear him, the brother must be talking to himself. He is not speaking but thinking these unspeakable thoughts, and the elimination of punctuation adds to the sense that all inhibition has been removed. The brother's stream of consciousness represents the unheard protest of all victims of a ruthless amoral economy that rewards greed and self-interest. Everything in the irreverent style and tone of "The Brother" contributes to the theme. Blasphemy is the ultimate critique of pseudo piety.

Drawing from the Well
Theological Themes

What does Robert Coover do with the story of Noah and the Flood and the Parable of the Two Sons? The biblical story is told from the perspective of Noah; Coover tells it from the perspective of the brother left behind in the flood. "The Brother," though modeled on biblical parables, has a different focus and theological message. Coover adopts the biblical literary device of midrash by inventing a story to interpret a story. By employing this method, Coover challenges us to hear stories, especially biblical ones, from a variety of perspectives, and especially from the perspective of the disenfranchised.

In the Old Testament story, Noah leaves no brother behind. Coover invents an abandoned brother and makes him the narrator. This choice on Coover's part allows us to view Noah's escape from a contrasting point of view: this flood's innocent victim. Furthermore, in postmodern fiction, there are no heroes. Rather, the protagonist or the narrator (or both) is likely to be an anti-hero. Hence, Coover refuses to applaud Noah as "the just man" favored by God. By telling the story of the flood from the perspective of the brother left behind, Coover transforms Noah into a character more familiar to us as the CEO of a failing bank or corporation. A twenty-first-century audience will recall more than one celebrated case of a person who saved his own skin and left others to drown.

Placing the story in the left-behind brother's voice also deepens the contrast by a subtle allusion to the New Testament Parable of the Two Sons. In this way, Coover has cleverly inverted Jesus' parable to make it a critical New Testament midrash on the Noah legend. The dominant theological theme of both stories then becomes a critique of human relationships as they mirror humanity's primary relationship with God, metaphorically portrayed as "father."

Of all Jesus' fictive surrogates for God, the most appealing father figure appears in the Parable of the Two Sons. The story offers an obvious example of both a forgiving God's ideal relationship with sinners and our flawed relationships with God and with each other. Moreover, though it has a joyful ending for one son, the parable can be described as an "unjust saying" since it implicitly condemns the "good" son and leaves him miserably resentful. The story's ending stimulates a thoughtful redefinition of genuine goodness or godliness.

In Genesis, once Noah has obeyed God's command, everything is in divine hands. In "The Brother," Robert Coover reinterprets the Old Testament legend with more emphasis on human relationships and human responsibility. Coover implies a different and more complex foundation for human morality. His version of the story reflects the postmodern oxymoron of a secular theology. Furthermore, Coover suggests that the ones in need of conversion are most likely to be those who think of themselves as good and, therefore, as entitled to divine favor and attention. In this respect, we can say that the author anticipates a twenty-first-century critique of the ultra-patriotic conceit known as "American exceptionalism."

Conventional American morality implies a connection between virtue and prosperity. As a "virtue," American individualism tends to separate private from public moral responsibility. Coover was ahead of his time in emphasizing that the two cannot be separated. For example, "The Brother" implies the ethical question: "Considering the ecological impact of the flood, how private is personal morality?" "The Brother" presents an unsettling version of the story, which also stimulates theological questions like "Whose side is God on?" "Who is really good?" In this respect, Coover is here imitating the practice of Jesus, who never lost an opportunity to align himself with outcasts and to challenge the authenticity of those his society considered virtuous.

In retelling the Jewish legend of Noah, Coover stands on its head the traditional belief in God's protection of the righteous. By doing so, he is reviving the practice of his biblical mentors and masters. Throughout her multivolume study, New Testament scholar Barbara Reid stresses how this deceptively simple literary form is designed to challenge and disturb its audience with a message that subverts the complacency of those who consider themselves morally superior to others.[16] In both Jesus' Parable of the Two Sons and Coover's retelling of Noah and the Flood, the endings force a thoughtful audience to redefine genuine goodness or godliness. A parable has succeeded when we recognize the hero—or more likely, the villain—in ourselves.

Wading Deeper on Your Own

Questions for Reflection and Discussion

1. What seem to be the author's assumptions about the audience for: (a) Genesis 6–9 and (b) "The Brother"?
2. What were your assumptions about the story of Noah before you opened this chapter? Have any assumptions changed?
3. How much of the story of Noah and the Flood is true? On what kind of evidence is your answer based? How much of this evidence was available to the author(s) of Genesis? Why does it matter?
4. Cite an event during your lifetime which provoked the question: "Whose side is God on?"

5. In the Parable of the Two Sons, the figure representing God as the father forgives all the younger son's sins. Why didn't God forgive the sinners in Genesis at the time of the flood?
6. In both biblical parables, the moral lesson is clear. In the twentieth-century parable, "The Brother," the theme is more ambiguous. How do the literary choices of the author contribute to that ambiguity?
7. Is "The Brother" a Christian or an anti-Christian parable?
8. Which of the selections explored in this chapter did you find yourself thinking about more deeply? Why?

Suggestions for Writing and Journaling

1. From a recent edition of the newspaper or other current events medium, choose an account of a situation that seems related to one of the parables considered in this chapter. In an essay, summarize the article and then compare and contrast it with one of the parables from both theological and literary points of view.
2. Write a short original parable in which you create a protagonist who responds differently to a natural or "human-made" disaster.
3. Rewrite Genesis 7:1–24 as told by Noah in the first person.
4. Rewrite the Parable of the Two Sons as told by the mother or the elder son.
5. Twenty-first-century moral theology stresses human responsibility more than divine design and control. Write an essay commenting on the selections in this chapter as they either exemplify or challenge this emphasis.

Irrigating Other Fields

Biblical parables, by questioning conventional values, maintain an ongoing dialogue with human culture. Give some thought to the three stories in this chapter as critiques on the dominant values in family, in educational systems, in work professions, and in different societies and cultures.

4
DRAMATIC POETRY
The Book of Job
Job 1:1–42:6
J.B.
Archibald MacLeish
The Trial of God
Elie Wiesel

Introduction

The Book of Job has inspired more literary works than any other text in the Old Testament. From classical to modern times, secular authors have interpreted and reinterpreted Job's story, meditating on its themes in works that reach across all genres—novels, poems, plays, screenplays, and even a graphic novel. Apparently, the ancient scriptural drama of this man's feisty confrontation with God resonates across the ages with the spiritual lives of many writers who would agree with Matthew Fox that "Art, not theology, is the proper language for uttering our God experience and our absence of God experience."[1]

Writers have long acknowledged that writing fiction in the form of a novel or a play has been for them a way to search for meaning and to explore unanswered questions. Classical literature of the past often strove to make positive statements in response to these questions. Literary classics since the twentieth century tend to keep those questions alive—and hurting. The ancient biblical Book of Job makes clear that unanswerable theological questions did not originate among atheists in recent intellectual history; rather, such questions have tormented people of faith in all ages. Biblical scholars today often suggest that the biblical authors themselves were exploring questions rather than recording divinely-inspired answers. Although many good people have tried not to ponder the incomprehensible dimension of God's silence and the futility of all human efforts to dispel it, events in the twentieth and twenty-first centuries, in particular, have forced such questions to the forefront of human consciousness.

Of all literary genres, the one exceptionally appropriate to conflict is drama. American playwright Arthur Miller has remarked that every time a curtain goes up onstage, a trial begins. In the Book of Job, the little "satan" puts a good man on trial. In two modern plays based on the biblical story of Job, poet Archibald MacLeish and Holocaust survivor

Elie Wiesel dare to put the Creator of the universe on trial. In reality, however, what the audience witnesses in all three dramas is the trial of humanity's idea of God and the way it has been and continues to be manipulated to remake the deity in the image of humanity's values.

The mass extermination of the Jewish people by the Nazi government provoked a twentieth-century challenge to the popular idea of a benign and all-powerful God. As the supreme crisis of a people's belief in a loving God, the Holocaust has inspired numerous creative adaptations in which the historic testing of the Jewish people's faith serves as a vivid symbol for the perennial battle between faith and reason. Commenting on his own version of the Job story, Archibald MacLeish has said: "I intend no trespass on sacred territory. When you are dealing with questions too large for you, which nevertheless will not leave you alone, you are obliged to house them somewhere."[2]

Archibald MacLeish staged *J.B.* in 1958, a decade after World War II. Elie Wiesel did not publish *The Trial of God* until 1979, thirty-six years after, at the age of fifteen, he had actually witnessed the trial of God acted out by fellow prisoners in Auschwitz. In the first section of this chapter, we will go through the Book of Job to see its theological themes, and then compare and contrast all three works in relation to their dramatic genre, theatrical features, literary styles, and theological themes.

Drinking from the Spring
The Biblical Text
The Book of Job

Why do innocent people suffer? Why do the just and righteous experience misfortune at the hands of others? These two compelling questions are at the heart of the story of Job, a text that is part of Israel's ancient wisdom tradition and literature. The story of Job testifies to excruciating pain, makes a plea for justice, and offers a lively and heartfelt debate about the experience and causes of suffering. As part of Israel's wisdom tradition, the Book of Job has a rich historical, social, cultural, religious, and theological context. As a work of literature, the book's use of irony leads to surprise after surprise and evokes many human emotions such as pity, compassion, anger, frustration, and awe as the dialogues among the book's characters reach deep down into the experience of what being human really means in the midst of fear, doubt, adversity, and tragedy.

Historically, no one knows for certain when the Book of Job was written, though the general tendency is to date it sometime during early post-exilic times when, under King Cyrus, the Persians ruled Israel.

During the Persian period, the Jews (as the people of Israel were now called) experienced a number of hardships. New taxations caused economic difficulties. These taxations forced some Jews to go into debt and to mortgage their property so that they could meet their financial obligations. The Jews were also subject to the exploitation of large landowners, some of whom included people from their own group. Furthermore, some of the wealthy Jews who loaned money to their own people charged high interest rates and thus forced some of their own community members to foreclose on their homes. Those like Nehemiah who were benevolent within the community granted the people some latitude and relief to ease the struggle of debt payment. Even though Cyrus freed the Jews from exile, which was a moment of great liberation for them, the people themselves lived under a new climate that was not altogether easy for them. Thus, they were a community familiar with suffering, an experience that extended as far back as the time of the Exodus. The Book of Job reflects the experience of the Jewish community and their questions about God and justice in the aftermath of the Babylonian Exile.

From a literary standpoint, the story of Job takes place in pre-Mosaic times. According to the setting of the story, Job lives within a tribal culture. The story depicts him as a patriarch of a tribe, and as such, he is concerned about the tribe's needs and growth, as well as his own descendants, land, possessions, and prosperity. Family ties are close, and Job can expect to live on in the memory of his descendants long after he has passed away.

Job lives in an oral culture. The spoken word is of utmost importance, and what people say about themselves and others is not taken lightly. Within the Book of Job, the exchanges among Job's friends are often heated, bombastic, and even insulting at times. Job's self-understanding becomes the impetus for debates and arguments among his friends, and results in their disdain for him largely because they all live in a culture where honor and shame are of utmost importance. These two values are pivotal to the culture and to understanding the story of Job. Job's culture as reflected by the text is predominantly a shame culture. Shame was a communal judgment, and one's behavior or attitude was seen as bringing shame to the community at large. Shame included being disrespectful of others and being disrespectful of the basic values of the community. The opening lines of the story describe Job as an honorable person, but his disasters soon cause him shame, which in turn causes him to be isolated from his friends. According to his friends, Job is in the wrong and that is why disaster upon disaster has befallen him. Thus, Job suffers on account of his ill fate and because of others' attitudes toward him. Once a reputable and upright person in the community, Job soon becomes a man scorned and condemned; he is a living symbol of shame; his good name becomes horribly tarnished.

The Book of Job also reflects many religious traditions of the ancient biblical world. In ancient Israel, three sources of religious guidance and leadership were available to the people: the law and its teachings by the priest, the word of the prophet, and the counsel of the wise. The Book of Job belongs to the third category. According to wisdom teaching, those who live wise and righteous lives enjoy wealth, prosperity, longevity, and offspring. Those who are unjust and unrighteous suffer the loss of good fortune. Such a belief was part of the Deuteronomic theology of retribution found particularly in Deuteronomy 28. This theological theory states, in essence, that those who act justly and are blameless will be rewarded, but those who act wickedly or have sinned will be punished and cursed. Job's experience presumes the latter, but in reality, the story undermines and calls into question this ancient belief and, in fact, acts as a corrective to it. Thus, the Book of Job functions as a religious and theological polemic against the Deuteronomic theology of retribution. The book is also a polemic against another popular religious belief of the day, namely, that sin and suffering went hand-in-hand and that suffering was the direct result of sin.

Theologically, one of the book's main concerns involves questions about the roles of God and human beings in the cause and experience of suffering. The story raises the poignant question of whether or not a relationship with God can continue in the midst of excruciating pain and suffering. The story also provides us with a glimpse into the reality of when bad things happen to good people. Does God cause bad things to happen to the righteous? Is God at fault for not intervening in the midst of human tragedy? What kind of a God remains silent and at a distance, watching a person become completely engulfed in anguish, loss, and sorrow? How are people to understand God's silence in the face of human pain and suffering? Such questions only lead to deeper questions: What is one's image of God? What is one's understanding of God? The story of Job pushes the envelope with regard to one's belief in and about God while challenging many common assumptions, presumptions, and teachings pertaining to the Sacred Presence.

As a great work of literary artistry, the Book of Job belongs to a group of biblical books called Wisdom Literature that includes Proverbs, Sirach, Ecclesiastes, Psalms, the Song of Songs, and the Wisdom of Solomon. The story of Job is not one unique to Israel. Other cultures such as Sumeria, Mesopotamia, and Egypt had stories and a main character similar to the biblical Job. Composed of prose and poetry, the story contains several characters in conflict with one another and with Job, the main character. Discordant speeches capture the dynamic personalities of the various characters who move the story's drama forward, from one scene to the next. Much of Job's speech takes the form of lamentation, a spontaneous response to the presence of the realm of death and brokenness. Job's argument with God draws heavily on legal imagery which also appears when Job protests his innocence and calls for a third party to stand with him (see, e.g., Job 9:33; 16:19; 19:25). Additionally, irony is the primary literary technique used throughout the book. Job can be divided into seven sections:

- The Prologue 1:1–2:13
- First Round of Speeches 3:1–14:22
- Second Round of Speeches 15:1–21:34
- Third Round of Speeches 22:1–31:37
- The Elihu Speeches 32:1–37:24
- The God Speeches 38:1–42:6
- Epilogue 42:7–17

The stage has been set; the characters are poised to begin their interaction. God is in the heavenly court having a conversation with the one who is about to cause havoc in Job's life. Let us now enter into the world of Job whose story contains wisdom to last a lifetime and invites us to ponder some of life's most enduring questions about God, justice, fidelity, friendship, courage, and suffering. Let us reflect upon our own life experiences and discover Job as a friend who understands what it means to be misunderstood, to be judged wrongly and accused falsely, and who knows what it takes to be faithful to one's self and one's God even when reason fails and the spirit pales. In the dramatic and poetic story about Job, we will come to know God's "servant" who waits to befriend us all.

Setting the Stage: The Prologue
Job 1:1–2:13

The Book of Job opens with a beautifully crafted "Prologue." One by one, some of the main characters come into view and assume their roles on the stage of life in this timeless drama about suffering, silence, bewilderment, and fidelity. Like the classic stories of old that began "Once upon a time," the story of Job opens in a similar manner: "There was once a man in the land of Uz . . ." (Job 1:1). The Prologue can be divided into five units:

1:1–5	Job and His Family
1:6–12	An Attack on Job's Character
1:13–22	Job's Loss of Property and Children
2:1–10	An Attack on Job's Health
2:11–13	Job's Three Friends

We enter into Job's world, meet his friends, and journey with him through all his trials and tribulations as we reflect on our own lives and our struggle to trust God when everything seems to be imploding around us, and true friends are nowhere to be found.

Job and His Family (Job 1:1–5)

In these opening lines of the Prologue, the biblical writer gives us an exquisite portrait of a man who is richly blessed and whose righteousness seems to have been unsurpassed by anyone else in his community. Job is blameless and upright; he feared God and turned from evil. Here the notion of fearing God implies love and awe and not fright. Job's possessions and prosperity are great. He has seven sons and three daughters, 7,000 sheep, 3,000 camels, 500 yoke of oxen, 500 donkeys, and very many servants (v. 2). The author's use of numerical hyperbole in relation to Job's possessions captures Job's great prosperity. This prosperity is a sign that God favors Job. In the wisdom tradition, of which the Book of Job is a part, such righteousness and blessedness that characterize Job also mark him as being exceptionally wise in handling his daily affairs, which has rendered him wealthy to the point that he becomes the greatest of all the people of the East. So righteous a man is Job that he even offers sacrifices to God on behalf of his children just in case any of them had sinned or cursed God in their hearts. Thus, Job is a man of great faith who loves his family dearly. Just when life seems like it could not get any better, Job experiences an abrupt turn of events in his life that leaves him utterly destitute and bewildered yet confident in his own integrity and innocence. The unraveling of Job's prosperity and his excruciating pain begins in Job 1:6–12 when the hassatan, "the satan," comes on stage, and Job is never the same after his chance encounter with this adversarial force.

An Attack on Job's Character (Job 1:6–12)

In the next part of the story, the focus shifts from earth and Job to the realm of the Divine wherein God and the host of heavenly beings dwell. Now we meet not only God but also the satan who is about to play havoc with Job's life. The figure of the satan is not to be equated with such images as the devil of the New Testament sense of "Satan" or Lucifer, one of the so-called fallen angels. Here the figure merely represents someone who is an adversary. One by one, the heavenly beings present themselves to God, and so does the satan.

From the response the satan gives to God, we learn that this creature has been surveying the entire earth, roaming around aimlessly to see what sort of mischief could be stirred up and what kind of havoc could be created. Without a second thought, God poses a simple question to the satan, "Have you considered my servant Job?" Clearly, the phrase "my servant Job" connotes a sense of fidelity and intimacy that exists between God and Job, and especially on Job's part toward God.

The give and take conversation between God and the satan that follows next sets up the wager. The satan challenges God to stretch out the divine hand to touch negatively everything that Job possesses that in turn would be the impetus for Job to curse God, so the satan asserts. God, however, is quite clever. God turns the whole situation around and places all that Job possesses in the satan's power, with the caveat that the satan not stretch out his hand against Job. Job's life is to be spared. What we see here is God's absolute trust in Job and confidence in Job's steadfast love for his God. God is going to let the events of life run their course. God is neither going to control Job's life and life's choices nor control the actions of the satan, whom God also trusts will uphold the parameters marked out with respect to Job's life.

God gives divine freedom to Job and to the satan, and God's sacred presence remains in the midst of all, even when Job may not be able to sense or perceive it. And so Job becomes like a puppet in the hands of a puppeteer, a Gumby figure who will be poked and prodded to the point of excruciating pain. But Job is not being "tested" by his God. Job is the pawn in the hand of one who has waged a bet with God, who does not play the game but rather allows the game to be played by the satan—only to have the satan defeated by the game itself.

Job Loses Property and Children (Job 1:13–22)

In four swift episodes, we see what happens to Job as the satan begins tinkering with Job's possessions in an attempt to prove God's knowledge of Job false and Job's fidelity to God imperfect. The scene now shifts again to a family gathering of Job's children. Job, not present at the gathering, receives a series of messages from various messengers. Job learns that his oxen, donkeys, and camels have been carried off, his sheep burned up, his servants killed, and worst of all, his children are all dead as well, because the house had collapsed on them when a great wind blew across the desert and shook the house right off its foundation. Such horrific news is both unbelievable and unbearable, especially when the news of such tragedies is delivered in rapid succession. The repetitious phrase, "I alone have escaped to tell you," makes the loss even greater for Job.

Why should the messenger escape turmoil but not any of Job's livestock? Why should a perfect stranger escape calamity and none of Job's family members? Where was the saving hand of God in these times of tragedy? Why did God not intervene to change the course of history? After all, Israel's God is Lord of Creation and Lord of History. Why should Job, a man of unsurpassable righteousness, be the prey of such insidious wickedness?

Job's response to his tremendous loss is striking. He assumes the role of a mourning penitent: he tears his robe, shaves his head, falls on the ground, and worships God. Thinking that God has caused him to suffer loss on account of some sort of transgression that he or his family may have committed, Job accepts God's divine chastisement without any malice or curse directed toward God. Job simply states:

> Naked I came from my mother's womb, and naked shall I return there; the Lord gave, and the Lord has taken away; blessed be the name of the Lord. (1:21)

The story's narrator adds a single comment that accents Job's righteousness and fidelity: "In all this Job did not sin or charge God with wrongdoing" (1:22).

For the ancient Israelites, no separation existed between faith and everyday life. Daily life was lived in the context of their faith, and their faith was shaped by their life experiences. The ancient biblical people also believed that life could be either blessed or cursed by God, which would bring prosperity or calamity, respectively. At this point in the story, the audience realizes that God is not the one creating weal and woe—the satan is. Job, however, thinks that God is responsible for the great losses incurred, which befits the theology of Job's day, but against which the Book of Job instructs, thereby shedding light on the truth about God and God's ways.

Despite this important theological lesson, do not people today still feel the way Job does, namely, that God is the one responsible for causing calamity in their lives or for causing them undeserved and unbearable suffering? What we will see later on as the story continues to unfold is that the theology of Job's day, and his belief in it, is precisely what causes Job so much pain and angst. This continues until he has the actual experience of God, which is far greater than all the theological discourse he has learned or which is being given to him by his friends throughout the book.

Attack on Job's Health (Job 2:1–10)

Just when we think things could not get any worse for Job, they do. The opening lines of Chapter 2 reiterate what was heard in Job 1:6–8, except that now God highlights Job's enduring integrity and fidelity. In this section of the Prologue, God and the satan go head-to-head, and God, still trusting completely in Job, continues to allow the satan to play the game with Job. Of interest, we learn that the satan has even tried to turn God away from Job to the point where God would destroy Job's life. As the story unfolds, we will see that God is the one who restores Job's fortunes and essentially his life.

The satan has no power over God or Job, but this force of nature does increase Job's suffering. Now Job is covered head to toe in sores, and still he assumes the position of a penitent: he sits among the ashes from his own scraped sores (2:8). Even when confronted by his wife, who tries to persuade him to curse God and die and thus be freed of his misery, Job persists in his integrity and continues to accept readily whatever comes to him from God, even if it is misfortune: "Shall we receive the good at the hand of God, and not receive the bad?" (2:10b). Once again the narrator's comment highlights Job's integrity and fidelity: "In all this Job did not sin with his lips" (2:10c). Job has been conditioned by the theology of his day, and we, the audience are being enlightened about such ancient beliefs as the story unfolds. As ancient as these beliefs are, do we not see these ancient beliefs still operative today?

Job's Three Friends (Job 2:11–13)

The Prologue closes on a note of consolation, at least at this point in the story. Job's three friends hear of his travails; they come and console him; and together they all adopt the position of penitents. They all sit in silence with Job. In silence, they bear Job's pain with him. They offer no word, for no word could bring comfort. Job's experience of suffering is unspeakable. Their greatest gift of compassion is just to be present to him.

Summary

The Prologue has introduced us to a series of main characters: God, the satan, Job, and Job's three friends. We also meet Job's wife. Several of these characters interact with one another in such a way as to showcase

Job's magnificent character and the solid relationship that exists between Job and God, despite what Job may think about God and God's ways gleaned from his own tradition and its theological teachings. The Prologue not only has set the stage for the rest of the drama to unfold but also opened wide the doors for theological discourse so important for today as we try together to discern the ways of God and God's abiding presence in the midst of the ever-changing human condition. Will Job remain as accepting as he is throughout his life and his story, or will we be treated to a glimpse at a person who is bold and courageous enough to question and confront his God in a way that redefines faith and gives hope to us all?

First Round of Speeches
Job 3:1–14:22

The first round of speeches presents us with many insights into Job, his situation, and his friends. The main theme in this first round of speeches—of all the rounds of speeches—is suffering. Early in the book, the biblical writer presented Job as a patient person, but now Job is no longer patient. In this section of the book, we hear Job pouring out his lament to no one and to everyone. He does not curse God on account of his suffering, but he curses the day of his birth and the night of his conception (similar to Jer. 20:14–18). Job has prayed for darkness and now he prays for death:

> Why did you bring me forth from the womb?
>   Would that I had died before any eye had seen me,
> and were as though I had not been,
>   carried from the womb to the grave. (Job 10:18–19)

Thinking that all this suffering is from God, he wants death to deliver him from God, the taskmaster (3:18–19).

Job's friends now abandon their silence (13:5) and thus begins three rounds of speeches. Job's friends are shocked at Job's interpretation of his own life. In the first two rounds, Job's friends speak and Job responds. The third round of speeches is a conglomerate of statements by Job's friends with his responses interspersed.

In this first round of speeches, Eliphaz reminds Job that suffering comes from human activity and is also a divine punishment for wicked living. He also thinks that Job's suffering could be a divine discipline (4:1–21). In giving Job advice, he tries to comfort him (5:1–27), but his words only bring Job more aggravation and make him feel more and more misunderstood (6:8–30).

Job's response to Eliphaz, in which Job also directs his speech to God, is striking. Job has a strong emotional outburst (3:1–7:21); he says that his calamity and anguish are too great to be measured (6:1–3), but that they must be spoken aloud (7:11); and he makes known that he perceives God to be a divine hunter who pursues him with poison arrows (6:4). Eliphaz's advice is too much for Job to take in. Job eventually turns to prayer and expresses his longing for death as a relief (7:1–21).

The next friend to be introduced in this first round of speeches is Bildad, who gives Job some theological recommendations (8:1–22). He argues that God is just and therefore God cannot be the cause of suffering (8:1–3, 20–22), and that humans cause their own suffering because of the choices they make that lead to unpleasant consequences (8:8–19). Bildad suggests to Job that his children died prematurely because they committed sin (8:4). Like Eliphaz, he advises Job to live uprightly, to turn to God, and to repent (8:5–22). Through his speech to Job, Bildad indirectly makes the claim that Job has brought on his own pain; Job is the one who has distorted justice; and therefore, Job needs to make amends with God.

In Job's response to Bildad (9:1–10:22), we see the book's drama beginning to intensify as Job's speech becomes bolder and bolder. Thus far, Job's friends have argued that mortals cannot be righteous before God. Eliphaz's words to Job, words that Eliphaz heard that came to him from a voice that he heard during an experience he had one night, communicates this sentiment:

> Can mortals be righteous before God?
> Can human beings be pure before their Maker?
> Even in his servants he puts no trust,
> and his angels he charges with error;
> how much more those who live in houses of clay,
> whose foundation is in the dust,
> who are crushed like a moth.
> Between morning and evening they are destroyed;
> they perish forever without any regarding it.
> Their tent-cord is plucked up within them,
> And they die devoid of wisdom. (Job 4:17–21)[3]

Eliphaz's words suggest that all are sinners (4:17–21), and Bildad's words follow suit. Although Job agrees with their questions, he understands his own suffering in a way that is completely different from his friends' understanding. He continues to assert his innocence while seeing his situation with God as a "no-win" situation because he is the one vulnerable and condemned, and God is the powerful one robed in justice and righteousness (9:1–35). For Job, one cannot be justified when the judge and defendant are the same and extremely powerful. God can overturn the order of creation just as God has established it (9:5–12). Thus, Job turns to lamentation (10:1–17). He does not know what else to do, so he complains to his God. He wants to know

> Why did you bring me forth from the womb?
> Would that I had died before any eye had seen me,
> and were as though I had not been,
> carried from the womb to the grave.
> Are not the days of my life few?
> Let me alone, that I may find a little comfort
> before I go, never to return,
> to the land of gloom and deep darkness,
> the land of gloom and chaos,
> where light is like darkness.

Once again, Job receives no comfort from his friends.

Zophar is the next friend to be introduced into the drama, and he too offers a response to Job. He says that Job's complaints are babbling nonsense (11:2–4). He claims that God's ways are incomprehensible to humans and that God recognizes the worthlessness of certain people (11:5–12). He tells Job that if he would set his heart aright and put iniquity far away, then security and joy would return and life will be better than noonday (11:13–20).

The dramatic dialogues between Job and his friends continue as Job next offers a response to Zophar. Job remains somewhat unfazed by Zophar's accusation, namely, that Job has spoken out too much (12:1–2). Job then launches into his longest speech in the book (12:4–14:22).[4] In the speech Job delivers as a response, we see that he continues to be taunted by the sarcasm of his friends but he does not cower to them or their sarcasm. He responds boldly (13:4). He admits that all that has happened to him is not haphazard and pointless, that God's might and strength go together with wisdom and prudence (12:13–25), but the problem is trying to figure out God's wisdom and prudence. Thus, Job wants to take God to court (13:3)! Job has made up his mind that he will not be intimidated or silenced by the empty and ashen aphorisms of his friends. He will speak out of the depth of his experience (13:12–13). Most importantly, Job demands an answer from God; he demands to know what his transgression is that has caused him to be afflicted in the way that he is. Hence, while the friends advocate silence, Job refuses to be silent in the midst of his misery. He complains, cries out, wails, laments, and takes a firm stand against the persuasive arguments and accusations of his friends, and he will not be silent until he also receives an answer from God.

Second Round of Speeches
Job 15:1–21:34

In this second round of speeches, the drama continues to intensify, as Job's friends become more accusatory and as Job becomes bolder and bolder. Eliphaz's speech opens this second round of dialogues. Earlier in the book, Eliphaz was gentle and encouraging but now he changes his tone. According to Eliphaz, if Job were not as wise as he claimed (13:1–2), then he would not have replied with so much hot air (15:2–3). In his speech to Job, he attacks Job's wisdom and sarcastically asks Job if he is some mythic, primordial sage begotten in some certain way before creation took place (15:7), and here the poet's use of a series of rhetorical questions makes Eliphaz's speech sharp, pointed, and cutting (15:7–9). Appealing to ancient tradition (15:7–8), Eliphaz then offers a description of the blessings of the righteous, but a harrowing, admonitory account of the fate of the wicked (15:17–35). He reminds Job that the wicked live in constant inner torment and turmoil and anxiety (15:20–24). Also, impending death lies heavy on their hearts (15:23b-24). He ends his address to Job by commenting on the futility of folly (15:30–35). Implied here is Eliphaz's indirect accusation of Job, namely, that he is not righteous and needs to own up to his transgressions.

Once again, Eliphaz's speech does not go unchecked by Job. Once again, Job does not keep silent. He is growing tired of the advice of his so-called "comforters" who bring him weariness and not the rest that he so desperately needs and longs for. In a spirit of lamentation, Job talks about the assaults of his enemies, which he now sees as being his three friends, as well as God. He describes them as traitors (16:8, 11), ferocious beasts (16:9–10a), bullies (16:10b), muggers who assault and batter him (v. 12a), and an archer and fencer who have pierced his kidneys and have caused him excruciating pain. The words are descriptive; the imagery is vivid; the pain is overbearing. Job's sense is that he is fast approaching death (16:18–17:2), and he hopes that even after death has sealed his lips from crying out, his blood will not be silent, for he is an innocent victim in his own eyes, who deserves to be vindicated. He hopes for an intercessor from on high to hear and help him, but his hope remains only a hope, for there is no divine word, no intercession or intervention to be had. No one in the heavenly realm seems to plead Job's case. He only encounters silence, silence, silence. He feels forsaken, mocked, alone, and he cries out:

Where then is my hope?
    Who will see my hope? (Job 17:15)

Following Job's response to Eliphaz, Bildad once again enters the picture. Bildad rebukes Job and asks him when he will be quiet. Then he says:

How long will you hunt for words?
    Consider, and then we shall speak.
Why are we counted as cattle?
    Why are we stupid in your sight?
You who tear yourself in your anger—
    shall the earth be forsaken because of you,
    or the rock be removed out of its place? (Job 18:2–4)

Bildad then continues to describe in very detailed language the fate of the wicked, which was similar to what Eliphaz said to Job. Again, the implication is that Job has sinned in some way. Bildad then describes the horrible fate of the wicked (18:5–21).

In Job's response to Bildad, Job puts his friend on notice by telling him that even if he, Job, were guilty and at fault for something, Bildad has no right to gloat over him. Job again states that God has dealt with him in a crooked way (19:6). Once again, Job does not keep silent in the face of his tremendous suffering. He puts the blame on God. He recounts the ways that God has mistreated him. When he cries out, his cries fall on deaf ears (19:7). God has stripped him of his honor (19:6). Job repeats his charge that God's anger is turned against him (19:11a). He again states that God has forsaken him and as a result of God's forsaking him, all his friends and relatives have followed suit (19:13–22).

Alone and close to death, Job looks for a vindicator. He continues to maintain that he is innocent, and thus there must be a kin who will stand up in court and deliver him, but he finds no one to vindicate him. He concludes his reply to Bildad by stating that those who persist in blaming him and holding him guilty will ultimately have to face judgment themselves (19:28–29).

Following Job's response, Zophar once again addresses Job (20:1–29). Zophar is rather curt with Job and demands that Job "Pay attention!" (20:2). Like Eliphaz and Bildad, Zophar also gives Job a description of the fate of the wicked (20:6–29), and he emphasizes that the wicked ignore God and are proud and arrogant (20:6). He reminds Job that God with mighty wrath will assail the wicked, and thus Job can expect even more than what he is currently experiencing.

Job's response to Zophar is direct and filled with ironic twists. He makes clear to Zophar and to his other friends that if they cannot offer him their silence (13:5), then they can at least pay attention to what he is saying (21:2). Here is the irony: Job wants his friends to keep quiet, but he wants a response from God.

Job refutes all that Zophar has said to him and then he makes some pointed comments to his friends:

> Oh, I know your thoughts,
> and your schemes to wrong me.
> For you say, 'Where is the house of the prince?
> Where is the tent in which the wicked lived?'
> Have you not asked those who travel the roads,
> and do you not accept their testimony,
> that the wicked are spared in the day of calamity,
> and are rescued in the day of wrath?
> Who declares their way to their face,
> and who repays them for what they have done?
> When they are carried to the grave,
> a watch is kept over their tomb.
> The clods of the valley are sweet to them;
> everyone will follow after,
> and those who went before are innumerable.
> How then will you comfort me with empty nothings?
> There is nothing left of your answers but falsehood.
> (Job 21:27–34)

Third Round of Speeches
Job 22:1–31:37

This third round of speeches is not as clearly organized as the other two rounds. In the face of Job's rebuttal, Eliphaz flies back at him with a series of rhetorical questions meant to show how wrong Job's position is. He accuses Job of a series of serious sins (22:6–11). Once again, he tells Job that he is suffering because he must have committed these sins; he also accuses Job of thumbing his nose at God. Eliphaz, however, does not give up on Job. He keeps telling him that if he comes to terms with what he has done and then repents, all will go well for him and he will again enjoy prosperity (22:23).

What we now see in Eliphaz is a sad picture of a degeneration of a religious person who has too easily confused his own attempts to understand God with divine revelation itself. Eliphaz relies on his own theological beliefs and teachings and does not consider that something else might be going on here that he cannot understand and which defies the theological understandings of the day and culture.

Job's response to Eliphaz (23:1–24:25) indicates his annoyance at Eliphaz and once again, Job expresses his desire to take God to court (23:4–7), but God is nowhere to be found (23:8–17). Job is left to wonder why God does not have scheduled times for holding court and rendering decisions (24:1). Job questions why God does not intervene in the plight of the poor who suffer on the streets every day; the wicked are not punished and the poor are not rescued (24:2–25). After Job delivers his response, Bildad begins his speech in a different way: he does not offer sarcastic remarks to Job but instead begins with words of hymnal praise of the Creator God who establishes peace (25:1–6). He makes clear that Job's innocence is impossible because there is no such thing as an innocent human being.

Job's final reply highlights God's unsearchable majesty, beginning with a solemn oath, "As God lives" (27:2). Then Job goes on to maintain, yet again, his innocence (27:3–23). He makes clear that God is the one wronging him. Unlike his friends, Job insists that he will not serve God with lies and falsehoods (27:3–4) and he will not concede to his friends' position (27:5). He reminds his friends that under Israelite law, one convicted of false witness against an innocent person is subject to the same penalty that the innocent party would have undergone (27:7). To Bildad and his other friends, Job proceeds to offer a teaching concerning "the hand of God" (27:11–23). What follows next is a lengthy poem filled with imagery, metaphorical language, and rhetorical questions. Here Job focuses on wisdom whose way God alone knows (Job 28).

Finally, in Job 29–31, Job makes clear that his plea for arbitration has fallen on deaf ears; God cannot be found to receive a subpoena that Job would like to give him; and his friends are false witnesses who refuse to tell the truth on the witness stand. Thus, in these three chapters, Job reviews his case, expresses his final lament, and reasserts his innocence. His hope is that someone, somewhere will hear him and take heed of his voice. Not surprisingly at this point, no word from God comes forth.

Elihu Speeches
Job 32:1–37:24

Elihu comes in out of the blue. He is an angry young man who has been following Job's case closely. He tells Job that Job is wrong, that God does speak and that perhaps he, Job, has missed what God has been saying all along, and he reminds Job that God uses dreams and nightmares and sickness to warn sinners and to get them to return to the path of life (33:14–22). He concludes his speech by taunting Job like Job's other friends. He also rebukes him and hurls a series of questions at him, all of which are not helpful to Job and instead cause him more pain. Elihu's questions, however, prepare the way for God, who like Elihu, will hurl similar questions at Job.

In all the dialogues between Job and his friends, a presumably compassionate God remains distant and silent, leaving us to wonder if God genuinely cares about those who cry to the heavens for relief.

The God Speeches
Job 38:1–42:6

The setting for Job's encounter with God is a tempest, a whirlwind of a fierce storm (38:1). In the ancient Near East and in the Old Testament, storms are oftentimes the setting for theophanies—the appearances of God to human beings (Exod. 19:16–20; 1 Kgs. 19:11–13; Ps. 18:7–17; Hab. 3:14). The storm conveys divine power and mystery and also symbolizes Job's stormy life of suffering and the loss of his children's lives in "the great wind" (1:19). Finally, in the midst of his horrific and chaotic world, Job encounters God who speaks about all sorts of things that do not pertain to Job's plight, suffering, or anguish. Making sense of this divine response has generated much speculation in biblical literature, especially after God has been so silent and so distant.

While the speeches do not explain the suffering of Job, they do present his anguished state as the place of divine encounter, which suggests the following key points:

1. God does not abandon us in the midst of our pain and suffering. God enters into the chaos of it all.
2. In trying to involve Job in a question and answer schema, God is trying to involve Job in the learning process and trying to help lead him out of his own small context into the larger world.
3. In trying to get Job to focus on something greater than himself, God is trying to put the pain and suffering in a larger context; God is pleading with us to see the beauty in life even in the midst of all our own misery.
4. Through the Book of Job, we see that suffering is mysterious. God does not cause us pain and suffering; the stuff of the human condition does, as well as our own sometimes ill-made choices. We have been given free will, and when we exercise that free will in ways that are not healthy, then we will experience ill consequences.

5. For Job, the greatest pain comes from his confusion about his relationship with God, and is that not the case for many of us today? In reality, God has been listening all along the way.
6. Just as Job calls upon God and calls out to God, and challenges God, so we do too in the midst of our struggles; we have to call out to God and give the pain to God, but like Job, we have to wait on God, and surely God will come to us in ways we least expect it to grace us and to enter into our suffering and struggles and pain.
7. The key is patience and, in the case of Job, one wonders if God's silence is a sign of God "bearing with." Perhaps we need to reimagine God not as one who has power over and is in control and intervening to stop horrific situations, but instead as one who suffers with, who bears with, who dwells in full communion with us in the midst of all that life brings.
8. Finally, Job has shown himself to be a true friend of God but not so his friends. Job gets angry, but never curses or forsakes God. In the midst of his pain and suffering, he constantly seeks God, and in the end, God responds to Job in an unexpected yet transformative way, and both Job and we as his audience remain shrouded in the mystery of God whose presence remains ever constant, ever faithful.

Epilogue

Job 42:7–17

At the end of the dramatic story of Job, we see that the God who indicts the friends and restores Job seems more fickle than a just and compassionate God. This God seems more arbitrary than predictable. If Job was indeed a faithful "servant" (1:8; 2:3) who has "spoken what is right" (42:7–8), then why must seven sons and three daughters, along with countless livestock die, before God restores all of Job's fortunes to him? Furthermore, those who have died are not restored; Job receives new sons and daughters and livestock, but he still suffers the loss of the ones he first loved. Is this truly divine justice? The Epilogue leaves us with many unanswered questions.

Final Conclusions

What we see in the Book of Job is innocent suffering, and rather than explain why such suffering exists, the book offers us a feast of understandings and interpretations on the matter. Through its portrayal of Job's life, the book presents us with injustice, losses, grief, and the collapse of worlds. The story of Job is capable of embracing the sufferings of individuals and communities alike. Job is the one who is homeless, frightened, broken displaced, hungry, and feeling alone and abandoned. Job's story calls us to face our responses to suffering—in our own lives and lives of humans and nonhumans around us, and to make a note that even the most righteous of people will share in this experience of innocent suffering at some point in time. The story also reminds us that those who suffer are not abandoned by God but will be favored by God in the midst of the suffering. One has only to hope in God and wait, wait, wait. Even though we are left with unanswered questions, we need to remember that the text is a polemic against the Deuteronomic theology of retribution. All we can do is enter into the mystery of God with wonder and awe, realizing that when we come face-to-face with the transcendent Divine as Job did, we will be speechless, and we will most certainly feel our smallness. Yet, the sheer joy is knowing that our God loves us enough to dare to reveal God's self to us no matter what our condition or state in life may be.[5]

Having highlighted the main points in the various speeches within the Book of Job, we turn now to two contemporary works of literature that have been either inspired by the Book of Job or that reflect some of the main themes of the book.

Playing in the Fountain
The Literary Texts
J.B.
The Trial of God

About the Authors

Archibald MacLeish (1892–1982)

To say that the life and works of Archibald MacLeish span the entire intellectual and emotional history of the twentieth century in which he lived and died is no exaggeration. In his poetry, drama, and essays, he ruminated again and again on the theological and philosophical questions that preoccupy thoughtful men and women during periods of global upheaval like our own. MacLeish's friends, enemies, and colleagues included many of the best-known figures of history. He had letters from presidents like Franklin Delano Roosevelt, John Kennedy, and Ronald Reagan. Among his literary friends he numbered Ernest Hemingway, James Joyce, Robert Frost, Ezra Pound, Robert Penn Warren, Richard Wilbur, and Louise Bogan. First hailed as a handsome football hero, he went on to be condemned as a dedicated pacifist and investigated by the FBI as a communist spy. Besides winning awards for poetry and drama, he excelled in a succession of careers as a lawyer, journalist, college professor, editor of *Fortune Magazine*, Librarian of Congress, and Secretary of State. Most remarkably of all, MacLeish's life harmonized with his ideals. Poet Richard Wilbur eulogized him: "Not all poets are good men, but Archie was always both."

As a young man, MacLeish considered becoming a minister. He was discouraged, however, by his inability to resolve the very theological questions that form the theme of *J.B.* While visiting the ruins of devastation wrought upon civilians during World War II, the poet's faith in God began to be tormented. "How is it possible to believe in the justice of God in a world in which the innocent perish in vast meaningless massacres?" he asked. Then he offered the answer he would later dramatize in *J.B.*: "Only in man's love does God exist and triumph."[6] This conviction that God needs humanity to bring about a just world was the basis for the deeply sensitive social conscience which, according to his biographer, MacLeish displayed long before it was popular for poets to do so.

Elie Wiesel (1928–present)

Holocaust survivor Elie Wiesel has dedicated his entire life and international career as an author and lecturer to the task of assuring that the world does not forget what happened in the death camps of Hitler's regime. After witnessing many atrocities firsthand, including the crucifixion of a child, Wiesel writes in his most famous novel, *Night*, "Never shall I forget that night . . . which has turned my life into one long night . . . Never shall I forget that smoke. Never shall I forget the little faces of the children whose bodies I saw turned into wreaths of smoke beneath a silent blue sky. Never shall I forget those flames which consumed my faith forever."[7] These lines are often quoted to identify Elie Wiesel as an avowed atheist. Hence, Wiesel's later testimony to the contrary comes as a shock: "I never stopped praying. I never divorced God. It is because I believed in God that I was so angry at Him—and still am. The tragedy of the believer, it is deeper than the tragedy of the nonbeliever"[8]

In 1985, Wiesel visited Berlin and for the first time met with German men and women whose contemporaries had served and tolerated Hitler. "I had never before considered that it could be as painful to be the children of those who ran the camps as to be the child of those who died in them. . . . I don't believe in collective guilt."[9] In 1986, Wiesel was awarded the Nobel Peace Prize.

Reflecting on Genre

Dramatic Poetry

As a component of Old Testament wisdom literature, the Book of Job serves as a model for what one critic considers the ideal genre for troubled times: "literature in which God . . . is present in his absence, is hidden, and has to be sought."[10] The Book of Job features a whole array of literary devices for exploring the problem of evil and the suffering of the innocent. Scholars have found this variety both fascinating in its rich complexity and exasperating in its inconsistencies. Hence, literary critics identify the book generically as a folk tale, as an allegory, and as a drama in verse, a poetically elaborated version of a tale handed down in the oral tradition long before the Bible was written.

As a folk hero, Job probably had a real existence that predated the Book of Job by several centuries during which his story grew bigger with each telling. Eventually, Job assumed the status of a wisdom figure and a model of patience. Job's story fits the familiar archetypal plot pattern known as "The Testing of the Hero." As a drama of intense spiritual conflict and unresolved tension, however, Job's story is more complicated. Job's personal misfortunes serve as metaphor for the universal problem of evil and the question of God's complicity in it. Hence, the story of Job could also be classified as an allegory, that is, a story with two levels of meaning, one specific and the other universal.

In the book, a prologue and an epilogue in prose create a "framework narrative," while almost thirty-nine chapters of poetry constitute the body of the book. Prose is chosen for the prologue and epilogue to establish statistical "facts." The use of a prologue and epilogue is a common literary device with which an author of fiction establishes a tone of verisimilitude. We are told that Job's enormous wealth consists of 11,000–12,000 animals, sufficient grain acreage to maintain these huge herds, and a staff of servants large enough to reap the grain and tend the animals. Because the land of Uz did really exist historically as an ancient trade hub, these statistics suggest that Job's wealth derived from agricultural trade.

The thirty-nine chapters of poetry in the Book of Job are sometimes dramatic and sometimes lyric. Poetry is defined as dramatic when it is in the form of monologue or dialogue, or when it presents other features of a theatrical production. Literary critics classify Job as a precursor of the modern psychological drama, where the stage is the arena of a person's mind. Here the voice(s) of Job's conscience and his interior conversation with his creator, whether they take the form of dialogue or monologue, always presuppose an audience. The audience for the monologues and the partners in the dialogues are alternately God, the satan figure, or one of Job's friends.

Poetry is classified as lyric when it expresses personal emotions or meditations, and sometimes, reactions to events. Lyric passages, predominantly in Hebrew verse, record Job's emotional reactions to the disasters that befall him and to his friends' attempts to console him. Hence, the biblical text itself, like modern plays inspired by it, combine characteristics of works composed for the theater with passages of lyric poetry.

Two modern dramas based on Job fall into somewhat different genres. While MacLeish is satisfied to have the ending of *J.B.* leave some ambivalence as to its classification as either tragedy or comedy, Wiesel's stage directions specifically designate that *The Trial of God* creates a unique genre, emblematic of life itself: "tragic farce." Despite differences in genre, all three works are poetic and all three works capture the drama of the human-divine relationship in all its mystery and ambivalence.

Reflecting on Structure

First, let us consider the Book of Job from the standpoint of its overall dramatic structure. As mentioned earlier, its forty-two chapters are divided thus:

- The Prologue 1:1–2:13
- First Round of Speeches 3:1–14:22
- Second Round of Speeches 15:1–21:34
- Third Round of Speeches 22:1–31:37
- The Elihu Speeches 32:1–37:24
- The God Speeches 38:1–42:6
- Epilogue 42:7–17

A classical drama, whether in three or in five acts, follows a pattern based on three phases of conflict, moving from exposition of characters in conflict through complication, to climax and final resolution. Job's progress from affliction by God, through intellectually wrestling with God, to a final reconciliation, fits loosely into this pattern. Another way of looking at dramatic structure called "The Tragic Rhythm of Action" has been summarized in the formula: Purpose, Passion, Frustration or Fulfillment, and Final Perception. Following this structural pattern in the Book of Job, the Prologue states the satan's purpose: to put the just man on trial. Then the chapters of poetry trace the hero's passionate fidelity to God through many debates and temptations. Finally, frustration becomes fulfillment as Job utters a wise perception that leads into the humiliation of his friends and his fortunes being restored: "I had heard of You by the hearing of the ear, but now my eye sees You" (Job 42:5–6).

As we proceed to examine *J.B.* and *The Trial of God*, we see that the decisions made by both playwrights favor theatrical devices that present the deity in a harsh light. The first of these choices is the structural feature of a play within a play. (In *The Trial of God*, the play becomes a Purim spiel within a Purim spiel, a traditional Jewish play, often using satire.) By making God appear on stage as an actor and as a spectator, both modern authors subtly embody a significant theological question heard earlier in the Book of Job: Of which crime is God guilty—of participating in human suffering or of passively watching it?

All of the playwrights' other choices support a satirical mood. Like some of the existentialist playwrights of the post-World War II era, MacLeish chooses to comment sarcastically on the human condition by costuming his characters as clowns in a circus. His directions reduce stagecraft to a minimum and replace soft lights with an unflattering bare bulb. Using masks, the playwright acts out the confusion between good and evil and humanity's tendency to attribute both to God. Without putting it into words, these theatrical devices communicate the play's ultimate question: "Can absolute good appear in the mask of absolute evil?" In *The Trial of God*, Elie Wiesel raises a similar question when he has the priest recommend that the Jews put on the mask of a convert and act out a conversion to Christianity as a Purim spiel.

Reflecting on Other Literary Devices

The Use of Theater Language

Although MacLeish and Wiesel examine the same themes as the Book of Job, the playwrights had more tools at their disposal than the biblical author. In the theater, words are not the only language. Set, costumes, and props communicate as much to the audience as dialogue. In both plays, setting in time and place communicate a universal theme: In *J.B.* the stage setting says, "All the world's a circus." This metaphor was popular with the post-World War II philosophers known as "existentialists." One of their principal premises was that the world is "absurd." Hence, their works became known collectively as Theater of the Absurd. Playwrights like Beckett, Ionesco, and Pinter were often witty, but deeply serious—often disturbing. Nothing could be more serious than the subject matter of *J.B.* MacLeish chooses to relax the audience so that when their guard is down, he can deliver a knockout punch to the face of religious complacency. Elie Wiesel's choice of setting is also important. The Jewish village that has been wiped out by a pogrom is not in Germany, as we might expect, but in Ukraine. Thus the playwright draws attention to the global scope of anti-Semitism. Everyone knows about the Nazi

Holocaust, but we need to be reminded that, historically, it was far from unique.

Masks and costumes add to the playwright's theatrical vocabulary. Masks worn in carnival time and on the Feast of Purim provide anonymity for mischief makers. In *J.B.*, they allow the playwright to ask one of the play's biggest questions in a way that implicates the audience: "Do human beings use both God and Satan to 'mask' human responsibility?" In *J.B.* costumes also communicate time. Circus costumes have remained almost the same throughout the ages. Hence, time in *J.B.* is the universal present. The time setting for *The Trial of God* is more specific: during a historic seventeenth-century pogrom. Placing *The Trial of God* in the seventeenth century is a distancing device for Wiesel who needs something to make it possible for a Holocaust survivor to deal with this very personal material. Distance also allows him to dramatize the dilemma of Judaism in its historical continuity. The play is set not only in historical time, but also in liturgical time: the Feast of Purim. Like the mood of Mardi Gras, the mood for Purim is playful and irreverent, even though it commemorates the cyclical persecution of Jews which goes back to the biblical era.

Characterization

When an author makes a descriptive statement about a person's character, that statement is called direct characterization. For example, the Book of Job, as well as the stage directions preceding the texts of both *J.B.* and *The Trial of God,* offer brief direct characterizations: "There was once a man whose name was Job. That man was blameless and upright, one who feared God and turned away from evil" (Job 1:1). In the Prologue before his script, MacLeish describes Nickles as "gaunt and sardonic," and both Nickles and Zuss as "in carriage and speech the broken-down actor."[11] In like manner, in the information for the play's director, Wiesel stipulates that Sam, the Stranger, is "diabolical." The audience for the play, however, does not know this fact until Maria accuses him of diabolical action.

When characters reveal themselves unwittingly on stage through their own words, actions, and reactions to each other and to events, this situation is called dramatic characterization:. Although the ancient Book of Job differs in style from the plays of MacLeish and Wiesel, the biblical author does share with *J.B.* and *The Trial of God,* the stylistic element of dramatic characterization. In addition to dialogue and action, the author of Job uses a minor character as a foil or contrast to expose a major figure's strengths and weaknesses. Thus, Job's three rationalizing friends serve as foils to his strong faith that transcends human reason.

In *J.B.*, Sarah's bitterness brings out the unconquerable good- nature of her husband, *J.B.* In *The Trial of God*, Wiesel expects his audience to recognize the cranky Berish as foil to the patient, long-suffering Job of the Bible. Temperamentally, Berish is the total opposite of both the biblical Job and of MacLeish's *J.B.* Maria's function as a foil to Berish's bitterness draws attention to how complacently a gentile reacts to the mistreatment of Jews.

Critics have pointed out that characterization is the weakest feature of MacLeish's *J.B.* Because the playwright chose to make *J.B.* an Everyman, he sacrificed the subtleties of a convincing, individual personality, not only for his protagonist but for everyone else in the play. Drama critics label MacLeish's characters "flat," or "two-dimensional" because they are simply stereotypes, not fully realized characters. On the other hand, Wiesel's dramatic characterization in *The Trial of God* succeeds in creating distinct individuals who can delay our recognition of their crucial symbolic dimension.

Reflecting on Literary Style

The Book of Job, *J.B.*, and *The Trial of God* are each literary masterpieces whose writers used a variety of literary techniques to bring their dramatic works to life. Among the literary devices commonly used by the ancient biblical poets, the most prominent ones were nature imagery and similes and metaphors drawn from the natural world. These two devices feature prominently in the Book of Job. For example, the biblical poet features Job drawing on the natural world to teach an important lesson:

> But ask the animals and they will teach you;
> the birds of the air and they will tell you;
> ask the plants of the earth and they will teach you;
> and the fish of the sea will declare to you.
> Who among all these does not know
> that the hand of the Lord has done this?
> In his hand is the life of every living thing
> and the breath of every human being. (Job 12:7–10)

Elsewhere, the character of Job meditates wistfully on the fragility of both human life and the natural world. Similes and metaphorical language capture Job's sentiments:

> A mortal, born of woman,
> few of days and full of trouble,
> comes up like a flower and withers
> flees like a shadow and does not last.

Do you fix your eyes on such a one?
    Do you bring me into judgment with you?
Who can bring a clean thing out of an unclean?
    No one can.
Since their days are determined,
    and the number of their months is known to you,
    and you have appointed the bounds that they cannot pass,
look away from them, and desist
    that they may enjoy, like laborers, their days.
For there is hope for a tree
    if it is cut down, that it will sprout again,
    and that its shoots will not cease.
Though its roots grow old in the earth
    and its stump dies in the ground
yet at the scent of water it will bud
    and put forth branches like a young plant.
But mortals die, and are laid low;
    humans expire, and where are they?
As waters fail from a lake,
    and a river wastes away and dries up,
so mortals lie down and do not rise again;
    until the heavens are no more, they will not awake
    or be roused out of their sleep. (Job 14:1–12)

Perhaps the most beautiful use of natural world imagery occurs in Job 38:1–40:1, where God finally responds to Job. In these chapters, the images capture the mystery, the beauty, the power, and the majesty of the Divine whose continued response from the whirlwind in Job 40:6–41:34 leaves Job humbled. This divine speech from the whirlwind uses not only natural world imagery but also similes and metaphors from the natural world, all of which reveals the magnificence of creation and the magnificence of God.

Like the writer of the Book of Job, MacLeish also draws on imagery, similes, and metaphors from the natural world. For example, J.B. in response to Sarah blurts out:

God is God or we are nothing—
Mayflies that leave their husks behind—
Our tiny lives ridiculous—a suffering
Not even sad that Someone Somewhere
Laughs at us as we laugh at apes.

> We have no choice but to be guilty.
> God is unthinkable if we are innocent.[12]

J.B.'s response to Sarah is straightforward; the lesson embedded within it is profound.

Distinctive to the Book of Job as dramatic poetry is the literary device called "anaphora" which is the repetition of the opening word, phrase, or grammatical element in a series. This anaphora creates a vibrant beat unrestricted by numerical meter. This device is the ancient poet's chief means of creating a poetic rhythm. Prominent in many chapters of the Book of Job, this device achieves an incremental intellectual and emotional emphasis. It is particularly effective when Job describes God's attributes of wisdom, strength, counsel, and understanding, beginning in Job 12:13–25. This device is also effective when God challenges Job with the voice out of the whirlwind in the series of rhetorical questions beginning with: "Where were you when I laid the foundations of the earth?" (Job 38:4).

Elsewhere the cut down tree that renews itself from its roots (Job 14:7–9) becomes a metaphoric foil for humankind's irrevocable death. Humankind's kinship with maggots (Job 17:14) and jackals (Job 30:29) becomes an image of alienation and isolation. The movement of a weaver's shuttle (Job 7:6), a runner in flight and a swooping eagle (Job 9:25–26) serve as similes for the quick passage of a lifetime. All of the poetic images add vividness and clarity to the writer's work and awaken the imagination of the reader.

Elie Wiesel expects the audience for *The Trial of God* to recognize allusions to Chapter 38 of Job several times. Early in the play, we recognize that the playwright has reversed the roles of Job and his counselors: Berish attacks God and the players defend him. Then in an exchange between Maria and the players we hear this parody:

> Are you God's confidante?
> Better yet, He is your confidante! He asks for your advice!
> You tell Him what to do and when—and to whom! You even
> order Him around! Right?[13]

Later Berish, the "reverse Job," begins to defend himself and abruptly cuts off the parody: "And now you want me to feel sorry for Him? Where was He when. . . ."[14] In *J.B.*, Sarah's comment "curse God and die"[15] is a direct allusion to Job's wife's comment in Job 1:9.

Another literary device popular with Hebrew poets that remains popular today is hyperbole, or deliberate exaggeration. Many misunderstandings of the biblical text would be avoided if readers recognized hyperbole, not as the literal thought or sentiment of the speaker, but as a simple strategy for intensifying importance or emotion. Sometimes Job's hyperboles express an extravagant confidence in God's kindness and solicitude:

> At destruction and famine you shall laugh
>   and shall not fear the wild animals of the earth.
> For you shall be in league with the stones of the field,
>   and the wild animals shall be at peace with you.
> (Job 5:22–23)

At other times, Job uses hyperbole to express casual contempt: "But a stupid person will get understanding when a wild ass is born human" (Job 11:12). Other examples of hyperbole can be found in the description of Job's restored fortunes and his earthly longevity (see Job 42:12, 16).

One of the literary devices most important for understanding Elie Wiesel's *The Trial of God* is symbolism. If we miss the symbolic function of every character and action in *The Trial of God*, we risk missing the whole point of the play. Berish, although a unique medieval Jew with a dramatically developed personality, functions symbolically as the bitter, disenchanted Jew of the twentieth century whom the God of the covenant abandoned to the atrocities of Auschwitz. As we have already mentioned, Maria, Berish's foil, is more than herself; she functions as a transparent symbol for the average indifferent gentile. The lecherous priest who repeatedly attempts to seduce Maria serves as the avatar of Christian anti-Semitism throughout the ages. The playwright expects Christians in the audience to respond to the priest with visceral repugnance and honest embarrassment.

The ultimate seducer in *The Trial of God* is, however, The Stranger, who remains in shadow until he emerges as Sam. Sam's self-description as one whose favorite pastime is to meet a variety of people, to please them, to gamble with them, and to win reveals not only the character of Satan but also the weaknesses of his victims who are, of course, the audience for the play.[16] When Sam, as God's defense attorney, presents all the rational explanations for God's apparent complicity in evil that religious people have offered throughout the ages, he becomes the symbol for all those who have tried to offer reasons for God's silence in the face of human injustice. All prove insultingly—diabolically—unsatisfactory.

> Independently of each other, many contemporary Christian theologians have concluded that the only god worthy of human worship is one who suffers wherever humanity suffers.[17] Such

> a concept involves, not a mere "defense" of God, but rather a radical revision of the traditional image of God as "impassible," that is, immune to suffering. When the gentile Maria identifies Sam as her seducer, screaming "Don't trust him!," she challenges Christians to re-examine the deception of their most cherished, consoling images of God.[18]

Above all, through symbolic actions in *The Trial of God*, Wiesel communicates his principal thematic statements. The most shocking and brutally effective symbolic action, the rape of the innocent Hannah, serves as a powerful symbol for the violent desecration of all Jews. The rape, however, is more than a powerful symbol. The kind of violence we see in the perpetrators of such crimes is always a rape of God's image in humanity. As in Greek tragedy, the atrocity against Hannah is not enacted onstage but is reported little by little and reaches its climax when Maria reveals that Berish, the father, was forced to witness his daughter's violation.[19] This symbolic action raises the rhetorical question: Does not humanity force God to witness the rape of innocence every day? Like the witnesses to the rape of Hannah, the Divine witness is rendered mute.

One literary technique that all three authors use is irony. In the Book of Job, the main literary technique is irony. In the Prologue, the readers and the heavenly court share knowledge that neither Job nor his friends and family possess. Job is being tested by the little "satan." Job is innocent of any wrongdoing, but ironically, his friends see him as a transgressor whose transgressions have resulted in his excruciating loss and pain. God puts a protective hedge around Job so that he will not die (Job 1:10), but Job bemoans the fact that God had placed a hedge around him. The hedge that prevents Job's death (cf. Job 2:6) and which is intended for good is, ironically, conceived as a hedge intended for evil. Job speaks ironically about the hedge, this "guard," in Job 7:12. Job's question to God is full of irony when Job asks God if he, Job, is so dangerous as the Sea or a Dragon that he has to have a guard over him continuously. Job has no idea that the guard is for his own benefit. Even the storm in Job 38:1–42:6 symbolizes a deity who is free, wild, beautiful, and deeply unsettling.

Job's supposedly comforting friends also use irony in a subtle attempt to prove that Job is wicked. The friends aim their words at the wicked man with whom they implicitly identify Job by means of verbal irony. Repeatedly, they twist Job's words in an attempt to incriminate him.[20] In Job 12:2, Job retorts sarcastically that his friends have such a monopoly on wisdom that wisdom would cease when they die. Then Job states, ironically, that what they say is common knowledge to all people (Job

12:3c). Job also makes clear to his friends that he is not inferior to them in knowledge (Job 12:3b and 13:2b). Additionally, all of God's speeches are filled with ironic comments that border on sarcasm (see, e.g., Job 38:4–5, 18, 21). These examples are just a few of the many examples of irony within the Book of Job. The biblical writer's use of this technique is what makes the text a dramatic and poetic masterpiece. Let us turn now to irony in *J.B.* and *The Trial of God.*

The best opportunity for dramatic irony comes when an author is retelling a story presumably familiar to his audience. Because the audience knows something that the speaker on stage does not know, his or her words have double meaning—one in the present for the speaker and another in the inevitable future for the audience. Thus dramatic irony is often linked to foreshadowing. In the first scene of *J.B.,* where J.B. and his family are celebrating Thanksgiving, Sarah, bubbling over with gratitude for all the good things God has given her family, gushes: "I feel/ my happiness impending like a danger."[21] MacLeish expects the audience to wince, for he assumes that everyone knows—even those who haven't read the Bible lately—that all these things will soon be cruelly taken away from this good, God-fearing couple. Then, when Sarah goes on to assure J.B. that he *deserves* everything he has received from God, the irony deepens as their conversation foreshadows J.B.'s coming theological dilemma. When he insists that no one deserves God's goodness, the audience anticipates the multiple misfortunes he will not deserve:

> J.B.: It's not a question of deserving.
> Sarah: Oh it is. That's all the question.
> J.B.: Nobody *deserves* it, Sarah. Not the world that God has given us.[22]

In this little exchange of domestic dialogue, MacLeish has introduced one of the huge theological questions of the play: Does suffering come because we deserve it? To this he adds another question rarely asked: Does anyone deserve to be born into this beautiful world to begin with? What is ironic here is that the mood will soon darken while the audience watches the senseless violence heaped on J.B. and silently repeats: "Nobody deserves it."

In *The Trial of God*, Wiesel also employs irony. In a village where all Jews have recently been exterminated, the play within the play is performed on the Jewish Feast of Purim. The Jews in the audience know that the feast celebrates a Jewish victory over anti-Semitism.

MacLeish's play was written in verse because poetry engages us at a deeply emotional level. The immediate and enduring popularity of the work attests to the success of this intention. By contrast, Wiesel's *The Trial of God* is written in a brusque prose style, addressed principally to the intellect, climaxing in what can be described almost as an assault on all emotional religious conviction.

As a poet, MacLeish was especially sensitive to the overall tone and tempo of the language in *J.B.* He knew that a drama in verse had to be both poetic and conversational. His first director instructed the actor playing Nickles to try to sound like Jack Kerouac reciting Shakespeare. *J.B.* went through relentless revisions during a year of rehearsals before winning a Tony Award on Broadway. Creating dialog for Wiesel's *The Trial of God* was also a challenge since the language had to sound convincingly seventeenth-century, yet be accessible to a twentieth-century audience. Both works, written for the theater, can be appreciated fully only when experienced in performance.

In summary, every great piece of literature, whether biblical or contemporary, employs the skills of highly gifted writers who use a variety of techniques to engage readers and to open the horizons of their hearts and minds. The Book of Job, *J.B.*, and *The Trial of God* are three examples of works that exhibit a variety of literary techniques to enhance the dramatic quality of their timeless message.

Drawing from the Well
Theological Themes

As a story—a poetic and prosaic drama—the Book of Job is a theological polemic against the Deuteronomic theology of retribution that states, in a nutshell, "if you are good, then God will reward you; if you are bad, then God will punish you" (see Deuteronomy 28). The book is also a polemic against the popular belief of its time, namely, that sin and suffering went hand-in-hand, that suffering was the direct result of sin. Furthermore, one of the main theological points in the book involves the questions about the roles of God and human beings in the cause and experience of suffering.

The book also raises the question of whether or not a relationship with God can continue in the midst of such excruciating pain and anguish. Additionally, the silence of God throughout most of the book causes us to wonder about the relationship shared between God and Job. On God's part, how intimate is this silence? How caring is it? How sustaining is it, and what, then, is our understanding of God? Is God the cause of bad things? Is God guilty by association? In other words, does not God have a responsibility to intervene in tragedy to change the course of human experience instead of merely standing by and letting pain and sorrow and anguish almost completely engulf a person?

Questions such as these and others move us forward to consider further one of the aforesaid principal theological themes in the Book of Job, namely, the perennially unresolved question of divine complicity in the face of human suffering and its relationship to sin.

This theme of human suffering and sin is explored throughout the dialogues between Job and his "comforters" and in Job's own conversation with God. Job's friends offer him every logical reason for his affliction. Despite all his afflictions, Job remains faithful to God, and his fidelity results in all his lost goods being restored to him by God. This conclusion seems to affirm that material prosperity is a reward for virtue. In their dramas, both MacLeish and Wiesel retain the debate, but reject this conclusion. In both their dramas, the setting, costumes, dialogue, and action, underscore the same theological theme using every theatrical means to retain questions for which there is no definitive answer: Why do bad things happen to good people? Is God just? Is God all powerful, or does the gift of human freedom render the Creator powerless?

Of the two authors, MacLeish is the more confident, yet is ultimately and unsatisfactorily sentimental. He chooses a humanistic, ultimately romantic tone: "Human love conquers all." For some critics, MacLeish's conclusion seems like a sentimental cop-out, even less realistic than the theological capitulation in the Book of Job. In fact, one sarcastic drama critic asserted: "MacLeish has not been able to avoid the greatest cliché of the fifties: that love cures boils!" MacLeish tries to have it both ways. According to MacLeish's thinking, if we cannot believe in God, we must believe in love, for that is to choose life over death. Love, like faith in a loving God, is ultimately irrational. MacLeish asserts that a human being is not the animal that thinks; the human being is the animal that—against all odds—loves. MacLeish writes in poetry because poetry focuses not on intellectual precision, but on emotional truth. Sarah's final speech, however, also suggests that love is a mode of perception unavailable to the intellect: If we love long enough, "We'll see by and by." For most people, human love is simply not enough to compensate for an atrocity like the Holocaust.

Wiesel, the more harshly cynical author, offers no such easy answer. In fact, through the episode of Maria's seduction, Wiesel defines evil as the perversion of love. Martin Buber also rejects all attempts to soften God's image. He criticizes Job's three friends for offering him a reasonable God. He condemns them as tempters who urge Job to revise his experience of God into a comfortable religion.[23] Wiesel resists the biblical temptation. As Matthew Fox asserts in the epilogue to *The Trial of God*, "This play lays bare how human evil breaks our most cherished images of God."[24] Wiesel's whole play, like the Book of Job, compels humanity to let go of the false anthropocentric God made in our own image.[25]

In *The Trial of God*, the rape of Hannah renders its witnesses mute. Wiesel seems to say that when God witnesses human evil, he too seems rendered mute. Hence, much twentieth-century literature after World War II has been labeled a "literature of silence." One example of this theme can be found in the existentialist Ingmar Bergman's film, *Virgin Spring*. A knight traveling through a forest comes upon the violated body of a young virgin. He raises his fist to the sky and cries out: "I don't understand You! You watched them do it!" Then he falls on his knees and prays: "Because I cannot understand You, I will worship you." Here Bergman attempts to recreate Job 38:4–12 and 40:4–5.

Neither MacLeish nor Wiesel chooses to allude to the revelation of divine compassion incarnated in Jesus Christ, whose ultimate image of the nature of God is known as The Passion. Yet, the playwrights' chief source of inspiration, the Book of Job, contains one of the historically earliest references to the need for a redeemer. Chapter 33, Elihu's monologue, contains the theological heart of the Book of Job. Another notable anticipation of Christian doctrine comes in Job's apparent belief in an afterlife (Job 14:12).

Finally, the climax of the Book of Job comes when the overwhelming voice from the whirlwind silences Job. Poetry conquers debate.

Wading Deeper on Your Own

Questions for Reflection and Discussion

1. What does the Book of Job tell us about the human-divine relationship in our lives?
2. How are we to understand the Divine Silence in the experience of human suffering in our world today?
3. What does the Book of Job tell us about the role of God in the midst of suffering?
4. What are the biblical author's assumptions about the reader?
5. What does MacLeish assume about the audience for *J.B.*?
6. Do MacLeish's assumptions assist or impede the characterizations of Zuss, Nickles, J.B.?
7. What does Wiesel assume about his audience? Does the play justify or challenge these assumptions?
8. What does the play *J.B.* communicate by having both God and Satan wear masks? Who does more talking in *J.B.*—God or Satan? What does this suggest?

9. Why do you think MacLeish chose to make the first death reported in the play so tawdry?
10. How does Nickles' definition of piety resemble that condemned by Coover in "The Brother"?
11. Does Nickles ever say anything with which you agree?
12. Compare Nickles with Sam in *The Trial of God*. Which version of Satan do you find more thought provoking?
13. What ideas about the relationship of sin to beauty and to freedom does MacLeish convey?
14. Can you think of any situation during your lifetime comparable to any situation in *The Trial of God*?
15. Elie Wiesel personifies Satan as evil which masquerades as good. Can you think of any current circumstance where this is true today?
16. "As long as there are Jews, they will inspire hate." Is this true of some other group today? Is hate a form of fear?
17. Who or what does Mendel symbolize? What does he mean when he says, "I fear for God"?

Suggestions for Writing and Journaling

1. Write an essay comparing the Book of Job with one of the following: the graphic novel by Kim Deitch; a novel by C. S. Lewis; the verse drama by Robert Frost; the Coen Brothers' film, "A Serious Man." Point out how the author either distorts or enhances the biblical theme.
2. Compare and contrast the themes of *J.B.* with those of "The Brother."
3. "Accept. Endure. And say Amen. This is what the powerful say to the powerless to keep them that way." Write an essay—or a short documentary script—showing how these words are acted out somewhere today.
4. From the works studied in this chapter, select one statement (or question) that disturbed you most. Then select the statement (or question) that most inspired you. Write a unified essay using both of them to support a conviction of your own.
5. Both playwrights created characters to personify their idea of evil in conversation with an "average" person. Try your hand at doing the same thing. Write a script for stage or screen with dialogue between a good person and some temptation personified.

Irrigating Other Fields

Each of the three authors studied in this chapter found it useful to explore conflicted feelings about God, sin, prejudice, and injustice in their worlds by inventing characters and composing imaginary dialogs in which they argued different positions with each other. As you encounter conflict situations in other fields of learning—history, political science, criminal justice, art history, computer science, language—experiment with writing short scenarios based on what you have learned in this chapter.

5

LYRIC POETRY AS PRAYER

Psalms of Lament

Psalm 22:1–21; 44

Selections from African-American Spirituals

Introduction

As we have just seen in the Book of Job, the authors of the Bible, besides telling stories in narrative prose, often chose to heighten the aesthetic and emotional impact of their words by rendering their message in the literary genre of poetry. In every poetic tradition, oral poetry precedes a written literature. The Book of Psalms is a collection of lyric poems in the form of prayers. In both Hebrew and Greek, the word "psalm" denotes a lyric to be sung to accompaniment by a stringed instrument. No one knows exactly how many psalms were sung in the original oral tradition before they were written down, and none of the ancient music has survived. Throughout the centuries since the music disappeared, however, the lyrics have inspired numerous composers to set the psalms to new melodies as varied as Gregorian chant, Leonard Bernstein's *Chichester Psalms*, and Steve Reich's *Tehillim*.

The Book of Psalms, the prayer book of the Israelite people, can and has been read by secular scholars in every age as an anthology of passionate poetry which preserves the values and emotions of one ancient people and, in translation, has continued to express the deepest religious feelings of people from generation to generation all over the world. In imagery and metaphor, these poems record intellectual and emotional reflections on nature, on good and evil, and on the ultimate mystery we call God whom the poet often describes in metaphorical language.[1] The psalms also refer to historical events of the Jewish people such as the crossing of the Red Sea and the entrance into the Promised Land. Some psalms even describe personal struggles and hopes.

Although some other biblical books contain prayers, the Book of Psalms is the only book in the Bible that consists entirely of prayers. These prayers record the community's relationship with a vividly imagined deity, a relationship both tender and stormy. Feelings of awe and reverence before God do not preclude the psalmists' questions and complaints; but gratitude and joy usually triumph as the devout Jew continues to count on God's faithfulness to the covenant. In all lyric poetry—sacred and secular—the strongest impulse is the urge to praise. Poet Mary Oliver often sums up the whole vocation of the poet in some version of this simple formula: "Pay attention. Be astonished. Say so." Nature's beauty impels many poets to praise its author and to see in human individuality a mirror for divine ingenuity. Gerard Manley Hopkins' lyric sonnet "Pied Beauty," for example, echoes the sentiment of many psalms: "Glory be to God for dappled things . . . All things counter, original, spare, strange; . . . He fathers-forth whose beauty is past change: Praise him."[2] In the biblical psalms, this celebratory spirit usually manages to prevail over more dismal emotions. In fact, although the preponderance of psalm prayers are classified as "laments," the whole collection is called *tehillim*, "praises."

Honoring the lyric impulse to praise, the total composition of the Book of Psalms is subdivided into five books, each of which concludes with a doxology, an exclamation of worship. In the final psalm, praise seems to grow in intensity until the clamor of trumpets, tambourines, and cymbals joins David's harp to culminate the Book of Psalms with the exclamation: "Let everything that breathes praise the Lord" (Ps. 150:6).

In the United States, the oral poetry most consistently influenced by the Bible was the poetry sung by African slaves. This musical genre that developed among African slaves resembles in many ways the content and spirit of the biblical psalms. Called "spirituals" or "sorrow songs,"[3] these lyrics also preserve the history of a people with God, a history of suffering in which faith in the goodness of God is severely tested. While most spirituals begin in sorrow, they usually conclude on a note of hope or trust, and even occasionally, a defiant "halleluiah!" The poetry of both psalms and spirituals springs from a unique attitude: no matter how desolate the situation you are in, singing God's praises lifts you above that desolation. For the African-American slave, the door to hope was music, and that music's distinctive style was homage to the God who was glorified in human individuality. In performance, the sorrow of the spiritual is often drowned in clapping, shouting, and exuberant halleluiahs. The African-American choreographer Alvin Ailey captured this spirit in his modern dance sequence, *Revelations*. This signature masterwork of the Alvin Ailey Dance Company inevitably brings a secular audience to its feet in a rhythmic act of praise.

Like the Israelites, the African slaves brought their culture with them into exile. Hence, after Native American oral poetry and dance, African-American spirituals—organized around the repetitive rhythms of Africa—are the oldest indigenous poetry and music in the United States. Spirituals were the precursors of the musical genres we know as jazz, blues, and gospel. For a while, many children and grandchildren of American slaves abandoned their oldest music because it enshrined an experience of shame. After the civil rights movement in the 1960s introduced "Black Pride," African performers, both classical and popular, revived the spiritual. In both content and style, the spirituals bear many resemblances to the psalms. First of all, their content assumes familiarity with the characters and stories of the Old Testament. Like the Book of Psalms, spirituals transmitted to a pre-literate congregation, not only sacred scripture, but also a shared history, for what attracted the African-American community to the Old Testament was the story of the Israelite exile, enslavement, and liberation. Secondly, the combination of joy and sorrow, worship and complaint, evident in the psalms, also characterizes the lyrics of the African-American spiritual. Ironically, when we consider that more people are physically enslaved in the twenty-first century than at any time in history, and then add to that the number of those enslaved spiritually, both the psalms and the spirituals are now relevant to more people than ever. The two specific psalms to be addressed in this chapter are Psalm 22:1–22 and 44. Elements of the psalms and African-American spirituals are examined together, and insights on their genre, structure, style, and theology are highlighted.

Drinking from the Spring
The Biblical Text
Psalm 22:1–21 and Psalm 44

Of the numerous psalms in the oral tradition, the 150 collected in the Hebrew Scriptures have been divided into several general classifications, which include hymns of praise, songs of thanksgiving, songs of lament, instructional psalms, royal psalms, liturgies, acrostic poems, historical psalms, and festival psalms, among others. Psalms of praise and thanksgiving each comprise a little over 15 percent of the total. Although the sixty others include some passages of praise and thanksgiving, by far their predominant mood places them in a category of lament or complaint. About one-third of all the psalms belong to the category of lament, which is one of the oldest and best attested literary genres in the ancient Near East. The lament psalms are subdivided into individual and communal laments, that is, the voice in the poem is that of either a person or a community. Toni Craven notes:

> Laments bespeak the knowledge that the individual or the community is not in control, that God is an agent of powerful change. Laments call God to act to bring order out of chaos, to restore the peace and wholeness of shalom. Spoken by those whose world is out of order to a God whose covenant offers the hope of renewed order, laments are powerful testimonies to the

> faith of a people who believed it appropriate to praise God from the depths of human distress with honest words of complaint.[4]

Both the psalm of lament and the sorrow song bespeak a sturdy relationship with God. Though reverence is an appropriate tone in prayer, excessive politeness can signal fear of shattering a fragile relationship. Neither the Israelite people nor the African authors of the spirituals felt the need to be polite with their God.

A Lament of an Individual
Psalm 22:1–21a

Psalm 22 is a prayer of lamentation. Part of the larger psalm (vv. 1–31), verses 1 to 21a capture the uttermost depths of suffering and pain, a suffering that is gripping and heart-wrenching as the psalmist cries out to God, wondering where God is and why God has not responded (vv. 1, 2). Wearied and downtrodden, the psalmist remains hopeful because the memory of God's intervention and saving help in times past on behalf of the psalmist's ancestors brings a sense of consolation, expectation, and even of certitude (vv. 3–5, 19–21).[5]

The lament section of Psalm 22 can be divided into six units:

vv. 1–2: A Cry of Despair
vv. 3–5: A Confession
vv. 6–8: An Expression of Grief and a Taunt
vv. 9–11: An Address to God
vv. 12–18: A Statement of Anxiety
vv. 19–21a: A Plea

The remaining verses, 21b–31, are words of praise and thanksgiving after the psalmist's troubles have been resolved. In some lament psalms, the final word can be one of praise, thanksgiving, and gratitude. Psalm 22 is thought to have been proclaimed in the worship of the cult community (v. 25) after the prayer has been answered (v. 24).

A Cry of Despair (vv. 1, 2)

Using a double address that is both personal and intimate, the psalmist calls on God and raises two poignant questions:

> My God, my God, why have you forsaken me?
> Why are you so far from helping me,
> From the words of my groaning?[6]

Verse 2 continues the psalmist's poignant sentiments. This time, the psalmist addresses God by means of a personal vocative, "O my God" and then confronts God as to why God has not answered. Israel's God is silent in the face of agonizing, perpetual pain and suffering that leaves the psalmist unable to find any rest or consolation whatsoever.

A Confession (vv. 3–5)

To the God of silence who has yet to respond to the psalmist's cry of despair, the psalmist now confronts God directly by first mentioning God's primary attribute and regal position and then by describing how God interacted with Israel in the past when the people had cried out. Israel's God did hear the cry of the oppressed in the past, and the people were delivered, saved, and not put to shame. The psalmist's ancestors had a dynamic and mutual relationship with their God, and now the psalmist is perplexed by the lack of response on the part of God.

An Expression of Grief and a Taunt (vv. 6–8)

A person of profound grief, the psalmist feels less than human (vv. 6–7). Walter Brueggemann and William H. Bellinger, Jr., highlight the effectiveness of the poetic language in these verses that communicate the extraordinary desperation of the psalmist: "Informed by three derogatory terms—scorned, despised, mocked—the speaker is abased and ashamed, and reduced in terms of social identity to a subhuman condition. In that condition of shame, the petitioner is helpless in the face of ridicule."[7] The psalmist then suffers the taunt of others who mockingly say:

> Commit your cause to the Lord; let him deliver—
> Let him rescue the one in whom he delights! (v. 8)

The irony here is that God will eventually deliver the psalmist from all the pain and suffering being endured because the psalmist has already committed his or her cause to the Lord.

An Address to God (vv. 9–11)

Shifting the focus away from the personal suffering being endured, the psalmist once again confronts God. Here the psalmist's words stand in stark contrast to what was spoken in verses 6–8. In verses 9–11, the psalmist acknowledges his or her relationship with God from the time of the womb. This human-divine relationship has been marked by great love, care, and fidelity, and thus, God should now answer the psalmist in this time of need. Implicit in these verses is the psalmist's reproach of God.

A Statement of Anxiety (vv. 12–18)

Exquisite metaphorical language in verses 12–18 describes either the adversaries of the psalmist or what the psalmist is feeling internally, or both. The adversaries are like "many bulls," "strong bulls of Bashan" (v.12). These "strong bulls of Bashan" whose opened mouths are like a "ravening and roaring lion" (vv. 12–13) reside in the fertile pastureland east of the Jordan. This fertile pasture was well known for its strong race of breeding cattle. This experience of either actual adversaries or horrific feelings causes the psalmist to have a physical response:

> I am poured out like water,
> and all my bones are out of joint;
> my heart is like wax;
> it is melted within my breast;
> my mouth is dried up like a potsherd;
> and my tongue sticks to my jaws;
> you lay me in the dust of death. (vv. 14–15)

The sense of being overcome and overwhelmed racks the poet's entire body to the point of feeling as if God has laid him or her "in the dust of death" (v. 15). Clearly the psalmist is deteriorating, a state that the poet attributes to God's lack of protection.

The psalmist's expression of anxiety continues in verses 16–18. Raw feelings and real or imagined adversaries are like dogs that surround the psalmist (v. 16a).[8] Once again the psalmist feels exceedingly vulnerable, a condition that triggers a physiological response:

> My hands and feet are shriveled;
> I can count all my bones.
> They stare and gloat over me;
> they divide my clothes among themselves,
> and for my clothing they cast lots. (vv. 16b–18)

The psalmist's lament is ever so poignant because in the midst of such inner and outer turoil, a response from God has yet to come forth.

A Plea (vv. 19–21a)

Shaken to the core, the psalmist once again addresses God directly:

> But, you, O Lord, do not be far away!
> O my help, come quickly to my aid!
> Deliver my soul from the sword,
> my life from the power of the dog!
> Save me from the mouth of the lion! (vv. 19–21)

Image after image reveals the psalmist's acute turmoil and the utmost trust being placed in God, whom the psalmist knows has the power to change the course of the tide, and in so doing, bring relief from peril, comfort from anxiety, and an end to fear and humiliation. In the second half of Psalm 22, specifically vv. 21b–31, relief does come to the psalmist from God, which evokes praise.

Thus, through graphic imagery, rhetorical questions, poignant statements to God, repugnant metaphors, terrifying similes, and persistent, commanding pleas, the psalmist in Psalm 22:1–21a invites us into the world of pain and anguish that flows into lamentation as one searches for the seemingly distant Sacred Presence. Paradoxically, that Presence remains forever present in the midst of turmoil even when we, overwhelmed by anxiety and adversity, cannot seem to feel or recognize God's nearness, to the point where we too, like the psalmist, cry out:

> My God, my God, why have you forsaken me?
> Why are you so far from helping me,
> from the words of my groaning? (v. 1)

The lament song of the psalmist is the same song sung by generations down through the ages, and it finds its home especially among African-American spirituals that convey similar sentiments as we will see later in this chapter.

A Communal Lament
Psalm 44

Israel's laments were not only personal; they were also communal. Psalm 44 is a communal lament where the community not only recounts God's past salvific deeds while recalling God's present deeds, but also laments, grieves, and protests what seems to be a national calamity, most likely a defeat in war. This communal lament is the first in a series of eleven that express the prayers of the people who are in various distressing situations.

The psalm can be divided into three units:

- vv. 1–8: A Celebration of the Memory of God's Saving Deeds
- vv. 9–22: A Defeat Lamented
- vv. 23–26: A Plea for Divine Assistance

Artur Weiser, in his classic commentary on the Psalms, offers a succinct summary of the events that take place in Psalm 44. He also offers striking parallels that Psalm 44 has with some other texts of the prophets.

The nation has been defeated by an enemy in battle (v. 10); the prisoners have been deported to a foreign country (v. 11; cf. Amos 1, 6, 9); Israel suffers from the scorn of her neighbors (v. 14f); and jackals have made the ruins of destroyed cities their abode (v. 19; cf. Jer. 9:11; 10:22; 49:33; Isa. 13:22; 34:13). Yahweh, the Lord of hosts and God of wars, who once had gone out to war at the head of the Israelite armies (1 Sam. 4.33ff.; 2 Sam. 5.24), has refused his help (vv. 4, 9); now the people prostrate themselves before God—probably in the sanctuary—(v. 25) and complain to him of their material and spiritual afflictions in order to beg for his help and for their deliverance.[9] Let us now take a closer look at Psalm 44.

A Celebration of the Memory of God's Saving Deeds (vv. 1–8)

This communal lament begins with the first person plural pronoun "we" which draws the community into listening to the psalm being proclaimed by an individual within the community and on behalf of the community. In verses 1–3, the poet recounts in general the marvelous deeds that God has done throughout history. The stories of these deeds have been passed down through the ages by generations of ancestors and have also been told to the poet of this psalm. Israel's God is the one who rescued the people from Egyptian oppression and bondage (Exod. 1–15), who drove out the nations (see 1 Kgs. 1:14, 24; 2 Kgs. 16:3, 6 and 17:8), but planted Israel (Isa. 5:1–7), who afflicted people (see Exod. 7:14–12:42), but set Israel free (Exod. 14), and who brought the Israelites into the land that was promised to them, which, according to the biblical text, they took possession of by means of a series of conquests (see Josh. 8–12), the success of which they attributed to the power of God interceding on their behalf. And why did God do all these marvelous deeds for Israel?—because God "delighted" in the Israelites (v. 3b).

Such experiences of divine benevolence and assertion of power lead the poet to make a personal statement on the community's behalf: "You are my King and my God . . ." (v. 4). Throughout vv. 4–8, the voice of the poet and the voice of the community come to the fore as both the poet and community acknowledge that all past victories achieved have been merited through God and God's power working within the community. Such feats became reason to boast in God continually and to give thanks to God's name forever.

A Defeat Lamented (vv. 9–22)

The tone and situation of Psalm 44 shift in verses 9–22. The poet, speaking on behalf of the community, moves from past memories to present realities. Verses 9–22 describe defeat in battle. Although no specific enemy nations are mentioned, the ones implied probably include Assyria, Egypt, and Babylon, among others. The backdrop to these verses is most likely the fall of the Northern Kingdom of Israel to the Assyrians around 722 BCE and the fall of the Southern Kingdom of Judah to the Babylonians in 587 BCE, along with the destruction of the Temple and the holy city Jerusalem. Following the fall of Judah, the people were exiled to Babylon and Egypt. Thus, the setting for this psalm may well be the exile or, if post-exilic, then the text reflects the community looking back on its not so distant past and recalling the events that led up to the exile. Quite possibly the poet could also be recounting a defeat in a battle that happened between 722 and 587 BCE. The actual setting and dating of the psalm, however, are uncertain.

The poet and community's anguished lamentation becomes most poignant in verses 9–12 through the use of the literary technique known as "cataloguing." Here the poet lists all the horrific deeds God has done to the community to the point where they have become the taunt of their neighbors (vv. 13–16; cf. Mic. 2:4–5).

In verses 17–22, the poet sets up a contract that showcases Israel's fidelity to God that stands in complete opposition to God's harsh treatment of Israel. Even though God has seemingly rejected Israel (v. 9), Israel has never forgotten its God (v. 17), has remained faithful to covenant (v. 17), and has never forgotten the name of its God or worshipped another god (v. 20). Through these contrasting images, the poet indirectly blames God for all of Israel's misfortune, a claim that comes to the fore in verse 22, where the poet makes a harrowing direct charge against God:

> Because of you we are being killed all day long,
> and accounted as sheep for the slaughter.

Thus, according to the poet, the community has been faithful to God and faithful to covenant, but God has not been faithful to the community or to covenant, which is why the poet and the community now lament. Lamentation, however, is not the final word.

A Plea for Divine Assistance (vv. 23–26)

Words of lamentation, frustration, and accusation turn to petition in verses 23–26, where the poet and the community call God to responsibility, beckoning God to take action on behalf of the community. With a series of imperatives and rhetorical questions, the poet and the community confront God directly:

> Rouse yourself! Why do you sleep, O Lord?

Awake, do not cast us off forever!
Why do you hide your face?
Why do you forget our affliction and oppression?
For we sink down to the dust;
our bodies cling to the ground.
Rise up, come to our help.
Redeem us for the sake of your steadfast love.

The poet and the community place an extra burden on God: God has to come to the aid of the suffering community if God's steadfast love is to remain the cornerstone to God's relationship with Israel and, by extension, with God's relationship with all the nations and all creation. Just as the community remembers, so now God is called to remember (v. 24). The psalm closes on a note of petition. The community must wait on hope.

Summary

Psalm 22:1–21 and Psalm 44 are two lyrical poems that function as prayer. These psalms express the heartfelt sentiments of the Israelite people, and the poems portray the theme and power of lament. In spite of all their hardships, losses, pain, and suffering, the Israelite people never lose hope, as these two texts portray. The people remain in conversation with their God, and they remain expectant that the God of their ancestors will act as in the days of old to deliver them from their fears, anxieties, and sufferings. For now, they have to wait on their God, knowing that in time, their lamentation—their prayer of the heart—will be answered and will one day become a song of joy. These lyrical prayers of lamentation expressed by the psalmist in Psalm 22:1–21 and Psalm 44 find a thematic and emotional echo in African-American spirituals that we shall now explore.

Playing in the Fountain
The Literary Text
African-American Spirituals

About the Authors

Identifying the authors of the spirituals, like naming the psalmists, is impossible. According to the Library of Congress, there are approximately five thousand spirituals extant, including fragments. Not one of them has a written text signed by an author. At the time spirituals were being composed, there was far less of a distinction between performer and audience. Hence, lines and variations interjected by one audience were often adopted permanently. Many lyrics developed interactively through the "call and response" style that remains popular in African-American churches.

Reflecting on Genre

The Lyric Lament

Like the psalms, spirituals also can be divided into individual and communal laments. In some lyrics, the individual expresses a simple self-pity:

Sometimes I feel like a motherless child,
A long way from home.
O Lord, what shall I do?
Trouble done bore me down.
I'm a child of misery.
Trouble done bore me down.
I'm sometimes up and sometimes down;
I'm sometimes level with the ground
Trouble done bore me down.

For the slave, the deepest personal affliction is to feel separated from the praying community:

Chilly waters in the Jordan.
Crossing over into Canaan.
And I couldn't hear nobody pray.
O way down yonder by myself,
And I couldn't hear nobody pray.

At other times, the individual lament becomes a call to personal responsibility:

Oh you got to walk-a-that lonesome valley,
You got to go there by yourself;
No one here to go with you.
You got to go there by yourself.

When you reach the river Jordan
You got to cross it by yourself
No one here may cross it with you.
You got to cross it by yourself.

When you face that judgment morning
You got to stand your trial in judgment.
You got to live a life of service.
You got to live it by yourself.
No one here to live it for you.
You got to live it by yourself.

In the lament psalms, the call for help is often cleverly embedded in a reminder of how God has acted powerfully for the Israelites in the past. Psalm 44, for example, begins:

> We have heard with our ears, O God,
>   our ancestors have told us,
> what deeds you performed in their days,
>   in the days of old:
> you with your own hand drove out the nations
>   you afflicted the peoples but them you set free.
> (Ps. 44:1–2)

Elsewhere, however, the same God is accused of acting harshly against the Israelites:

> You have made us like sheep for slaughter
>   and have scattered us among the nations.
> You have sold your people for a trifle,
>   demanding no high price for them. (Ps. 44:11–12)

Taking their cue from these psalmists, the African poets also set their call for help in the context of historical interventions, whimsically reminding God, as if God might have forgotten:

> Didn't my Lord deliver Daniel, deliver Daniel,
>   deliver Daniel?
> And why not every man?
> He delivered Daniel from the lion's den,
> Jonah from the belly of the whale,
> and the Hebrew children from the fiery furnace.
> And why not every man?

Yet, unlike the psalmists in Psalm 44:9–16, the slaves do not blame the invisible God for their affliction. The slaves hold their powerful slave masters accountable before God and warn them:

> I'm gonna tell God how you treat me,
> I'm gonna tell God how you treat me,
> Some of these days, Halleluiah!
>
> You're gonna wish that you'd-a-bin ready;
> God's gonna set your sins before you;
> God's gonna bring this world to judgment;
> Some of these days, Halleluiah!

Finally, the halleluiah is what distinguishes the spiritual from a secular blues song. The blues song savors pain and aims to keep it alive; the spiritual song always aims toward hope.

Reflecting on Structure

Typically, psalms of lament are constructed to feature three or more of the following elements in which complaint or lament alternates with sentiments of faith in God's goodness, concluding always in an act of praise or thanksgiving:

- a call for help addressed to God
- a confession of faith
- a lament
- a prayer of confidence
- an extended lament—sometimes an accusation or even
- a curse
- a promise of repentance
- an act of thanksgiving and/or praise[10]

Since the spiritual lyrics are very short—sometimes no more than two repeated lines—they do not follow the structural pattern of the individual psalms, but they do seem to take their cue from the psalm pattern in the sense that, collectively, the spirituals alternate the psalms' required elements. A typical religious service might begin with a confession like:

> I bin 'buked and I've been scorned,
> I've been talked about sure's you're born.
> But ain't goin' to lay my religion down.

This confession would then be followed by the plea, "Fix me Jesus, fix me." Next the leader would provoke a promise to change in a song like, "Changed mah name," and the service would conclude with an act of faith "Children, we shall be free."

Reflecting on Literary Style

The Hebrew psalms in general and the lament psalms in particular, and the African-American spirituals derived from them, present many interesting comparisons and contrasts. Although the psalms are quite ancient, by the time they were written and collected in the Old Testament, their literary craft was by no means primitive. From a poetic standpoint, the psalms' most appealing feature is imagery. In Psalm 22:12–13 the psalmist uses elements from the natural world to describe a perilous situation:

> Many bulls encircle me,
> strong bulls of Bashan surround me;

> they open wide their mouths at me,
>   like a ravening and roaring lion.

Another technique that the psalmist uses is metaphorical language that captures the strong sentiments of the poet's lament:

> You have made us like sheep for the slaughter
>   And have scattered us among the nations. (Ps. 44:11)
>
> You have made us the taunt of our neighbors,
>   the derision and scorn of those around us.
> You have made us a byword among the nations,
>   a laughingstock among the peoples. (Ps. 44:13–14)

Such language draws us into the psalmist's experience and invites us to share in the pain and suffering that evokes lamentation.

Another stylistic technique distinctive to the lament psalms and the psalter in general is *parallelism*. Parallelism creates symmetry in a Hebrew poem. The three main kinds of parallelism are synonymous parallelism, antithetic parallelism, and synthetic parallelism. In synonymous parallelism two lines say approximately the same thing in different words. Antithetic parallelism juxtaposes one statement with its antithesis. Synthetic parallelism involves the completion or expansion of the idea of the first line in the second line. Psalm 22:1–21 and Psalm 44 use two of the three types of parallelism. Psalm 22:16 is an example of synonymous parallelism:

> For dogs are all around me;
>   a company of evildoers encircles me.

Psalm 44:9–12 offers a rich example of synthetic parallelism:

> Yet you have rejected us and abased us,
>   and have not gone out with our armies.
> You made us turn back from the foe,
>   and our enemies have gotten spoil.
> You have made us like sheep for slaughter,
>   and have scattered us among the nations.
> You have sold your people for a trifle,
>   demanding no high price for them.

Parallelism serves two functions in Hebrew poetry. First of all, reflecting the musical origins of psalmody, parallelism is the primary source of rhythm. This becomes apparent when we read a psalm aloud and hear how, even when two synonymous phrases have a totally different number of syllables, they sound metrically alike. Secondly, by contrasting one thought with its opposite, the poet achieves a dramatic emphasis, just as an artist draws attention to an image by placing it against a contrasting background.[11]

With respect to the literary style of the spirituals, one cannot expect the unschooled African slaves to have their poetry at the level of the verbal sophistication and metrical intricacies that one finds in the Hebrew psalms. What literary scholars have found in the spontaneous African-American art, however, is remarkable in many ways. One of the first striking differences from the psalms is the spirituals' scarcity of nature imagery. Since slaves rarely enjoyed a leisurely, contemplative experience of nature's beauty, one can see and understand that their references to nature are so fleeting and sometimes negative. In "I Want to Go Home," for example, the slave enumerates forces of nature along with the harsh conditions from which he wants to escape:

> I want to go home
> Where there's no rain to wet you,
> O yes, I want to go home,
> . . . no sun to burn you,
> . . . no whips a-cracking
> . . . no tribulation
> . . . no slavery in the kingdom.

Like the psalmists, the slave poets interacted with the natural world by way of personification, often endowing it with negative powers or sympathies:

> O, I went to the rock to hide my face,
> The rock cried out, "No hiding place!". . .
> The rock cried out 'I'm burning too.
> I want to go to Heaven as well as you.

By far, the most effective literary device was symbolism. The circumstance of their captivity brought about their most ingenious use of this technique. Throughout the centuries, as all three Abrahamic religions have prayed the psalms daily, almost every figure in them, from nature imagery to historical allusion, evolved into a symbol for spiritual reality. For the slaves, however, these same symbols became an elaborate code for social reality, a secret communications system. Often when the slaves sang in the company of their owners, the song was a musical mask for an escape script. "Egypt" meant the South, "Hell" meant the Deep South; and "Pharaoh" referred to the slave master. The "Red Sea of Exodus" became the wide Atlantic that separated the Africans from their homeland. Depending on the immediate escape plan, words like "campground," "Promised Land," and "Heaven" symbolized Africa, Canada, or the Free States. In both the psalms and the spirituals, one of the most important symbols is "land." From Genesis, where a garden is the locus for unmitigated bliss and alienation begins with expulsion from a fertile paradise, to the Promised Land that culminates the exodus, "land" symbolizes freedom, integrity, fulfillment, union with the Creator. For the slaves, references to paradise and to the Promised Land were a way to talk about escape in the presence of their masters while the latter heard only pious hymns.

Another recurrent symbol is the "river." Egypt, the land of exile, was across a river, and every river reminded the Israelites of home:

> By the rivers of Babylon—
> there we sat down and there we wept
> when we remembered Zion (Ps. 137:1).

Hence, the slaves used the symbol of the river to express their yearning to cross all the waters that separated them from freedom and from their homeland. In the popular spiritual, "Deep River," we see how the terms "campground," "home," and "heaven" become synonymous symbols of freedom.

> Deep River, my home is over Jordan;
> Deep river, Lord, I want to cross over into camp ground. . . .
> Oh, don't you want to cross over to that Gospel feast,
> That Promised Land where all is peace?
> . . .
> And when I get to Heaven, I'll walk all about;
> Nobody there for to turn me out.
> Deep river, Lord, I want to cross over into camp ground.

In the slaves' encoded songs, any agency of travel symbolized escape: wheels, chariots, trains, even shoes. Hence, the raucous gusto of a song that sounded like a harmless wish to be fully dressed concluded with the chorus "Going to Shout All Over God's Heaven."

> I've got shoes, you've got shoes,
> All of God's children got shoes.
> When I get to heaven,
> Going to put on my shoes,
> Going to walk all over God's heaven.

And in another:

> What kind of shoes are those we wear, O my Lord!

That you can ride upon the air, O my Lord!
These shoes I wear are gospel shoes
And you can wear them if you choose,
O my Lord!

"Swing Low" originally a funeral song—often sung when a child died—asked God to send a golden chariot to escort the beloved to a better home. Eventually as "home" came more and more to symbolize freedom, the song was used as a rallying cry for the living. Here we see a cluster of symbols associated with escape to freedom.

Swing low, Swing low, Sweet Chariot
Coming for to carry me home.
I looked over Jordan and what did I see?
Coming for to carry me home
A band of angels coming after me
Coming for to carry me home.
If you get there before I do
Tell my friends I'm coming up there too.
Swing low, Swing low, Sweet Chariot
Coming for to carry me home.

In the increasingly secular culture that dominates postmodernist literary analysis, critics now focus almost exclusively on deciphering the encoded messages in the spirituals and deliberately suppress reference to any authentic faith experience. Even though some slaves regarded their songs purely as clever instruments of covert communication, not everyone singing in church and in the field traveled the Underground Railroad. Many slaves had no understanding of the code. For them, the lyrics were an unalloyed act of religious faith.

Finally, we can observe another persistent and unusual feature of the spirituals for which no literary term exists: a unique treatment of time. For the Africans, so united with their ancestors by music, the act of singing seemed to create a new "tense" in which past, present, and future become indistinguishable. This lack of a sense of time is especially noticeable when the poet addresses Jesus directly. Here, for example, the singer speaks in the present of a "someday" which has already happened:

O, poor little Jesus,
This world gonna break your heart.
There'll be no place to lay your head.
Come down, all you holy angels,
Sing round Him with your golden harps;
For someday He will die to save this world.

Probably, this treatment of time derives from the fact that the slaves so completely appropriated the Israelite experience of slavery and derived hope from the story of their eventual deliverance. Hence, while many of the psalms reflect past events, the spirituals tend to transpose them into a present or future reality.

Drawing from the Well
Theological Themes

As the prayer book of the Israelite people, the Book of Psalms as a whole, and specifically the lament Psalm 22:1–21 and Psalm 44, offers us a further glimpse into the ancient biblical community's theology. The prayers of a people embody answers to two basic theological questions: What was this people's dominant image of God? What kind of relationship with that God did they experience both in their personal reality and in the history of the liturgical community? This is true for us today. Our own understanding of who God is modifies the image of the one to whom we pray. Our personal history and humanity during our lifetime also influences our ability to resonate with the divine-human relationship embodied in the psalms. The image of God conveyed in Psalm 22:1–21 and Psalm 44 is that of an all-powerful male deity who is responsible for everything that happens in this world. Moreover, the God to whom the psalmist prays is one who has made an unbreakable covenant with his people, a covenant that they believe he has confirmed by frequent intervention in the life of their community. Remembrance of this covenant grounds the future hopes of those who pray in a confidence based on God's past performance:

> We have heard with our ears, O God,
> our ancestors have told us,
> what deeds you performed in their days,
> in the days of old:
> you with your own hand drove out the nations,
> but them you planted;
> you afflicted the peoples,
> but them you set free;
> for not by their own sword did they win the land,
> nor did their own arm give them victory;
> but your right hand, and your arm,
> and the light of your countenance,
> for you delighted in them. (Ps. 44:1–3)

Looking at the Psalter as a whole, which provides a context for the lament psalms and of which the lament psalms are a part, one can see that some of the psalmists' images of God and of Israel's relationship with God oftentimes reflect those experiences and images found in the Torah. For example, in the Book of Exodus, the deity is addressed as "merciful and gracious, slow to anger, and abounding in steadfast love" (Exod. 34:6). This image seems to have been sustained during many years of Israelite exile and enslavement and evolved into an image of God as liberator. The description of God's steadfast love for the Israelites comes into full view in Psalms 107 and 118, and especially in Psalm 136, where after each rehearsal of all the magnificent deeds that God has done on behalf of the Israelites, the psalmist repeats "for his steadfast love endures forever." This becomes not only the psalm's refrain but also a reassuring mantra for the community and for those who later receive and read the text.

In the psalms, the psalmist also presents us with a picture of a trusting relationship that alternates with feelings of oppression and even of abandonment, for example, "My God, my God, why have you forsaken me?" (Ps. 22:1). Thus, we can see from the biblical text that passionate but contradictory emotions seem to have pervaded the relationship that the Israelites had with the One whom they experience simultaneously as creator and protector, lover and judge. Many psalm prayers express a plaintive longing for daily interaction with a paradoxical God who seems both present yet unreachable, distant yet intimate. In some cases, terms like "Lord," the "Most High," and "King," all of which are reflective of the psalmist's royal theology, can be seen as establishing a respectful distance. Other psalms, however, seem to eliminate that distance, as in the case of Psalm 18:6–19, where the psalmist poetically re-tells the story of being rescued by the Most High:

> In my distress I called upon the Lord;
>   to my God I cried for help.
> From his temple he heard my voice,
>   and my cry to him reached his ears.
> Then the earth reeled and rocked;
>   the foundations also of the mountains trembled
>   and quaked, because he was angry.
> Smoke went up from his nostrils,
>   and devouring fire from his mouth;
>   glowing coals flamed forth from him.
> He bowed the heavens, and came down;
>   thick darkness was under his feet.
> He rode on a cherub, and flew;
>   he came swiftly upon the wings of the wind.

> He made darkness his covering around him,
> his canopy thick clouds dark with water.
> Out of the brightness before him
> there broke through his clouds
> hailstones and coals of fire.
> The LORD also thundered in the heavens,
> and the Most High uttered his voice.
> And he sent out his arrows, and scattered them;
> he flashed forth lightnings, and routed them.
> Then the channels of the sea were seen,
> and the foundations of the world were laid bare
> at your rebuke, O LORD,
> at the blast of the breath of your nostrils.
> He reached down from on high, he took me;
> he drew me out of mighty waters.
> He delivered me from my strong enemy,
> and from those who hated me;
> for they were too mighty for me.
> They confronted me in the day of my calamity;
> but the LORD was my support.
> He brought me out into a broad place;
> he delivered me, because he delighted in me.[12]

The psalms also present a sense of a continual, unsatisfied quest for a God who is always both near and just beyond reach: "With my whole heart I seek you" (Ps. 119:10). Thus, theology's perennial question: "Is God transcendent or immanent—above all or within all?" recurs in the alternate experiences of God embodied in the psalms.

Finally, the psalms, and in particular Psalm 22:1–21 and Psalm 44, present us with a theology that is historically, culturally, and politically conditioned, especially in their portrait of God as a warrior. Such a depiction reflects an image of God derived from and which mirrors the culture of the day that was embroiled in battle after battle in the conquest for power and land. The biblical poets and storytellers had to depict Israel's God as stronger and more powerful than all the other gods and stronger and more powerful than the most powerful ruler of any one nation. Much of the biblical portrayal of God is steeped in metaphor, because the biblical writers and their various communities tried to communicate their living experience of the Divine, who defies human expression and is beyond all metaphor.

When reading the psalms, and for that matter the entire Bible, readers always need to hold up the text for ongoing critical reflection and be cognizant of the text's historical, cultural, political, social, and theological background contexts and settings. Readers also need to understand the agenda of the psalmist, the time in which the psalmist was writing the psalms, the communities for whom the psalms were being written, and those communities would later receive and re-read these texts.

In the twenty-first century, the preeminent authority on the spirituals was the African-American musician and scholar, Joe Carter, who died in 2007. The grandson of slaves, Carter became an internationally acclaimed cultural ambassador who performed the spirituals for audiences from Nigeria to Siberia. In a 2003 National Public Radio interview with Krista Tippett, Carter confirmed that the African-American spirituals can be regarded as the initial prayer book of the enslaved African community, and like the Book of Psalms, a resource for insight into their authors' theology. According to Carter, the spirituals convey "a potent mix of African spirituality, Hebrew narrative, Christian doctrine, and an extreme experience of suffering."[13] The authors of the spirituals, then, derived their image of God from the pages of the Old Testament. Listening to the spirituals, the slaves hear God making a covenant commitment to them, the same covenant commitment that God made with Abraham as recorded in the Torah. The image of God to whom they pray is capable of performing miracles for people who trust in God. Hence, the slaves live in hope.

Despite many similarities, the ways in which the spirituals differ theologically from the psalms are significant. African slaves' prayers are also addressed to a masculine deity, but their language evokes an image even more anthropomorphic than the God addressed in the psalms. While the psalmist hears the God of Israel communicating anger poetically through thunder and lightning, the spiritual's startling vernacular hears an angry God who "hollers louder." More importantly, in the spirituals, the biblical image of a powerful God who will brutally punish enemies is softened by the slaves' identification with Jesus Christ to whom their American masters had introduced them. Jesus, the "Man of Sorrows," appealed to the slaves as their appropriate representative—God who had walked their walk. Hence, they sang: "Nobody knows the trouble I've seen; Nobody knows but Jesus."

Through their music, the Africans internalized a Jesus who prefers forgiveness to punishment, and embraced a savior who was, above all, their companion in suffering. Hence, no mean-spirited spirituals exist. Another notable difference is that, unlike the psalmists, the authors of the spirituals entertain no theological debate over transcendence and immanence.

Just above my head, I hear music in the air;
there must be a God somewhere.
Just above my head, I hear music in the air;
There must be a God everywhere.

As expressed in the spirituals, another distinctive feature of the slaves' spirituality is that, although consciously rooted in the Old Testament, it is a Christian spirituality. In the history of Christianity, the average churchgoer does not immediately feel a close kinship with Moses and his people, but from the beginning, African-American slaves felt a strong bond with a people who had known exile from their native land. Carter tells us that African religions (there were many) had in common a belief that the way to contact God was through the ancestors. African-Americans "understood biblical characters as ancestors in the African tradition and assumed that at death all their spirits would be reunited at home in Africa."[14] When the African slaves were torn from their land, they believed they were torn from their ancestors. Music became their bridge to reconnect across the miles.

According to the biblical story, the Egyptians enslaved ancient Israelites for some time. Throughout the centuries, however, when other monotheistic religions adopted the Hebrew psalms, they have interpreted slavery metaphorically, as the spiritual bondage to sin from which every believer prays to be delivered. Only the African-American slaves identified literally with the Israelite experience of physical bondage and the later exile from their native land. The spiritual "Go Down Moses" encapsulates the African-American identification with God's chosen people whose leader—himself a slave—led his people out of Egypt into freedom:

When Israel was in Egypt land:
Let my people go,
Oppressed so hard they could not stand.
Let my people go,
Go down, Moses, way down in Egypt land.
And tell old Pharaoh, Let my people go.

The slaves also felt closer to the covenant with Abraham than they did to any religious affiliation with the white slave masters who originally introduced them to the Bible. Their lyrics often place Abraham and Jesus together as if they were contemporaries. Hence, many lyrics straddle Old and New Testaments. For example, the refrain: "Rock-a-my soul in the bosom of Abraham . . . O Rock-a-my soul" leaps immediately to verses expressing belief in Jesus as redeemer:

I never shall forget the day,
When Jesus washed my sins away.
I know my God is a man of war
He fought my battle at Hell's dark door.
If you don't believe I'm a child of God,
Follow me where the road is hard.

Rock-a-my soul in the bosom of Abraham
O, rock-a-my soul.

In "God's Going to Trouble the Water," the lyrics conflate a healing episode in the fifth chapter of John's Gospel with the miracle at the Red Sea, both of which inspire confidence that God will again lead his people through troubled waters to freedom:

Wade in the water, children,
Wade in the water, children,
Wade in the water, children,
God's going to trouble the waters.[15]

See that host all dressed in white.
The leader looks like the Israelite;
See that band all dressed in red,
Looks like the band that Moses led.[16]

Richard Newman's comment on this song suggests how the slaves' association with the Bible encouraged them in their many attempts to escape: "The message is that it is safe, even necessary, to step out into a 'troubled' situation, even the Red Sea, because God's action in agitating events may be disruptive, but it is ultimately redemptive."[17]

Accepting the popular assumption that the author of the psalms was David, a slave in exile, the African-American slaves associated with him as the underdog who slew the mighty giant Goliath:

I say to David, come play me a piece.
David says to me: "How can I play,
When I'm in a strange land?"

For the slaves, David became the epitome of hope that, with God's help, the weak would conquer the strong.

A confidence in God's promise of deliverance to the Israelites formed the basis of the slaves' belief in eventual deliverance by the same God: "I have observed the misery of my people who are in Egypt; I have heard their cry on account of their taskmasters. Indeed, I know their sufferings, and I have come down to deliver them from the hand of the Egyptians, and to bring them up out of that land to a good and broad land, a land flowing with milk and honey" (Exod. 3:7–8). Even now, though, in the midst of bondage, they experience the divine companionship promised to the Israelites: "I will be with you" (Exod. 3:12).

Most of the time, the spiritual alludes to the biblical text but does not directly quote from it. At least once, however, the refrain of "before this time another year" is taken almost directly from a psalm, where the psalmist is obviously expressing the sentiment of an Israelite whose patience is strained after many years in exile. The spiritual says:

> O Lord, how long?
> Before this time another year, I may be gone
> . . . O Lord, how long?

These words of the spiritual echo Psalm 13:1–2:

> How long, O Lord? Will you forget me forever?
> How long will you hide your face from me?
> How long must I bear pain in my soul,
> and have sorrow in my heart all day long?
> How long shall my enemy be exalted over me?

By incorporating the ideas and sentiments of Psalm 13:1–2 into a complaint, the singer of the spiritual seems to be invoking a scriptural endorsement for his or her resentment.

Another theological difference between the psalms and the spirituals relates to moral responsibility. As Toni Craven points out, "Although some of the psalmists admit human sinfulness as a cause of suffering, more often they impute someone else as the party responsible."[18] We see this point in the following two texts:

> Depart from me, all you workers of evil,
> For the Lord has heard the sound of my weeping.
> (Ps. 6:8)

> Even now they lie in wait for my life;
> the mighty stir up strife against me.
> For no transgression or sin of mine, O Lord,
> for no fault of mine, they run and make ready.
> (Ps. 59:3)

By contrast, while the slaves often blamed their masters for the sin of injustice, they accepted full responsibility for their own sins:

> It's me, it's me O Lord, standing in the need of prayer . . . .
> T'ain't my mother or my father,

But it's me, O Lord . . . .

T'ain't my deacon or my leader
But it's me, it's me, O Lord, standing in the need of prayer.

In accepting personal responsibility, the slaves refused to sacrifice their entire identity to that of mere victims. Just as the psalmist expressed honest sentiments as heard in Psalm 59:3, so also the writers of the spirituals express heartfelt sentiments. They acknowledge their guilt, which includes a bold prayer for conversion:

O, fix me Jesus, fix me right. Fix me right, fix me right.
O, fix me Jesus, fix me right. Fix me so I can stand.

One of the most intriguing features of early African-American spirituality is the fact that the uneducated slaves were able to separate genuine Christianity from the example of it given by their slave masters. As poet and scholar Sterling Brown asserts: "They taught you the religion they disgraced."[19] In spite of the slave masters' cruelty and hypocrisy, the slaves focused on the person of Jesus Christ, whom they revered as a God who suffered as they did. In his NPR interview, Joe Carter described the message of the spirituals as "a theology of suffering . . . that leans into suffering—and in surrender, transforms and rises above it."[20] At least for the duration of the song, this remarkable peace of soul enabled the slave to feel pity for his or her oppressor. "The ancestors knew that the worst kind of bondage takes place in the inside. . . . It was the master who was really the slave," asserted Carter.[21]

Concluding that interview, Krista Tippett summed up the human dividend that accrued from African-American spirituality: the paradox that when, in their music, the slaves gave themselves over to powerlessness, they "felt graced with a dignity their masters could neither enjoy nor destroy."[22] The same remains true for the psalmist of Psalm 44:20–26 whose lament turns to certitude, confidence, gratitude, and praise:

If we had forgotten the name of our God,
    or spread out our hands to a strange god,
would not God discover this?
    For he knows the secrets of the heart.
Because of you we are being killed all day long,
    and accounted as sheep for the slaughter.
Rouse yourself! Why do you sleep, O Lord?
    Awake, do not cast us off forever!
Why do you hide your face?
    Why do you forget our affliction and oppression?

For we sink down to the dust;
    our bodies cling to the ground.
Rise up, come to our help.
    Redeem us for the sake of your steadfast love.

Wading Deeper on Your Own

Questions for Reflection and Discussion

1. Were you aware that Muslims, like Jews and Christians, pray the psalms?
2. Besides having a common forefather, what beliefs unite all three Abrahamic religions?
3. Like the psalmist in Psalm 22:1–21, when have you felt forsaken by your God, and in that state, how have you cried out to your God?
4. Do you think that the slaves' spirituality contributed to their victimization? If so, how? If not, why not?
5. How do institutions and individuals use religion to control people today?

Suggestions for Writing and Journaling

1. Choose either Psalm 22:1–21 or Psalm 44 as discussed in this chapter. Read the psalm several times. Then record how either of these psalms speaks to you at this time in your life.
2. Describe the situation that makes either Psalm 22:1–21 or Psalm 44 meaningful to you. Write your story in a psalm. Then describe how you imagine God to whom you address your psalm.
3. Explain any change of mind or heart that you might have experienced as you sat with either Psalm 22:1–21 or Psalm 44.
4. Write an essay demonstrating the effect of parallelism in any of the psalms of your choice.
5. Listen to a recording of African-American spirituals. Write a profile of African-American spirituality based on what you heard. Listen to recordings of Handel's *Messiah* and of the musical *Jesus Christ Superstar*. Write a profile comparing and contrasting the Christian spirituality that inspired them.
6. Write an essay analyzing parallelism and symbolism in a psalm of your choice.
7. On the Internet, find a spiritual in which past and future are fused. Write an essay in which you quote the spiritual:
    - describe the effect of its fusion of tenses
    - explain how it brings about a similar effect.

Irrigating Other Fields

From psalms and spirituals, the prayers of the Israelites and the African American slaves, respectively, scholars have been able to reconstruct the theology of the praying community at a specific time in history. This chapter should make you aware that your knowledge of current events, today's news media, and your own conversations in the social media are constructing—or deconstructing—a theology.

Part Two

An Interplay of Biblical and Literary Themes

Part One of this text demonstrated how an understanding of literary *genre* can transform our interpretation of certain books of the Bible and how centuries after they were written, biblical stories continue to inspire novelists, dramatists, and poets to adapt these ancient works to dramatize the concerns of new audiences. Building on this approach, Part Two will focus on several of the themes within biblical literature and will point out how literary art embodies these themes afresh. The themes to be explored include the spiritual quest, love, war and peace, and liberation. These themes come to life in the selected biblical stories and contemporary literature that have been chosen for discussion in this next part.

6
THE THEME OF THE SPIRITUAL QUEST

The Book of Jonah
Jonah 1–4

Life of Pi
Yann Martel

Introduction

Although this chapter takes the title "The Theme of the Spiritual Quest," it can be said that all the human desires embodied in biblical themes require a lifelong quest. Thoughtful people of all religious faiths and people of no faith continually pursue a quest for truth, for intimacy, for peace, for ethical and meaningful relationships within the human family, and increasingly beyond humanity in relationships with the other-than-human. Not by any accident does the word "quest" form the root of the word "question." Many literary artists presented in these next few chapters seem propelled and perplexed by questions designed to compel the reader to continue a personal quest long after the story concludes. Two stories that engage the theme of the spiritual quest are the biblical story of Jonah and Yann Martel's marvelous novel *Life of Pi.* The incredible journey of Jonah offers an ideal introduction to a twenty-first-century counterpart, the fantastic adventures of a Hindu boy named Pi. Strains of the story of Jonah can be heard in the story of Pi as both characters embark on exciting and wisdom-filled journeys.

Drinking from the Spring
The Biblical Text
The Book of Jonah

One of the best-loved tales in the Old Testament is the story of Jonah, the man who flees from God's presence because he received a word from God that told him to go to the city of Nineveh to deliver God's judgment against the city because of the people's wickedness (1:1–3). His adventures take him to sea, where he is thrown overboard in a storm and then swallowed up by a big fish. He spends three days and three nights inside the fish's belly. He then goes on to fulfill his God-given vocation as a prophet, only to be part of an interesting turn of events that showcases God's cosmic plan of salvation for all creation.

Little is known about Jonah ben Amittai, the main character in the Book of Jonah, except that he prophesied during Jeroboam II's reign (around 786–746 BCE), as indicated by 2 Kings 14:25. The time of his ministry was a time when Assyria enjoyed a privileged position of power among the nations of the ancient world.

Although the book is fiction, specific factual references give it a historical flavor. One of the central historical places mentioned is Nineveh, the capital of Assyria. According to the text, God commanded Jonah to go to Nineveh to declare to its inhabitants their wickedness so that the process of repentance could begin. The king of Nineveh initiated actions and a decree calling for repentance so that the city might be spared divine judgment. Unfortunately, though, historical evidence shows that the city did fall (cf. the Books of Nahum and Zephaniah).

The Book of Jonah was probably composed sometime during the fifth century BCE, when the Jewish people were recovering from the Babylonian Exile and resettling in their land. This period found people engaged in active questioning and reflection regarding God's justice and mercy as the prophets preached repentance.

The Book of Jonah has the spiritual quest as one of its main themes, along with themes that include inclusivity, the greatness of God, repentance, and divine compassion. The story of Jonah also demonstrates how power can be both challenging and liberating. In the text, we see that the forces of the natural world pose dilemmas for human beings, but God's power has liberating effects for all creation. Didactic in style, the book proclaims a theological message that celebrates the care of God for all creation, including the reluctant prophet Jonah, whose spiritual quest leads him into a deeper knowledge of his God and himself. Comprised of four symmetrical chapters, the book can be divided into two parts: Jonah's Dilemma in Chapters 1–2 and Jonah's Mission in Chapters 3–4. Chapter 1 parallels Chapter 3, and Chapter 2 parallels Chapter 4. Chapters 1 and 3 focus on Jonah's experiences with a group of sailors (Chapter 1) and the Assyrians and their king (Chapter 3). Chapters 2 and 4 focus on Jonah's conversations with God and God's response.

A variety of literary techniques add creative, literary color to the story of Jonah. Direct discourse allows readers to enter into the book's characters and their simple yet complex lives. Repeated key words, for example, "great" (1:2; 3:2; 4:11), add cohesion to the story, while irony weaves humor into it. Personification (i.e., 1:4 and 1:15) and merisms (i.e., "days" and "nights" in 1:17; "great" and "small" in 3:5) contribute to the text's overall imagery and metaphorical quality. Phrases and ideas echo other stories; for example, Jonah 4:2 harks back to Exodus 34:6–7 and ties this story to other biblical stories and traditions that often stress a similar point. As a whole, the book is an intricately crafted story whose artistic nature supports its striking and profound theological message.

"Pick Me Up and Throw Me into the Sea"
Jonah 1

The Book of Jonah opens with a focus on Jonah who, fleeing from God's presence, boards a ship headed for Tarshish. Jonah receives a word from God to the city of Nineveh[1] to deliver God's judgment against it because of its people's wickedness (vv. 1–3). Jonah decides not to follow God's command and instead, sets out in an attempt to flee for Tarshish from God's presence and to avoid having to go to Nineveh to declare divine judgment upon the city and all its inhabitants.

Jonah's spirited adventures and spiritual journey begin after he goes to Joppa and boards the ship. Having set sail with his mariner companions, Jonah and crew are tossed and tumbled about by a violent storm at sea that threatens to destroy them. What readers see that Jonah does not realize is that God created the storm in response to Jonah's decision to flee from God's presence. Frightened, the mariners pray each to his god while Jonah lies fast asleep in the hold of the ship—but not for long. The captain wakes up Jonah and orders him to pray to his (Jonah's) god (vv. 3–6).

The sailors next cast lots to see what person among them is responsible for the calamity. When the lot falls to Jonah, the mariners confront him with all sorts of questions, and they hear from Jonah about his background and his god: "the Lord God of heaven, who made the sea and the dry land" (v. 9). Because the mariners knew that Jonah was fleeing from the God of Israel, the revelation of the identity of Jonah's god made them even more frightened (vv. 7–10).

The mariners then discern with Jonah what they should do with him so that the sea will subside and the great storm quiet down. Jonah tells them that he is willing to sacrifice his life: "Pick me up and throw me into the sea; then the sea will quiet down for you; for I know it is because of me that this great storm has come upon you" (v. 12). The mariners, reluctant to do such a thing, then pray to Jonah's god for pardon and mercy.[2] They do not want to perish themselves, nor do they wish to be made and declared guilty by ending Jonah's life. After finishing their prayer, they hurl Jonah into the sea. Immediately the sea stops raging. Seeing what has transpired, the mariners grow even more afraid of the power of God; they therefore offer a sacrifice and make vows to Jonah's god (vv. 11–16). Yet God takes care of Jonah. God makes provisions for a big fish to swallow up Jonah, who stays in the fish's belly for three days and three nights (v. 17).

Jonah and God's relationship is a dynamic one. God seeks out Jonah to carry out a special task, but Jonah tries to flee from God's presence in order to avoid doing the task he is being asked to do. Jonah's reluctant response to God causes havoc in the world around Jonah, in others' lives and in Jonah's own life, forcing him to being willing to be tossed into the raging sea so that the storm will quiet down. Ironically, Jonah is willing to sacrifice his life to the sea, but he is not willing to accept the divine challenge of declaring God's judgment in Nineveh, which would be difficult but not cost him his life. In seeking to guard his life at first, Jonah ends up being willing to risk his life, and he has now learned that a reluctant response to God will have far-reaching consequences. Jonah is relatively powerless in relationship to his God, but he does use his power of choice to produce liberating effects for others. Jonah chooses to allow the mariners to toss him overboard, which has positive effects for all except Jonah. He liberates the crew from their perilous state, but engulfs himself in the terror of a raging sea. The story shows us that God, however, understands Jonah's reluctance to act as a prophet, and instead of allowing him to be ravaged by the storm continually, which would have cost him his life, God provides Jonah a bit of respite inside a big fish. God gives Jonah a secure place for a brief time, even though Jonah probably does not think so. When Jonah gives up his life, God gives back his life.

"Then Jonah Prayed to the Lord His God"
Jonah 2

From the belly of the great fish, Jonah prays to God (vv. 1–8). Once wanting to be distant from God, Jonah now draws near in his moments of desperation. Jonah's psalm of lament attests to his confidence in God and reveals his innermost thoughts and feelings. He acknowledges to God what God has done to him. God has cast him "into the deep," "into the heart of the seas"; there the flood surrounded him "and all God's waves and billows passed over him" (v. 3). Jonah's experience makes him fear that he has been driven from God's sight (v. 4). Then Jonah reiterates to God what has happened to him: the waters closed in over him; the deep surrounded him; weeds were wrapped around his head. Jonah was overpowered by the forces of nature (v. 5). Yet when Jonah was on the threshold of death, Jonah's prayer reached God, and God rescued him (vv. 6–7). Jonah's profession of faith signals that Jonah's original audience struggled with idolatry: "Those who worship vain idols/forsake their true loyalty" (v. 8). Jonah closes his prayer with an expression of thanksgiving, a promise of sacrifice, and the proclamation, "Deliverance belongs to the Lord" (v. 9). Following Jonah's prayer, the narrator comments that God spoke to the fish, and "it spewed Jonah out upon the land" (v. 10).

Chapter 2 presents another side of Jonah. The one who tried to run away from God now surrenders to God, a most important move in the spiritual quest. Jonah acknowledges that God uses power to save the one in distress. What is troublesome, however, is that the text portrays God manipulating situations, people, and creation in a less than positive way; God's power dominates to accomplish God's purpose, in this instance when the person commissioned for the task had refused. The text prompts a critical reader to ask, "Is this truly God and the ways of God?" Might it rather reflect a theology permeated by assumptions of hierarchy, where creatures have no choice but to do what God wants? There is a difference between persuasion and control; here, the situation reflects God's control over the natural world; and yet, God also acts in a liberating way. Having created an oppressive situation for Jonah because Jonah did not do what God had in mind, God then liberates Jonah from it. The biblical writer's agenda, then, seems to be to establish God as Lord of creation and Lord of history.

"Get Up, Go to Nineveh, That Great City, and Proclaim to It the Message That I Tell You"
Jonah 3

Once Jonah is out of the belly of the great fish, God again commissions him to go to Nineveh to proclaim God's message. This time, Jonah sets out without any reluctance, and upon arrival at the city, pronounces to the community there a message of doom. Immediately the people proclaim a fast and begin to perform gestures of repentance (vv. 1–5).

When the news reached the king, he too began to mourn. He proclaimed a total fast and a time of mourning for both humans and animals. He decreed that all must turn from their evil ways and their violence in the hope that God would have a change of mind, turn from fierce anger, and spare them (vv. 6–9).

In the final section, the narrator comments that God observed the people's actions, had a change of mind, and did not bring disaster upon them (v. 10).

Jonah 3 illustrates how power can liberate. After surrendering to God's power, Jonah carried out his prophetic word and mission to Nineveh. The prophecy that Jonah proclaimed to the people was powerful, enabling the people to fast and mourn and helping them to take charge of their lives. When the king heard the word, he too was empowered by it to the degree that he decreed among the people a time of mourning, a fast, and a mandatory turning away from evil.

Chapter 3 presents a new vision of leadership. Here, leadership uses power to motivate and to mobilize the people for good so that their lives may be spared. And, God does spare them. While God is still depicted as someone who can either cause or eliminate pain and suffering, national leadership is now seen in a new light. The king could have ignored the prophetic word; he could even have had the prophet bound up or put to death. Instead, he uses his power to help liberate the people from their evil ways and "from the violence of their hands" (v. 8). Furthermore, the hierarchy of power is being transformed. Even though the king was considered to be the head of state, he defers to the prophet and God's message. Thus, power is shared.

From the text we see that: (1) God's work of liberation comes through people, and is associated with leadership, right judgment for all concerned, and cooperation on the part of all; (2) God's word is meant to liberate, even if it is a word of doom; and (3) God's overpowering of a person is not necessarily to make the person unfree but rather to set that person free to be a catalyst for others' liberation from evil and violence. When the perpetrators of evil turn from it, then those oppressed by it are liberated also. Of significance here is the fact that Nineveh is part of the non-Israelite world. God's word and care are meant for those who would believe (v. 5), regardless of ethnicity, class, or religious background. The fact that both humans and nonhumans enter into a fast and postures of mourning underscores the relationship and solidarity that the ancient people shared with the natural world.[3] All creation—not just human beings—is to be redeemed and liberated. Finally, we see that Jonah has been strengthened by his life experiences thus far, and he has learned to trust in God because he now knows that God cherishes his life. God has saved him once, and in Jonah's mind, God will do it again if the need arises.

"The Lord God Appointed a Bush, and Made It Come Up over Jonah, to Give Shade over His Head, to Save Him from His Discomfort"
Jonah 4

With the Ninevites on the right track with God and among themselves, one might think that Jonah would celebrate. Not so! Jonah is displeased with the outcome of events and becomes angry. In a heartwarming prayer to God, Jonah attests to his belief in God: "I knew that you are a gracious God and merciful, slow to anger, and abounding in steadfast love, and ready to relent from punishing" (v. 2). Jonah also admits to

God that this is precisely the reason he was running to Tarshish in the first place. God responds to Jonah by asking him if it is right to be angry. So Jonah departs out of the city toward the east, makes a booth for himself to provide shade, and then watches to see what will happen to Nineveh (vv. 1–5).

While Jonah is sitting in the shade, God causes a bush to come over Jonah to shade his head from the sun and alleviate his discomfort. Jonah enjoys the bush until God causes a worm to attack the bush so that it withers. God then causes a hot east wind to intensify the sun, so that Jonah becomes faint and asks God to let him die (vv. 6–8; cf. v. 3).

God responds to Jonah's complaint and request:

> You are concerned about the bush, for which you did not labor and for which you did not grow; it came into being in a night and perished in a night. And should I not be concerned about Nineveh, that great city, in which there are more than a hundred and 120,000 persons who do not know their right hand from their left, and also many animals? (vv. 10–11)

Jonah has grown spiritually, and in this chapter we see that a marvelous relationship has developed between Jonah and God. Jonah is so candid, so honest with God, and his prayer reflects those qualities. The fact that he "knew" God to be just and gracious presupposes experience. Jonah knows God not only from the tradition (see Exod. 34:6–7, where words and ideas similar to Jon. 3:2 appear), but also from his personal encounters. Jonah's call and his candid personal prayer both hint at a real relationship between God and Jonah that may have existed for some time. Jonah's ability to express his anger to God would also support the existence of such a relationship. Even though Jonah was reluctant to carry out God's directive the first time, God did not abandon Jonah. God continued to work with Jonah in all sorts of ways. When God reproved Jonah, it was never an experience that caused him harm; God's final reproof was verbal (4:9–11).

Jonah 4 proclaims a liberating God whose power is at the service of the Ninevites, Jonah, and even the cattle. Even though there are hints of God having "power over" creation, that is, the bush and the worm are both "appointed" by God, the predominate theme is God using divine power to empower Jonah to help transform the city of Nineveh. By means of the bush and the worm, God teaches Jonah about divine care and compassion not only for people but also for animals. What is so liberating about this text is that it attests to the breadth of God's plan of salvation that includes non-Israelites and animals. This text helps to liberate God from a humanly constructed identity that is predominately, if not exclusively, androcentric in its concerns.

Summary

The Book of Jonah is a fast-paced, heartwarming, and revelatory story about Jonah and his God, and how that relationship affects other people, animals, and elements in the natural world. Jonah's genuine candor allows readers to appreciate the dynamics of his very real relationship with God. On the journey through life, God and Jonah have found each other, and Jonah has grown in stature and depth.

Cosmological in its focus, the Book of Jonah breaks the boundaries of class and ethnicity to present a view of salvation and liberation that was prophetic for its day and remains so even now. The text affirms that God, the ways of God, and the power of God can be discovered in the midst of human life and all its experiences, as well as in and through the natural world and the cosmos, and that God uses all creation to bring about redemption and liberation for all. If the text reflects accurately God's care for human and nonhuman life even in the midst of humankind's sinfulness, then critical readers must ask, "How can people use the insights from the Book of Jonah to bring about liberation and transformation in a way that is nonviolent and inclusive?" Truly, the text of Jonah is a prophecy among prophets.[4]

Playing in the Fountain
The Literary Text
Life of Pi

About the Author

Yann Martel (1963–present)

In his own personal history, as well as in his most popular novel, Yann Martel has embodied the concept of spiritual odyssey through multicultural exploration. Born in Spain to French-Canadian diplomats, Martel was living and teaching in Germany when he received word that his playful novel about an Indian boy had won Great Britain's highest award for fiction, the Man Booker Prize. Immediately translated into French, *Life of Pi* took the French equivalent of the Booker Prize and soon captured similar awards in Asia and South Africa. For Martel, writing itself is an interior "Quest Journey." As he explained in an interview soon after the Booker triumph brought him international fame, "I'm not really interested in psychological novels. . . . I'd rather look out than in.[5] In *Life of Pi*, looking out means looking at the world and ourselves, not only through the vision of other religions, but even through the vision of other species. "It's through the eye of the other that we come to understand ourselves," Martel believes.[6] For this reason, in preparation for writing *Pi*, he consumed many volumes of solid information on religion, zoology, and animal psychology. He also read the work of psychologist Alfred Margulies, who had published a book giving a name to the creative gift of entering the consciousness of another: *The Empathic Imagination.*[7] Appropriating this term, Martel goes on to define empathic imagination as "the great solution" to intransigent political conflicts: "If you are an Israeli, you should imagine yourself a Palestinian . . . understand why they are angry. If you are a Palestinian, imagine you are an Israeli . . . understand why they are afraid."[8]

For Martel, human and animal interaction offers an opportunity to make this act of empathic imagination both entertaining and instructive. Encouraged by the success of this device, Martel attempted to duplicate its appeal with two other novels where he approaches serious subject matter, the Holocaust and the Crucifixion, respectively, through animal fantasies. So far, regrettably, both works have disappointed the critics.

Reflecting on Genre

Metaphysical Fable

Like the Book of Jonah, *Life of Pi* is a marvelous story of a young man on a spiritual quest. Both stories entail episodes on water, and both stories feature strong protagonists. To choose fantasy as the best vehicle for talking about spiritual truth might seem contradictory for Yann Martel, but this literary artist is convinced that fantasy can actually compel both writers and readers into a serious spiritual quest. His commentary on this process is worth quoting at length because it summarizes the essence of what happens when theology enters into a "dialogue with literature":

> I discovered in writing *Life of Pi* that, in a sense, religion operates like fiction. A good novel works by making you suspend your *disbelief*. When you read a novel that doesn't work, you sense that, "Oh, this happened and it was so improbable. That's not how they do it." Novels that don't work are emotionally dead. . . . A good novel—even though there are robots and flying dinosaurs—just takes us in. Religion works the same way; it makes you suspend your disbelief so that factual truth becomes irrelevant. . . . A religious person will not say that his belief contradicts reality. It's just that there's more to faith than facts. . . . Religion interprets the facts differently. . . . Maybe God's silence is an appeal to get beyond factuality . . . a trick to

call us through the imagination. If you don't have any imagination, you live a diminished life.[9]

Because of the novel's seamless blending of brutally realistic detail with totally implausible elements, a few literary critics prefer to assign *Life of Pi* to the category of "magic realism." The author's overt theologizing, however, places the work more surely in the genre of "metaphysical fable." As a fable, the novel can be considered exempt from the demands of psychologically complex characterization. The author has explained that what should be considered a weakness in the novel was his deliberate choice: "I don't find the ego that interesting. I would rather have a normal character face extraordinary circumstances than an extraordinary person face normal circumstances. . . . I find the good life is the one where you tend to shush the ego, where you forget yourself."[10]

Reflecting on Structure

In the novel, an "Author's Note" is followed by three parts that subdivide into a total of ninety-five short chapters. The preliminary "Author's Note" itself is actually an elaborate fiction. Everyone named there is invented, except Martel and Moacyr Scliar, whose book inspired *Life of Pi*. Readers familiar with literary style and technique will recognize that Martel is employing an ancient and typical framing device of fantasy literature by which an author attempts to persuade the reader that what follows is a true story.

At first glance, the novel's tripartite structure—before, during, and after Pi's sea journey—seems to be unnecessarily interrupted by italicized intrusions of time, place, and narrator. A closer look soon reveals that Martel's theological intent governs a complex structural composition. Martel is doing something more than pretending to deceive the reader. Although most of the tale does seem to be told by Pi himself, in fact, Martel will name no less than three narrators, as well as other sources for the story. Within a few pages, Martel, who is Narrator 1, speaks of meeting Narrator 2, "a spry, elderly man" named Francis Adirubasamy, who promises to tell "a story that will make you believe in God."[11] The novel is not Adirubasamy's own story but the story he heard long ago from a "main character" named Patel. The author then tells the reader that, over nearly a year, he met many times with Patel. Significantly, the author did not record these interviews; he listened and "took notes." Patel introduces another source when he shows the author his journal from the time of the main events. Patel's adult remembrances of these events are, of course, much more detailed and intellectually reflective than the journal a teenager was able to keep while struggling with starvation, storms, wild beasts. Finally, Martel names and thanks three Japanese professionals who supplied him with "official" documents and a tape recording to complete his research. We are told that Martel himself will combine all these sources to tell Mr. Patel's story, in the form of a first person narrative. Not until after finishing the novel will the average reader recognize how important this opening note is to the novel's theological theme.

The significance of narrators is further emphasized in the italicized introductions to Chapters 2, 6, 12, 15, 21, 30, 36, and 83, which describe each person from whom the story was heard. Again and again, Pi tells a story to listeners who retell his story that is eventually recorded and told to foreigners in words that are sometimes, but not always, his own and sometimes those of his translators. Inevitably, changes occur with each retelling. Through this elaborate and sometimes confusing method, Martel subtly emulates the way the Bible itself was originally transmitted.

The summary of the text's content is as follows: Part I, Chapters 1–36, describes Pi's account of his life in India from childhood to age sixteen, when the ship transporting his family and their zoo sinks, leaving him adrift in a lifeboat with wild animals. Like Jonah, who is thrown overboard into the sea, where he encounters a great fish, Pi's adventures begin at sea.

Part II, Chapters 37–94, covers Pi's account of his 277 days at sea with Richard Parker, a Bengalese tiger whom he comes to both love and fear. Part II concludes with Pi's rescue and Richard Parker's departure.

Part III consists only of Chapter 95, which occurs many years later and records the conclusion of the putative author's research. A summary of his conversations with several retired Japanese diplomats, who had questioned Pi as part of their investigation of a lost ship, authenticates the transcript of Pi's interrogation in the Benito Juarez Infirmary in Mexico. The tape includes Pi's two alternate versions of "the story" and his final defense of faith.

Reflecting on Literary Style

Martel's literary style seamlessly combines opposites of content and form. Paragraphs are by turns, charming and repellent, descriptively poetic and ruthlessly realistic, and like the author's style of the Book of Jonah, subtly ironic and overtly didactic. Yet, Martel himself likes to describe his style as deliberately simple and straightforward: "Something happens and you live through the consequences . . . It's an apparent simplicity. At one point you realize that with simple little strokes I am creating a more complex picture."[12] Martel also acknowledges his conscious desire to emulate the simple power of the Gospels: "The gospels are amazing texts. They're very, very rich . . . You know, the shortest gospel, the Book of Mark, I think in some editions is only twenty-six pages long, and yet it goes so deep. And the same with the Bhagavad Gita, with the Koran. They're really, really deep texts."[13] The story of Jonah is also a brief story and yet within its four short chapters lie tremendous wisdom and invaluable lessons.

An element of Martel's literary style that bears no resemblance to gospel simplicity can be described as literary shock treatment, which sometimes consists in simply piling on repulsive physical detail. In preparation for the novel, Martel immersed himself in numerous castaway stories and survival manuals for professional sailors. At times, when he seems determined to omit not a single sentence from his research, information overload can become tiresome. His second shock technique is more effective: juxtaposition. The author places passages of extreme realism side by side with lyricism; for example, a mouthful of animal feces is followed by a series of vividly beautiful metaphors. "The sea roared like a tiger . . . whispered in your ear like a friend telling you secrets . . . clinked like small change in a pocket . . . thundered like avalanches . . . hissed like sandpaper"[14] Again, in passages like this, we can discern a theological intent dictating style. Here and elsewhere Martel encapsulates not only the two opposite faces of nature, but also the two opposite faces of nature's creator.

At times Martel's style is overly didactic. Chapters 45–53, arguably the hardest of all pages to read, repeatedly describe animals eating animals. These relentless, deliberately disgusting assaults on the reader's stomach are clearly Martel's symbolic commentary on warfare. Having described the death throes of an orangutan in the jaws of a hyena, he doesn't trust the reader to get his message. So the author spells out the metaphor: "To the end she reminded me of us."[15] Martel intensifies his literary shock treatment with an even more sickening protest against war, and the ruthless economic Darwinism that supports it, in his descriptions of cannibalism.[16]

Like many postmodern authors, Martel's use of biblical allusion is tacit rather than overt. Besides the obvious allusion to Jonah in the novel as a whole, critics note other, subtler biblical references. For example, interpreting the mysterious island that rescues Pi from starvation, British professor Alistair Brown points out an allusion with an ecological warning: "the Eden myth is reconfigured in a chilling biological reversal where trees consume men. The natural environment is fluid and adaptable and man is anything but in perfect control or understanding of it despite his presumptuous arrogance."[17]

Drawing from the Well
Theological Themes

Yann Martel's principal theme is the value of theological pluralism. Early in the novel, the protagonist Pi tells us that, at the age of sixteen, although well-behaved in other respects, he became "transgressive" by practicing three religions simultaneously. The stranger-than-fiction fact here is that as homework for this novel, the author Yann Martel did a similar thing. He studied the foundational texts of Judaism, Christianity, Hinduism, and Islam. Then he immersed himself in writings by the mystics in each tradition, as well as expert commentary on them. Moreover, he even adopted prayers and practices from each religion. What becomes clear in the novel, however, is that for all his assiduous research, Martel seems to have resisted the intellectual rigors of formal theology to rest content with a purely aesthetic and subjective version of religious experience.

To a certain extent, the theme of salvation through theological pluralism, as well as the plot through which Martel enunciates it, can be considered autobiographical, for the author himself claims to be the survivor of spiritual shipwreck. Yann Martel started out in a sea of disillusion with organized religion. In an online interview with PBS, he later cautioned those who stop midway in this experience: "People who reject religion or are very cynical about it usually know just enough about it to reject it. So they know only the exaggerations, the excesses of that religion . . . what a lot of us do with Islam. . . . Now that I've put aside my criticism . . . of organized religion and gone to the texts . . . I see more of where they're coming from."[18]

As a result of his openness to all revelatory experiences of the divine, Martel concludes Pi's odyssey by having him embrace Gandhi's conviction that "all religions are true,"[19] which is similar to Jonah's seafarers' realization. Such a hospitable creed seems to have guided the author's choice in making his protagonist a Hindu: "The Hindus have a different approach—everything is an incarnation of the divine, whether it has a Hindu name on it, or whether it is called Jesus, Buddha, or Allah. To them everything is a manifestation of Rama, so they tend to be very inclusive."[20] Echoes of contemporary eco-theology in Martel's invocation of the Hindu tenet that "all sentient life is sacred" are easy to detect.

In the italicized introduction to Chapter 15, the physical setting expresses Pi's ultimate theology in metaphor. Here, years after the boy's rescue, the narrator finds the adult Pi living in a Pantheon where images of the elephant god Ganesh rub shoulders with the Virgin of Guadalupe, Shiva, Lakshmi, Shakti, and Christ. Pi's commodious religion embraces even atheists like his teacher Mr. Kumar, to whom he is grateful for igniting his own passion for truth: "The first avowed atheist I ever met," one of the teachers who ". . . came into my dark head and lit a match."[21] Martel puts his own sentiments into the mouth of Pi: "Atheists are my brothers and sisters of a different faith, and every word they speak, speaks of faith. Like me, they go as far as the legs of reason will carry them—and then they leap."[22]

Martel represents this leap many times throughout the novel, where Pi's adventures and arguments serve as the vehicle for a second pervasive theme: his belief that faith and reason, like fact and imagination, are not incompatible adversaries but simply different tools for interpreting what we call "reality." In Pi's final debate, neither he nor the Japanese businessmen convince each other: neither science nor faith alone is "reasonable."[23] Through Pi's conversation with the Japanese investigators, Martel directly lectures on the dogmatic post-modernist anti-dogma that facts do not exist in isolation. In pointing out that all talk about truth is a form of storytelling, Pi states the case for studying theology as one studies everything else: in context. No scientific or historical fact exists independent of its context. Who is reporting the fact? When and where? Why is it being reported—to answer a question or debate a point? To plead for the innocent or prosecute the guilty? "We want 'the straight facts' as you say in English. . . . Isn't telling about something—using words—already something of an invention? . . . The world isn't just the way it is. It is how we understand it, no? And in understanding something, we bring something to it, no? Doesn't that make life a story?"[24]

References like this to all truth as "story" have attracted the most negative and perceptive criticism of the novel, especially from scholars who believe in God. In Martel's conversations with them, he has tried to clarify that to say (as he has said) that religion operates like a novel, like fiction, in no way means that religion doesn't speak truth or that God does not exist. "It just means that God exists in a way that is accessed only by the imagination."[25] As one critic points out, however, for those who believe, "God transcends the subjectivity and transience of the reading experience . . . and suspension of religious belief involves a temporariness fundamentally at odds with the nature of faith."[26]

Martel's third theological theme concerns a perennial issue in moral theology: Is there such a thing as a just war? Throughout the pages of Pi's survival narrative, Martel carries on an unambiguous attack on the immorality of war. Sometimes the theme is hammered home heavy-handedly: "If goats could be brought to live amicably with rhinoceros why not orangutans with hyenas?"[27] At other times, the author counts on the reader to draw immediate analogies from the animal kingdom. For example, Pi's agony over killing a fish silently contrasts with modern superpowers' cold budgetary calculations when they estimate the cost of war. After describing several vicious murders, Pi sums up war's worst collateral damage, the desensitizing of human warriors: "It is simple and brutal . . . a person can get used to anything, even to killing."[28] When Richard Parker kills the blind castaway to feed his flesh to the dying Pi, Martel is characterizing "just war" as cannibalism. If we are too sickened by Pi's encounter with the remains of the victim to notice it on a first reading, when we have the courage to return to the text, we will surely wince at one eloquent detail: the man who died that Pi might live has no face.[29] Pi's reaction is that of a devout Hindu: "Something in me died then that has never come back to life."[30]

Martel makes sure to end his tale with a question that will provoke debate among his readers: Which is the "better story"? Pi rejects the kind of story the Japanese businessmen are looking for:

> I know what you want. You want a story that won't surprise you. That will confirm what you already know. That won't make you see higher or further or differently. You want a flat story. You want dry, yeast-less factuality. This is another way of saying I believe in a world ordered by a god whose presence can't be measured. You believe in a world ordered by rational science.[31]

According to the Japanese investigators: the facts in the two stories "match" perfectly.[32] Only one real difference exists, and that is the tiger. The tiger isn't a fact; he remains a mystery who disappears just before Pi is rescued. The businessmen are forced to admit that the story is better with the mysterious tiger. Is theirs a purely literary preference, a vote for art over journalism? Obviously, the novel's most important theme depends upon identifying the symbolic meaning of the tiger. Martel's own interpretation, that reality is better with religion, scarcely qualifies as exegesis for the most important figure in the novel. A far better revelation of the significance of the tiger will come when we ponder the power of the paradox to which Pi himself attests: "Richard Parker . . . it is the irony of this story that the one who scared me witless to start with was the very same who brought me peace, I dare say, even wholeness."[33]

In summary, both stories about Jonah and Pi and their life experiences, similar though somewhat different, contain invaluable theological lessons and insights. When these lessons and insights are heard together, we the readers of these two texts are invited to share in the greatest spiritual quest of all: the search for God, the search for Truth, and the search for self.

Wading Deeper on Your Own

Questions for Reflection and Discussion

1. Compare the element of irony in both the Book of Jonah and *Life of Pi*. What lessons are communicated through this literary device?
2. Describe Jonah's relationship with the Divine? How is this relationship similar to and different from Pi's relationship with the Divine?
3. How do images and figures from the natural world contribute to the development of each story—its plot and its themes?
4. What are the traits you admire most in Jonah and in Pi? Why? How are these traits embodied in your own life?
5. Jonah and Pi learned many invaluable lessons on their spiritual quests. What lessons have you learned thus far from your own spiritual quest?
6. Is Martel serious when he says that his story "will make you believe in God"? As you began reading, did you want to believe him or want to prove him wrong?
7. What does Pi mean when he says: "Every atheist is a potential believer"?
8. In what way did Richard Parker really save Pi's life?
9. What does the author suggest by having Richard Parker disappear after he and Pi have been rescued?
10. What additional meaning is added to the tale in *Life of Pi* by the origin of Richard Parker's name?
11. Comment on the exchange between Pi and the Japanese investigators as a humorous parody on a typical conversation about religion.

Suggestions for Writing and Journaling

1. Write an essay that details the wisdom gleaned from both the Book of Jonah and *Life of Pi*. What are the common threads of wisdom that run through both stories?
2. "My grim decision was taken. I preferred to set off in search of my own kind than to live a lonely half-life of physical comfort and spiritual death on this murderous island" (*Life of Pi*). Write an essay beginning with this quote in which you describe the

circumstances of what you would call a "lonely half-life of physical comfort and spiritual death."

3. Write an essay commenting on the meaning of Richard Parker and of his final disappearance incorporating either or both of the following quotations:
   - "It was natural that, bereft and desperate as I was, in the throes of unremitting suffering, I should turn to God."
   - "Then Richard Parker, companion of my torment, awful, fierce thing that kept me alive, moved forward and disappeared from my life."
4. Write an essay interpreting the story of the cook and the sailor's leg in *Life of Pi* as a critique of a brutal economic system.
5. Re-read Chapters 21 and 22. Write an imaginary conversation with Mr. Adirubasamy in which you debate the extent to which the novel does or does not succeed in its initial promise to "make you believe in God?"
6. Consider this quote from *Life of Pi*: "I am a Hindu because . . ." Write an essay that begins "I am a (Christian/Jew/Muslim/Atheist/Agnostic) because . . ."
7. Write an essay about the illusion of freedom in our permissive society beginning with "I know zoos are no longer in people's good graces. Religion faces the same problem. Certain illusions about freedom plague them both."
8. In Chapter 25 of *Life of Pi*, Pi condemns false religious values. Write an essay comparing his statements with those of Jesus in the Christian Gospels where the Gospel writers portray Jesus condemning false religiosity.

Irrigating Other Fields

In the Book of Jonah and *Life of Pi*, both novelists have used the techniques of fantasy (usually reserved for comedy) to induce readers to ponder serious questions. You might attempt to write (and perhaps perform) a fantasy that brings a similar approach to a serious subject of interest to another field of learning.

7

THE THEME OF LOVE

The Song of Solomon

Solomon 1:2–8:14

The Woman Caught in Adultery

John 7:53–8:11

The End of the Affair

Graham Greene

Introduction

Like *Life of Pi*, Graham Greene's *The End of the Affair* dramatizes a spiritual quest in the form of "a story to make you believe in God." But perhaps no two works in modern literature offer a greater contrast in the image of God to which the novelist invites belief. The more inclusive the faith that Pi declares, the less intrusive—that is, less intimate and demanding—his idea of God becomes. By contrast, Greene's Divine Lover who pursues Sarah and Bendrix through the very excesses of their passion acts like a very personal lover who would agree with the lover in the Song of Solomon that "love is strong as death, and passion as fierce as the grave" (Song of Sol. 8:6). So passionate is the language of these verses in the Song of Solomon that some biblical scholars wonder how a text like this one managed to be included in the biblical canon. No one knows the identity of the two lovers whose imagined ardor may have, perhaps, inspired this poetry. One thing is certain, however: this poem has enjoyed a rich interpretation that spans the gamut of passionate love between two ordinary people, to the love that God has for a person, to the love that Christ has for the church.[1] This poem has even inspired great mystics like John of the Cross to write "The Spiritual Canticle," a passionate love poem that describes the mystical experience of his God as lover, a poem that uses a literary style, tone, and storyline very similar to the Song of Solomon. The Song of Solomon and the story of the woman caught in adultery in John 7:53–8:11, along with *The End of the Affair* by Graham Greene, attest to the intensely human appeal of literature that embodies a credible image of a God who loves.

Although *The End of the Affair* was directly inspired, not by the biblical text, but by the author's own affair with the woman to whom the novel is dedicated, Sarah clearly resembles the biblical character of the adulterous woman in the John 7:53–8:11, and Graham Greene obviously wants his readers to remember how Jesus said that many sins are forgiven one who loves so much (Lk. 7:47).

Drinking from the Spring
The Biblical Text: The Song of Solomon
Solomon 1:2–8:14

Perhaps no other poem in the biblical text captures passionate, erotic love like that which is portrayed in the Song of Solomon, also known as the Song of Songs. Rich in interpretation and layered in symbolism, the work describes an intimate love, one that is passionate, playful, erotic, and simply divine, that exists between two people. In her commentary on the Song of Songs, J. Cheryl Exum observes that "The Song of Songs is a long lyric poem about erotic love and sexual desire—a poem in which the body is both object of desire and source of delight, and lovers engage in a continual game of seeking and finding in anticipation, enjoyment, and assurance of sexual gratification."[2] A rural, pastoral setting creates the backdrop for the Song, as metaphorical language attempts to capture the essence of love's passion and pleasure. The Song of Solomon is a marvelous interplay between the beauty of the natural world and the beauty of humanity. Clearly, the Song is a celebration of love and life that beckons us to remember that indeed beauty is in the eye of the beholder, for how one sees the natural world and nonhuman life is somehow related to how one sees human life, one another, and vice versa.

When we look at the Song of Solomon through the eyes of the Song's two lovers, we see that they look on life with the eyes of love. We receive a glimpse at the link that exists between the natural world and human life, and how such a link plays a significant role in the expression of love. Their loving gaze upon one another and upon the natural world is a divine gaze that sees, appreciates, and affirms beauty. We also see a vision of harmonious relationships reminiscent of Eden. This vision confronts us with the question: "Can paradise be regained?" Ponder the question as we discuss several examples of metaphorical language used in selected passages and verses of the Song of Solomon in an attempt to illuminate the relationship that exists between creation and love, and human love as part of creation.

The Song of Solomon can be divided into five cantos:

Canto 1: 1:2–2:7
Canto 2: 2:8–3:5
Canto 3: 3:6–5:8
Canto 4: 5:9–8:4
Canto 5: 8:5–14

Within the Song, many voices can be heard including those of the lover and beloved. Because the identity of these two main characters remains obscure, interpreters have seen the lover and the beloved in a variety of ways and assigned various genders to them. The interpretation that this analysis assumes is a classical one: the lover is a male; the beloved is a female. The focus is on the dialogue between the man and the woman.

"My Beloved Is to Me a Cluster of Henna Blossoms"
Canto 1: Solomon 1:2–2:7

The first canto (1:2–2:7) is a dialogue between the man and the woman in love. The speaker of 1:2–4a, 5–7, 12–14, 16 and 2:1, 3–7 seems to be the woman, the man's "beloved," while in 1:8–11, 15, 17 the man, the woman's "love" seems to be the one who speaks. Throughout the dialogue, images from the natural world color the speech of both the man and the woman as they express their deep love and admiration for each other. As we will see further on, some of these images become representative of the man and woman themselves.

In 1:7–8 and 17, natural world imagery creates two distinct settings or "landscapes" that are peaceful (1:7–8) and inviting (1:17). In 1:7 the woman's question directed to the man gives us the impression that her loved one is a shepherd. The phrases "where you pasture your flock" and "where you make it lie down at noon" conjure up a picture of a wide open green field, perhaps on a hill, with sheep gently grazing as the loved one stands with his staff, gazing on his flock. This shepherd image recurs in 2:16.

In pastoral poetry, the "noon hour" is *otium*, a time for rest. Here in verse 7, the woman sees this noon hour as a time when her loved one would make his sheep lie down. What may be suggested by this verse is the woman's desire for a rendezvous since, for a brief time, the sheep may not need the shepherd's full attention.

In 1:17, the phrases, "our couch is green"; "the beams of our house are cedar"; and "our rafters are pine" create a new setting. Here, the speaker, who is the lover, uses images from the natural world to describe metaphorically their home or their dwelling place of rest in the woods. Thus, we now find the two lovers in a wooded place. Othmar Keel suggests that "to place the lovers in a 'house' of cedars and junipers is to see them as more divine than royal. To have fresh greenery as a bed is the prerogative of the gods."[3]

The woman uses two metaphors in 1:13 and 14 to describe the person of her beloved: he is a "bag of myrrh" that lies between her breasts, and he is "a cluster of henna blossoms in the vineyards of Engedi." Myrrh, an oil, was used to anoint both the priests and the sacred vessels (see, e.g., Exod. 30:23). A henna bush is known for its rich, rose-scented white flowers that are arranged in erect clusters on the bush. Plant imagery continues in 2:3 where the woman points out that in relationship to other men, her loved one stands out as "an apple tree does among the trees of the wood." Apples are exotic fruits that offer refreshment (see, e.g., 2:5).

The woman also uses two images from the natural world to describe herself: she is a "rose of Sharon" and a "lily among thorns" (2:1). In 2:2, the man picks up the lily image in order to describe how striking the woman is among other maidens. Elsewhere, the man compares his love to "a mare among Pharaoh's chariots," and states that her eyes are "doves." These two images suggest power on the one hand, and peacefulness and gentleness on the other.

"My Beloved Is Like a Gazelle"
Canto 2: Solomon 2:8–3:5

The second canto (2:8–3:5) opens with the woman's description of what she sees: her loved one leaping upon the mountains, bounding over the hills, on his way toward her. She compares him to a graceful gazelle and a young stag (2:9) and later on, she holds up these two images as models for her loved one to embrace (2:17). A gazelle, a small antelope, is noted for its gracefulness. A stag is a mature male animal, more specifically, an adult male deer. The image of the loved one as a gazelle and stag suggests vigor and agility. The picture of a gazelle or stag leaping upon the mountains and bounding over the hills is a beautiful one indeed! And so is the loved one in the eyes of his beloved.

In 2:10–13, the woman quotes the man who invites her to arise and come away with him, for the winter is past and the spring has arrived in full bloom: flowers appear on the earth (v. 12); the voice of the turtledove can be heard in the land (v. 12); the fig tree spices her unripe figs (v. 13); and the vines are in blossom, giving forth fragrance (v. 13). With the arrival of spring comes the time for love and lovemaking. Spring is a season of fertility and new life. Such a delightful description of the spring season makes the loved one's invitation to his beloved all the more enticing.

In 2:14, the beloved continues quoting her loved one who now calls her a "dove." Earlier the woman's eyes were compared to doves (see 1:15); now her entire being is compared to a dove. This reference is both an endearing term, "O my dove," and a symbol. Doves, lovebirds par excellence, are associated with the love goddesses Aphrodite, Atagatis, and Ishtar.

"I Come to My Garden, My Sister, My Bride"
Canto 3: Solomon 3:6–5:8

A question with a reference to the "wilderness" (3:6; see also 8:5) opens the third canto (3:6–5:8). Here, the wilderness connotes not only a distant and inaccessible area but also an untamed, and "wild" place. Chapter 4:1–7 is known as a *wasf*. This is a particular genre that was used extensively in the Ancient Near East to extol praise for the physical beauty of either the beloved or the lover. In these verses, the beloved's beauty ravishes her loved one so much so that he gushes forth image upon image as he sees the beauty of his beloved mirrored by the beauty of the natural world. He exclaims, once again, that his beloved's eyes are "doves" (4:1); her hair is like "a flock of goats" moving down from Mount Gilead" (4:1); her teeth are like "a flock of shorn sheep that have come up from the washing-place" (4:2); her cheeks are like "the halves of a pomegranate" (4:3); and her two breasts are like "two fawns, twins of a gazelle that feed among the lilies" (4:5).

The loved one continues his graphic description of the beloved in 4:9–15. Here, the central metaphor is the garden. In the ancient Near Eastern world, a garden was one of the most beautiful and elegant pleasures one could have. References to a garden recall the idyllic state of Eden in Genesis 1–2; the prophets associate them with renewal and restoration. In 4:12, the man describes the woman as "a garden locked, a fountain sealed." These two images connote inaccessibility, and perhaps virginity. A variety of exotic, aromatic trees grow in the garden (4:13–15). Finally, in 5:1a, the loved one envisions the garden as the beloved herself:

> I come to my garden, my sister, my bride;
> I gather my myrrh with my spice,
> I eat my honeycomb with my honey,
> I drink my milk with my wine.

Succulent images from the natural world turn this canto into a most erotic love feast.

"You Are Stately as a Palm Tree"
Canto 4: Solomon 5:9–8:4

The fourth canto (5:9–8:4) opens with two questions that the daughters of Jerusalem pose to the woman with regard to why her loved one is so special. Her response takes the form of a *wasf* (see 4:1–5). Again, images from the natural world abound. The woman states that her loved one's locks are "wavy," "black as a raven" (5:11); his eyes are "like doves besides springs of water" (5:12); his cheeks are like "beds of spices, yielding fragrance" (5:13); his lips are "lilies, distilling liquid myrrh"; his appearance is "like Lebanon, choice as the cedars" (5:15).

The picture of a pastoral setting similar to that in 1:7–8 and 2:16 returns in 6:2–3; then there is a shift of focus in 6:4–10. Here, the man again compliments the woman for her loveliness (see 4:1–15). He expresses his singularity of heart in verse 9, and adds further that when the maidens, queens, and concubines saw the woman as a babe, so it seems, they questioned who this person was who "looks forth like the dawn" and is "as fair as the moon," and "bright as the sun,"and so on (6:9–10). As in previous verses, elements from the natural world and creation are used to express human beauty.

Scene and speaker shift again in 6:11–12. In these verses, the woman recounts an experience that she had when she went down to the nut orchard (6:11), during which time her fancy had set her in a chariot beside her prince (6:12). Her experience in the nut orchard seems to have freed her senses and imagination to envision herself with her beloved, who, through the power of her imagination, had become her "prince" (6:13).

Two more litanies of praise (7:1–9 and 7:10–8:4) spoken by the man and woman, respectively, close the canto. Images from the natural world continue to be a means for expressing human loveliness, as fields and vineyards (7:10–12) become the opportune place for desired lovemaking (7:12–8:3).

"Let Us Go Forth into the Fields"

Canto 5: Solomon 8:5–14

The fifth and final canto (8:5–14) presents a variety of images, many of which are, again, taken from the natural world. The canto closes with a passionate desire expressed by both the man and the woman. To his beloved, the loved one pleads:

> O you who dwell in the gardens,
> my companions are listening for your voice;
> let me hear it (8:13).

To his plea the beloved responds:

> Make haste, my beloved,
> and be like a gazelle
> Or a young stag
> upon the mountain of spices (8:14).

Metaphorical Language and Love's Expression in Perspective

The Song of Solomon presents us with many beautiful images and expressions of love. Language that is highly metaphorical accents the love that exists between the man and the woman. This love is at once human and divine. The natural world becomes a source of inspiration for both the writer of the Song of Solomon and its two main characters, and natural world imagery provides an avenue by which the man and the woman can express their mutual love and admiration for each other. Throughout the poem, the man and woman's sensitivity to the beauty of the natural world and their experience of it, enables them to see and appreciate the beauty of each other and vice versa. The garden of the natural world becomes the locus for their expression of love, and this garden becomes their own bodies upon which they feast in the course of exquisite lovemaking. Thus, the Song of Solomon is a celebration of love and life that invites us to see the beauty of the natural world and how that beauty becomes embodied in the lives of two lovers whose love is not only passionate but also an expression of the divine.[4]

The Biblical Text: The Woman Caught in Adultery *John 7:53–8:11*

Within the New Testament corpus, the story of the adulterous woman in John 7:53–8:11 teaches a lesson about love and compassion. The setting for this story is the temple area where Jesus is teaching the people who had gathered around him. The scribes and Pharisees bring him a woman found guilty of adultery. Under Mosaic Law, justice for this crime demanded that both the man and the woman engaged in the sexual relationship be stoned to death (Lev. 20:10; cf. Deut. 22:23, 24). Of note, only the woman stands accused; her partner is absent. Jesus deals directly with the scribes' and the Pharisees' hostility toward the woman and himself. When he is finally alone with the woman, he addresses her in a manner similar to how the biblical writer portrayed God's address to Adam, Eve, and Cain after their transgressions: He questions her: "Woman, where are they? Has no one condemned you?" (John 8:10). Her reply is simple and candid, "No one, sir," and Jesus' reply is complementary: "Neither do I condemn you. Go your way, and from now on do not sin again" (John 8:11). Like the God of the Old Testament who dealt with Adam, Eve, and Cain, Jesus neither accuses nor condemns the woman; nor does he condemn the scribes and the Pharisees.

By not condemning the woman and merely questioning her, Jesus allows her to reclaim her own personal integrity. His response to the woman's accusers is honest, just, and disarming: his response to the woman is compassionate. Strikingly and, unlike the God of the Old

Testament, Jesus does not mete out consequences. He simply tells her to go away and not to sin again. With no further comment from either party, Jesus leaves the woman free to work out the details of her life. Clearly, this story exemplifies not only how justice and compassion are interrelated and ultimately liberating but also a deep divine love for humankind and the human condition as exemplified by Jesus' attitude toward and response to the woman.

The theme of deep, passionate love expressed in the Song of Songs is a theme central to Graham Greene's novel, *The End of the Affair,* where Sarah, one of the novel's main characters, finds a kindred spirit in the adulterous woman of John's Gospel.

Playing in the Fountain
The Literary Text
The End of the Affair

About the Author
Graham Greene (1904–1991)

Born in Berkhamsted, England in 1904, the fourth of six children of a private school headmaster, Graham Greene suffered from bullying as a child and grew up to write what he called "entertainments" populated by "tough guys." The seedy world he created—the domain of gangsters, spies, and cynics—became known in literary circles as "Greeneland." As an outcome of his World War II career in the Secret Intelligence Service, Britain's equivalent of the American CIA, he developed a lifelong friendship with the notorious double agent Kim Philby and a taste for covert detective work that provided content for many novels and screenplays. Besides over twenty-two volumes of collected fiction and drama, a filmography of sixty-six titles attests to Greene's success as a screenwriter. These works of fiction, adapted for the screen, attracted stars like Orson Welles, Michael Caine, and Richard Gere. In addition to "potboilers," Greene produced a series of works that dramatize serious theological issues. His published memoirs, as well as Norman Sherry's meticulous three-volume authorized biography, demonstrate unequivocally that most characters and situations in Greene's fiction are autobiographical.

The End of the Affair is based on the author's relationship with the beautiful Lady Catherine Walston, to whom the novel is dedicated. Moreover, the novel records theological arguments and feelings related to Greene's youthful conversion from atheism to Roman Catholicism and quotes statements by Walston, who became a Catholic because of Greene's serious fiction. The lovers' behavior in the novel reflects Greene's own lifelong failure to live up to Catholic moral precepts. In the novel, when Bendrix argues with priests and with God, he sounds very like Greene, whose belief in Catholic doctrine failed to empower him to live a holy life. In reality, Greene once turned down an opportunity for a personal interview with the mystic Padre Pio saying: "I don't want to change my life by meeting a saint."[5] These words could be those of Bendrix, the novelist who narrates *The End of the Affair*.

A basis in autobiography does not guarantee literary excellence, but in Greene's case, it does argue for the authenticity of the faith experience in which the fiction is grounded. Throughout his life, human love seemed destined to draw Greene to religious faith. At the age of twenty-two, he became a Catholic under the influence of his fiancée, Vivien Dayrell-Browning, herself a devout convert. Eventually, however, the author became an intellectually engaged adult whose faith persisted long after he had to admit: "Continual failure or the circumstances of our private life, finally make it impossible . . . and many of us abandon Confession and Communion . . . a city of which we are no longer full citizens."[6] Because of statements like these and the fact that his most attractive characters are all somewhat flamboyant sinners, Greene polarized critics who both praised and condemned the implication in his most serious work that sinlessness is impossible and therefore not essential to genuine holiness. In 1952, despite widespread ecclesiastical condemnation for some of his work, The Gallery of Living Catholic Authors granted *The End of the Affair* its highest award for fiction.

With the paradox and perversity so evident in his literary style, Greene managed to be both a fully engaged and a "lapsed" Catholic. Even after his lifestyle rendered him ineligible for full participation in the sacraments, he remained devoted to the Eucharist and maintained friendship with scholarly priests who offered Mass for him in his home and in many hotel rooms. He pondered the works of leading post-Vatican II theologians, and when some of these latter seemed to him to be diluting Catholic doctrine, he staunchly resisted: "They have suddenly revived in me a deep faith in the inexplicable, in the mystery of Christ's resurrection."[7]

Reflecting on Genre

The Psychological Novel

Greene himself chose to divide his fiction into "serious novels" and the "entertainments" that eventually provided him with an affluent lifestyle. In *The End of the Affair*, he combines both genres. Book One begins like one of his famous detective stories and proceeds on the trail of the guilty until Book Three. From there on, the investigation evolves into a "mystery" story in the true sense, an exploration of the mystery of divine love.

In addition, the content of the novel can also be generically classified as "psychological fiction," even though the author does not employ any of the most sophisticated devices of that genre. The novel does exhibit several of the different concerns of psychological fiction. First of all, like psychological fiction, it focuses on the conflict between rational and nonrational knowledge, in this case, between faith and reason. Second, psychological fiction emphasizes internal mental and emotional states over external action. As we have already noted, these pages chronicle the author's own interior struggles in thinly veiled autobiography.

In this and numerous other works, the act of creating characters as surrogates for his own inner conflicts served the author as psychotherapy. Bendrix, Greene's fictional avatar, explains the process in Chapter 4 and elsewhere. Greene then attempts to generalize his experience by frequently interrupting the plot to indulge in psychoanalysis of emotions like love, hate, fear, jealousy, and egotism. "Hatred seems to operate on the same glands as love; it even produces the same actions. If we had not been taught how to interpret the story of the Passion, would we have been able to say whether it was the jealous Judas or the cowardly Peter who loved Christ?"[8] At the opening of Book Two, and throughout the following pages, Bendrix describes how compulsive possessiveness destroys both lover and beloved, which is just the opposite experience in the Song of Solomon where love is freely shared and freely given. In the final pages, he shows how not even death can end the agony. "You didn't own her all those years;" he prays to God. "I owned her. You won in the end; You don't need to remind me of that . . . but it was I who penetrated her not You."[9]

A third characteristic of psychological fiction is apparent when we see Bendrix acting out a process psychiatrists would identify as "projection," that is, when the tormented lover projects his self-hatred into verbal abuse of the beloved.[10] Greene inserts other insights from popular psychiatry when he suggests the influence of a dysfunctional childhood on Sarah's adult behavior. "Her mother had taught her effectively enough that one man was not enough for a lifetime."[11] These attempts by Bendrix to explain events through pseudo-science parallel his failures to escape theological explanations.

Reflecting on Structure

In deciding the design of a novel, an author's first important decision is always "Who will tell the story?" Greene chooses two first-person narrators: Bendrix, the novelist and jealous lover determined to identify his rival, and Sarah, the woman who has abandoned him for a higher love. By means of the first narrator, the author accomplishes two objectives, one literary, the other theological. First of all, as narrator of a detective story, he controls the flow of information to the reader to assure maximum suspense. Secondly, writing alternately as an atheist and as a reluctant convert, Greene is able to ponder the deeper "mystery story" as an outsider to the faith. Sarah's diary speaks in the voice of the second narrator. Three other related subject matters are woven into the plot: the adultery investigation; the psychology of love/hate/jealousy; the art of fiction itself. The choice of two narrators dictates the structure of the novel.

The narrative is divided into five books, each comprising seven to eight short chapters (except Book Four, which has only two). These chapters move forward and backward in time as Bendrix, the narrator, alternates between pursuing his investigation into the identity of his rival and recalling his own affair from its beginning to Sarah's death. In Book Three, the first person narrator becomes Sarah whose diary, addressed to God, explains how the affair ended. Book Three forms the theological heart of the novel. Books Four and Five return to Bendrix as narrator and move forward chronologically after Sarah's death. Events which can be interpreted as evidence that she is in heaven become the impetus for Bendrix' wrestling with a God he does not want to believe exists. Book Three makes one want to believe in a God as real and intimate as Sarah's lover, whereas Book Five makes one pray that believing in God does not require that one succumb to superstition and bad taste.

Reflecting on Literary Style

Everything, from the many-layered meaning of the title to the richly suggestive language of the opening paragraph, reveals the economy of Graham Greene's distinctive style. Consider for a few minutes the key words in the title. On the surface, the reader anticipates that "end" will mean "termination" and that the word "affair" connotes a temporary, tawdry relationship. Immediately, the opening sentence echoes the word "end" and draws attention to another, "chooses." Then as the story begins, we learn that the narrator is a lover who had no choice in ending his affair. Only after we have finished reading the whole story do we realize that "end" also means purpose, function, and ultimate fulfillment, that the choice that ended the affair was someone else's act of a pure love, the antithesis of temporary or tawdry. Even the definite article "the" we realize was carefully chosen to point, not only to the surface plot, but also to its theological theme: human love has "one end," to lead us inexorably to the fulfillment of existence, the divine love that is the source of all.

Greene's title and opening paragraph foreshadow the minute attention to words that will develop as the affair progresses. A prime example is the pronoun "you." In its first appearance early in the novel, the author subtly signals the egotism that is every lover's final undoing: "I imagined, like a fool, that there was only one 'you' in the world and that it was me."[12] After Bendrix identifies the one to whom "you" is addressed in the diary, his pain is replaced by bitterness. Gradually, as he begins to pray to the God in whom he refuses to believe, Bendrix uses the pronoun himself and at least once, he slips into a capital "You." In his last "prayer," the atheist cleverly maintains ambiguity by placing the pronoun at the beginning of each sentence, thus avoiding the theological implications of upper and lower case altogether.

Irony, one of the salient characteristics of Graham Greene's style, takes several forms: sarcasm, situational irony, and dramatic irony. Sarcasm helps Bendrix to feel superior to Henry, to Smythe, and to the priests in Sarah's life. Situational irony occurs whenever there is a contrast between expectation and reality. Early in the novel, Bendrix takes cruel delight in such an ironic contrast when he identifies Henry, the cheated husband, as Minister of Homeland Security. Later, Greene introduces comic irony when Parkis reports to Bendrix on Sarah's meeting with the secret lover who turns out to be Bendrix himself. Ironically, Parkis, whose "profession" places him at a moral level to which Henry cannot bring himself to stoop, is perhaps the most innocent character in the story. Dramatic irony occurs in conversations between Bendrix and Henry when one speaker knows something that the other does not know. For example, when Henry declines Bendrix' offer to spy on Sarah: "One can't spy on one's wife through a friend—and that friend pretend to be her lover."[13] Greene's stylistic choices mirror the overall irony of his protagonist's theological situation: "In proportion as he sins, his faith in Him against whom he sins is intensified."[14] C. C. Martindale's comment on *The Heart of the Matter* applies equally to *The End of the Affair*. In the end, the supreme paradoxical irony here is not in the novel, but in the autobiographical situation that inspired it. To Catherine Walston, Graham Greene wrote: "The only way to love God more than you is without you."[15]

Symbolism is not a highly developed element of Greene's usual literary style; in this case, when he does use it, the symbolic image appears only twice. First, Bendrix introduces it casually: "Then I closed the stained glass door behind me and made my way carefully down the steps that had been blasted in 1944 and never repaired."[16] Seventy-eight pages later when he is describing that fatal blast, the *stained glass* appears again. As an air raid severely damages, but does not destroy, the house in which Bendrix and Sarah make love for the last time, "Only the old

Victorian *stained glass* above the door had stood firm."[17] These ruins become sacred space when Sarah kneels and, pressing her nails into the palms of her hands, begins to pray. Then she symbolically places her body on an altar of sacrifice for the salvation of Bendrix, who lies beneath the door under the shatter-proof stained glass. The stained glass becomes the key to the easily decoded imagery of this scene symbolizing the novel's theological theme.

Drawing from the Well
Theological Themes

In all three works examined in this chapter, love is the primary theological theme that is portrayed through different lenses. In the Song of Solomon, love is passionate, erotic, and celebratory, surrounded by and embracing the beauty of creation. In the Johannine Gospel story of the woman caught in adultery, the love is forbidden, surrounded by judgment and the threat of death until divine love comes into play that is nonjudgmental and compassionate, opening the door for personal transformation. In Graham Greene's novel, the forbidden, adulterous love becomes a means of grace whereby the adulterous wife's pity for her husband keeps her from completely abandoning him in preference for the other. Through these stories, we are reminded of the Gospel teaching that God's grace rains on the just and the unjust (cf. Matt. 5:44–45). Love is a divine gift given to all, but how this gift is expressed and extended can be both rewarding and controversial.

Furthermore, in looking more closely at Graham Greene's work, one could say that for both the best and the worst of his theological themes, Graham Greene is indebted to the twentieth-century writers of the French Catholic Literary Renaissance.[18] At the beginning of his most controversial Catholic novel, he placed an epigraph from one of them, specifically from Charles Peguy. The epigraph reads: "The sinner is at the heart of Christianity."[19] All Greene's fiction inspired by his Catholic faith features a deeply religious sinner: a criminal, a whiskey priest, a suicide, an adulterer. Like his contemporary and lifelong friend Francois Mauriac, Greene liked to create fiction in which God's grace operates not from "on high," but from the murky depths of human corruption. His characters trust in the Jesus of the Gospels who assures us that he came "to save that which was lost." Greene's work was not, however, intended for an exclusively Catholic audience: "I write about situations that are common, universal . . . in which my characters are involved and from which only faith can redeem them, though often the manner of actual redemption is not immediately clear. They sin, but there is no limit to God's mercy."[20]

Faith in God's mercy, a theme also heard in the story of the woman caught in adultery, is the ultimate theme of *The End of the Affair*, for here the supernatural gift of faith involves belief not only in God's existence, but in God's unconditional love. Both protagonists struggle to refuse this gift, because belief in God's love makes "Him" a rival for theirs. In Sarah's case, belief in God begins when, kneeling beside Bendrix' lifeless body, she bargains with a God to whom she has never prayed before. If God will let her beloved live, she prays, she will give him up forever. Hence, she reasons, if God does not exist, her promise is not binding. For the same reason, Bendrix too is desperate to prove that the "you" to whom his beloved speaks in her diary is a delusion. By the final pages of the novel, however, Bendrix himself is addressing a personal God with a capital "You." For Sarah, relief would have been to believe in a less personal God: "I thought I could believe in some kind of God that bore no relation to ourselves, something vague, amorphous, cosmic, to which I had promised something and which had given me something in return."[21]

The object of this faith is not an abstraction. Sarah has come to believe in God as a lover of the unlovable. Here the story of the woman caught in adultery once again comes into view. And reading her diary, Bendrix is compelled to acknowledge the same ultimate "end" of human love: "It's a strange thing to believe that you are loved, when you know that nothing is here for anybody but a parent or a God to love."[22] Fighting desperately to believe that Sarah's sinfulness places her beyond God's love, Bendrix savagely attacks the priest's depiction of her as "a good woman."[23] Later he rejects Sarah's God because of its implications for all sinners: "For if this God exists . . . if even you —with your lusts and your adulteries and the timid lies you used to tell—can change like this, we could all be saints."[24]

Theologically and psychologically, everything else flows from belief in this love expressed in God's mercy toward the sinner. And sinners themselves can be instruments of this mercy. In all his religious novels, Greene seems obsessed with pity, the capacity to feel for another, as both a virtue and an obstacle to virtue. Greene believes the saving virtue of compassion is the chief quality of God's image in us. Pity motivates Sarah even when she feels no attraction to virtue. Longing for her lover with the same passion as the woman in the Song of Solomon longs for her lover, Sarah feels so kindly toward her husband that pity prevents her from leaving him. She goes to Smythe at first in the hope that his passionate atheism will destroy her faith. Yet when she realizes that, in fact, he is strengthening it, she continues the relationship out of pity. For Sarah, kissing Smythe's strawberry mark, is an act of prayer communicating the divine pity toward God's avowed adversary.[25]

Like the novelists of the French Catholic Literary Renaissance, Greene's serious novels challenged English-speaking Catholics of the twentieth century to reflect on their faith in relation to sinners rather than saints. Not all the notions that he absorbed from them were theologically sound. From Charles Peguy, for example, he learned of an act called "mystical substitution." Ostensibly an imitation of Christ's substitution of himself for sinners in his death on the cross, the offering of oneself for the salvation of another recurs in the lives of the saints. In *The End of the Affair*, Sarah's bargaining with God is a mild example of this exchange when she prays that God take away her peace and give it to Bendrix. Later Sarah desires to offer her whole self for him: "Dear God, if only You could come down from Your cross for awhile and let me get up there instead. If I could suffer like You, I could heal like You."[26] Although such an impulse seems fairly orthodox, Greene had previously, in *The Heart of the Matter*, carried the notion to the extreme of "voluntary damnation." Severe criticism from theologians was then understandable and probably guided Greene into safer theological waters in *The End of the Affair*.[27]

As an expression of genuine religious experience, the novel effectively ends with the triumph of faith and love in Sarah's diary. Books Four and Five, unfortunately, protract a theological anti-climax. Everyone including the author recognizes the essential weakness in the miraculous aftermath of Sarah's death in Book Five, not only as theology, but also as literature. In retrospect, Greene claimed that through the "miracles" he wanted to batter the mind of Bendrix and force him to a reluctant doubt of his own atheism.[28] The evidence of divine love and mercy in Sarah's life is miracle enough; miraculous cures are unnecessary, and so is the post-mortem revelation of the secret baptism that "took." What Greene does accomplish in Book Five, however, is to batter the reader with examples of the kind of superstition, devotional clutter, and bad taste in uneducated Catholicism that repels not only its critics but also potential converts. The best that can be said for Book Five is that it demonstrates how the essence of Catholicism survives all the institutional flaws and cultural accretions with which human weakness has burdened it.

When viewing these three texts together, we can see how the theme of love and lovers plays out in different people's lives. The Song of

Solomon provides us with a view of a beautiful, celebratory love. The lover in the Song is passionate, and the love shared between the lover and the beloved is a kind of playful, sensuous love that is at once human and divine. The woman in John's Gospel is guilty of passionate, adulterous love but the love extended to her by Jesus is an all-embracing compassionate love. Like the adulterous woman, Sarah experiences the same deep love and has an affair. Unlike John's adulterous woman who receives divine compassion, Sarah herself becomes the embodiment of divine compassion toward her husband. Moved by pity for him, she does not leave him even though her love for him has waned. Thus, the sinful Sarah becomes an instrument of God's love as the Gospel of John's adulterous woman becomes the receptacle of divine love. What these two women have in common is their passionate love for their lover, a love that resembles that of the lovers in the Song of Solomon. Thus, in these three stories we have seen the complexity and the beauty of love that can be not only erotic but also transformative.

Wading Deeper on Your Own

Questions for Reflection and Discussion

1. Discuss the theology of love embedded in the Song of Solomon.
2. The beloved in the Song of Solomon is the recipient of passionate love; the woman caught in adultery in John's Gospel is the recipient of compassionate love. Discuss how these two faces of love are innately "divine."
3. Identify the different "voices" in the Song of Solomon. How do they contribute to the development of the poem?
4. Is *The End of the Affair* "a story that will make you believe in God?" Does it make you want to? Afraid to? Afraid not to?
5. Were you surprised when you read Sarah's diary?
6. Why do you think that Graham Greene gives the reader so little in Bendrix to love?
7. What does the author seem to demonstrate through the character of Henry?
8. How does Sarah's idea of God compare with your own?
9. How does the image of God as Divine Lover compare with your other images of God?
10. Of what importance are the apparent cures of Smythe and Parkis's boy?
11. How does the character of Smythe contribute to the dialogue with theology?

Suggestions for Writing and Journaling

1. Write an essay that describes what the Song of Solomon teaches us about human, passionate love. Likewise, what does Luke's story about the woman caught in adultery teach us about love in relation to compassion?
2. Rewrite John 7:53–8:11 from the perspective of the adulterous woman. Describe how the adulterous woman is similar to and different from Sarah in Greene's novel.
3. Throughout *The End of the Affair,* Bendrix the narrator is writing another novel. Write an essay demonstrating how this book functions as a symbol for the interaction of divine love and human freedom.
4. Write an essay comparing and contrasting the literary styles of Bendrix and Sarah. How does the difference relate to their personalities?
5. Compare and contrast the choice of imagery in selections by each first-person narrator.
6. Bendrix describes his method of dramatic characterization: "I have never been able to describe even my fictitious characters except by their actions." Write a brief profile of each of the following according to their actions: Sarah, Smythe, Henry, Parkis.

Irrigating Other Fields

The *End of the Affair* has been made into a film twice. In neither version did the filmmaker capture the depth of Sarah's diary. Viewing the most recent version provides an excellent opportunity to critique the limitations of Hollywood's power to represent spiritual reality. When you discuss a current film with friends be sure to comment on how the film makers' choices either distorted, neglected, or undermined your own values.

8
THE THEME OF WAR
The Story of Cain and Abel
Genesis 4:1–16
The Wars of David
2 Samuel 8–18
A Sleep of Prisoners
Christopher Fry

Introduction

No desire is more elusive than peace, no activity more pervasive than war. These realities are as obvious in sacred history as recorded in the Bible as they are in human history as recorded in texts, memorials, ruins, and all the way to the gory images found in cyberspace. A few pages into the Book of Genesis, violence erupts between the first two brothers, Cain and Abel. Throughout subsequent chapters of the Old Testament, in numerous battles between families, tribes, and nations, such as the stories of the wars of David (2 Sam. 8–18), the God of Israel is presumed to take sides. In contrast to all of these events and stories, in *A Sleep of Prisoners*, playwright Christopher Fry shows a poetic version of humanity's proclivity to violence that appears to preclude the concept of divine intervention so often presumed in the Bible. This chapter traces the entrance of violence into the human condition by looking at the theme more deeply in relation to Genesis 4:1–16, the story of Cain and Abel, and 2 Samuel 8–18, the story of the wars of David. Interestingly, Fry's play *A Sleep of Prisoners* draws on the Cain and Abel story in Genesis 4:1–16 and the figure of David in 2 Samuel 8–18. This chapter also seeks to provoke a reconsideration of the taking of another's life as restitution for a life taken, as well as of the necessity for and reality of war.

Drinking from the Spring
The Biblical Text: The Story of Cain and Abel
Genesis 4:1–16

The story of Cain and Abel is part of Chapters 1–11, the first part of the Book of Genesis that speaks of mythological, primeval times prior to the formation of Israel as a people and a nation. Additionally, Genesis 4:1–16 is part of a series of stories that deal with transgression and chastisement (Gen. 3–11). The Cain and Abel story is attributed to the Yahwist source, who was writing sometime around 1000 BCE, which would have been during the early years of Israel's monarchy. Prior to the story of Cain and Abel is the story of Adam and Eve and their transgression (Gen. 3). According to the biblical text, Cain, the older child of Adam and Eve, follows in his parents' footsteps, except that his crime is much graver than that of his parents, and the transgression should have cost him his life.

The biblical writer opens the narrative in Genesis 4 with Adam and Eve living outside of the garden. Even though the couple is guilty of transgression, they remain graced because, after they have relations, Eve becomes pregnant and bears two sons, Cain and Abel (vv. 1, 2a). In the ancient world, fertility was a sign of God's grace and blessing. Abel becomes a keeper of sheep and Cain a tiller of the ground (v. 2b). As was customary in the ancient world, both boys brought offerings to God (vv. 3–4a). God chose Abel's offering instead of Cain's (vv. 4b-5). The point here is not that God has a preferential option for Abel and his offering; rather, the text celebrates the freedom of God. The divine choice sparks a sharp reaction from Cain: he becomes angry and crestfallen (v. 5b). Cain's reaction causes God to confront him (v. 6). In this moment of confrontation, God assures Cain that even though sin is lurking at Cain's door and waiting to overtake him, Cain has the power not to succumb to sin (v. 7). Despite his profound disappointment at God's choice, Cain is given a strong word of encouragement by God and a directive as to what he must do when he does come face-to-face with sin.

The high point of the narrative occurs in verse 8:

> Cain said to his brother Abel, "Let us go out to the field." And when they were in the field, Cain rose up against his brother Abel, and killed him.

Cain's attack against his brother was premeditated, spurred on by jealousy and anger. Unfortunately, Cain did not heed God's advice and did not respond to the grace of the moment. Instead, he allowed his own emotions to overtake his sense of conscience and reason, resulting in his act of aggression; he murdered his brother.

Now, according to the ancient Jewish law of retaliation known as *lex talionis* (see Exod. 21:24; Lev. 24:20; and Deut. 19:21), Cain's life was to be required of him for having taken a life. The law of retaliation was meant to be humane. For example, a life could not be required if someone violated the property of another. But if a life were taken, a life was required. Thus, Cain would by traditional law be put to death.

An interesting turn of events, however, occurs in Genesis 4:9–15. God's response to Cain's egregious crime is not to condemn him to death. Instead, God questions Cain, and Cain responds accordingly:

> Then the Lord said to Cain, "Where is your brother Abel?" He said, "I do not know; am I my brother's keeper?" (v. 9)

By questioning Cain, God gives Cain the opportunity to take responsibility for his actions, but Cain fails miserably and instead offers a deceitful and flippant response. God responds with yet another rhetorical question and then issues a chastisement:

> And the Lord said, "What have you done? Listen; your brother's blood is crying out to me from the ground! And now you are cursed from the ground! And now you are cursed from the ground, which has opened its mouth to receive your brother's blood from your hand. When you till the ground, it will no longer yield to you its strength; you will be a fugitive and a wanderer on the earth." (vv. 10–12)

The murder of Abel does not go unnoticed or unheard. Cain will have to suffer consequences for his crime. But Cain's response to God continues to be brash:

> Cain said to the Lord, "My punishment is greater than I can bear! Today you have driven me away from the soil, and I shall be hidden from your face; I shall be a fugitive and a wanderer on the earth, and anyone who meets me may kill me." (vv. 13–14)

God responds firmly but with compassion:

> Then the Lord said to him, "Not so! Whoever kills Cain will suffer a sevenfold vengeance." (v. 15a)

God then puts a mark on Cain "so that no one who came upon him would kill him" (v. 15b). The narrative closes with Cain going away from the presence of the Lord and settling in the land of Nod, east of Eden, where he takes a wife and fathers Enoch. Like his parents before him, Cain remains graced even though he has committed a heinous crime.

Significant in this story is Cain's punishment for the crime he has committed. If God were following human law in place at the time the Yahwist writer was composing this story, then God should have required Cain to be put to death. Cain's punishment, however, is not death. Instead, he will be a restless wanderer in the land, never experiencing a sense of peace and security, and for the rest of his life he will have to live with the reality that he murdered his younger brother and did not have the courage to take responsibility for this crime when he was confronted. This man who had the strength to enact such vengeance upon his younger brother is, in reality, a very weak person, lacking in character and moral stamina.

By not having God require Cain's life, the Yahwist who fashioned this text teaches his readers a profound and lasting lesson: God's justice is remarkably different from human law. Additionally, the story of Cain and Abel has an etiological purpose: it tries to explain the origins of sibling rivalry and, in the case of these two brothers, how such rivalry can lead to violence and murder within the family unit, leaving familial relationships in tatters and peace in shambles. Finally, the story of Cain and Abel sets the stage for the escalation of violence to be seen in 2 Samuel 8–18 that describes the many battles in which King David is engaged.

The Wars of David
2 Samuel 8–18

2 Samuel 8–18 is a block of material within chapters that imaginatively present some of the many battles that took place during the reign of David and introduce us to some of the main biblical characters who will also appear later in Christopher Fry's work, *A Sleep of Prisoners*. These selected chapters from the corpus of First and Second Samuel show us how violent the ancient world and culture had become since the biblical story of the murder of Abel. This next section presents not so much an analysis of the biblical texts, but rather traces the storyline and overview of the conflict and battles in which David and his family were engaged. The texts also introduce us to some of the important players in David's court.

To begin, 2 Samuel 8:1–14 provides a lengthy list of the battles in which David was engaged and which he won. His victories included the defeat of the Philistines, Moabites, King Hadadezer and his whole army, the Arameans, the Edomites, and the Ammonites, among others. In 2 Samuel 8:15–18, we hear that David reigned over all of Israel, administering justice and equity. We also learn who served in some of David's major posts, the most important one being Joab, the commander of David's army.[1]

2 Samuel 10:1–19 describes how David's military forces defeated the Ammonites and Arameans. The conflict with the Ammonites begins when David, in good faith, sends an envoy to Hasun, the son of the Ammonites' recently deceased king. Unfortunately, Hasun's princes incite Hasun against David and his gesture, which becomes seen more as a threat than a consolation, and Hasun acts accordingly by treating David's envoy with great disrespect (2 Sam. 10:1–5).

Such actions cause David to turn against Hasun and his people, which leads David to wage battle against the Ammonites and the Arameans, whom they had hired to fight alongside them. As commander-in-chief of David's army, Joab rises to the occasion and enters into a battle with the Arameans. Joab and his troops kill many of the Arameans and the survivors flee. Joab also wages battle with the Ammonites and successfully defeats them as well (2 Sam. 10:9–18). David's successful battles caused some kings to make peace with Israel, thus desiring not to enter into conflict with Israel and consequently risk being defeated by David's forces (2 Sam. 10:19).

In 2 Samuel 11:1–27, David's illicit and adulterous affair with Bathsheba, the wife of Uriah the Hittite,[2] results in Bathsheba becoming pregnant by David. In order to cover up his crime, David concocts a scheme in which he brings Uriah home from the battlefield to try and get Uriah to go back to his house to be with his wife, hoping that Uriah would then have sex with his wife so the pregnancy could then be attributed to Uriah. Uriah does not comply with David's scheme; he does not go back to his own house but, because he is loyal to David as his ultimate commander-in-chief, Uriah sleeps with the king's servants instead, which infuriates David even more. David then sends Uriah with a note to Joab. In the note David commands Joab to send Uriah into the front lines of battle and to make his slaying look like an accident. Joab, concerned about his own military reputation, entices the men of Rabbah to attack. In this attack, some of the Israelites are slain along with Uriah. David receives word of this and responds casually, sending a message to Joab telling him not to be dismayed by what has taken place, that such things happen in war, and that he should just press on with his attacks (2 Sam. 11:14–25). Bathsheba offers proper lamentation for her husband, and when the period of lament is completed, David takes Bathsheba as his wife. She bears a son from her and David's illicit union (2 Sam. 11:26–27).

In 2 Samuel 12:1–15a, the prophet Nathan eventually brings David's crimes to light; he confronts David about his wicked deeds; and David admits his wrongdoing. Nathan then assures David that God has forgiven him because he has finally acted with integrity and has taken responsibility for his crimes. Ironically, the child of David and Bathsheba is on death's doorstep. David pleads with God (2 Sam. 12:15b-23), but the child succumbs to death despite David's pleas and acts of fasting. David then pulls himself together, worships God again, and eventually has another son with Bathsheba, Solomon, who becomes David's successor to the throne (2 Sam. 12:24–25).

2 Samuel 12:26–31 continues the story of the campaigns that Joab and David waged against Israel's enemy nations. This time, the people defeated were the Ammonites who, though they battled with Israel earlier, were not totally defeated. This next round of battles that the Israelites fought against the Ammonites crushed the Ammonites, and those among the survivors of the enemy, David enlisted in labor on behalf of Israel and David's endeavors. When David took the royal city of Rabbah,[3] he also took the crown of Milcom, the national god of the Ammonites, and put the crown on his own head. This crown was quite heavy and contained a precious stone.

What follows next in the story of David and his battles are a series of episodes that involve conflicts within David's family, specifically among Amnon, David's firstborn son by Ahinoam of Jezreel (see 2 Sam. 3:2), Absalom, Amnon's brother, and Tamar, Absalom's sister (see 2 Sam. 13:1–18:33). Because Amnon desires his brother Absalom's wife, and because she refuses him, Amnon rapes her. David refuses to punish Amnon because he is David's firstborn son. This incident and David's response incites Absalom to so much rage that Absalom has Amnon killed. The crime deeply disturbs David, who eventually forgives Absalom. Absalom then in turn conspires to usurp the throne from David. When Absalom's troops wage battle against David and his troops, Joab's armor-bearers surround Absalom, strike him, and kill him (2 Sam. 18:15). These sections of the story about David and his national and family battles close with David lamenting the death of his son, Absalom (2 Sam. 18:33).[4]

The stories of Cain and Abel and those of the wars of David outside and within his family shaped the thought of Christopher Fry, who takes the biblical characters of Cain, Abel, David, and Absalom to develop a highly imaginative and poignant play about four prisoners of war locked up in a church in enemy territory. Their confinement magnifies their problems, and they struggle to understand themselves and their world. The action of the play takes place in a sequence of dreams, with the attempted murder of one soldier by his friend conjuring up themes and stories from biblical texts about the four, as well as well as about Abraham and Isaac. This next section focuses in on the highlights of Christopher Fry's play, in which we meet ancient biblical characters through the eyes of Fry's own characters.

Playing in the Fountain
The Literary Text
A Sleep of Prisoners

About the Author
Christopher Fry (1907–2005)

Christopher Fry witnessed a century of warfare. Born in Great Britain shortly before World War I, he survived the devastation of his homeland in World War II and lived to see his countrymen deployed in a third war throughout Afghanistan and Iraq before he died on July 5, 2005. Both a social conscience and high literary tastes developed at an exceptionally early age in this poet, playwright, actor, and director. Raised by a single mother, he was nourished on a steady diet of classical literature and encouraged in his early passion for theater. From his maternal grandmother, he learned of the family's Quaker pacifism and heard stories of his revered ancestor, Elizabeth Fry, a dedicated reformer of prisons. As a child of seven, the boy watched an almost daily funeral procession pass by his home bearing the bodies of military heroes to the local cemetery. Decades later, as a conscientious objector during World War II, he helped clear away fire bomb damage from streets, docks, and sewers, and removed bodies and rubble from devastated homes.

From the age of seventeen until twenty-three, Fry vacillated "between two poverties: of an actor and of a teacher."[5] At first as a theater amateur, he performed multiple tasks: actor, director, and producer. In addition, as musician and composer, he poured out songs for the stage. Then, at the age of twenty-seven, he brought all these skills to the professional level at Tunbridge Wells Repertory. Five years later, he became director of the Oxford Playhouse. World War II interrupted this promising career, but after the war, he returned to the theater. Fry's dedication to his art can be judged from the fact that his salary as director of the Oxford Playhouse was only $10.00 per week.

In the 1940s and 1950s, Fry was one of a small group of British playwrights (including T. S. Eliot) who enjoyed brief attention for restoring verse drama to the English stage. *A Sleep of Prisoners*, like Eliot's *Murder in the Cathedral*, was first produced in a church. Its premiere performance at St. Thomas Church, Regent Street, London, on May 15, 1951, was followed almost immediately by a New York City opening at St. James Church, October 16, 1951. Critics alternately praised and derided the poetic drama movement for attempting to revive Shakespearean eloquence at a time when playwrights of the "kitchen sink" school were popularizing slang and profanity. Nevertheless, between 1946 and

1956, five of Fry's verse dramas achieved critical and popular success when legendary stars of the Shakespearean stage, such as John Gielgud, Claire Bloom, Richard Burton, and Paul Scofield, assured an appreciative audience for dramatic poetry. Only a few of Fry's plays are classified as religious, but the poet's intentions were always more spiritual than commercial. Fry believed in a personal God and a world "in which we are poised on the edge of eternity, a world which has deeps and shadows of mystery and in which God is anything but a sleeping partner."[6]

A church a few miles from Fry's home supplied the realistic foundation for *A Sleep of Prisoners*. In this historic church, six soldiers had been imprisoned in 1649, and one of them had carved his name and date into one of its stones. Fry transferred the situation to the twentieth century and reduced the number of soldiers to four. Then he gave each actor a script with the kind of multiple roles that showcase a repertory actor's talents. As each man dreams a scene from the Bible, the characters go through a series of transformations. Cumulatively, the scenes dramatize the problem of human violence as a cause of suffering to God as well as to God's world.

Reflecting on Genre and Structure

Generically, *A Sleep of Prisoners* straddles several categories. First, it can be described according to its language as "verse drama." Then, as its structure moves in and out of sleep, it repeatedly creates a "play within a play." Finally, as each dream makes a series of mental states vividly visual, we recognize characteristics of the psychologically-based expressionistic drama. The terms "verse drama" and "play-within-a-play" are self-explanatory. Expressionism, the movement that began in visual art and soon spread to stage, screen, and opera, was an attempt to make states of mind visible.

In this play, Fry adapted expressionism's insights in their most accessible form, the expressionism with which we are all most familiar: the dream. Every dreamer is a playwright. Psychologists point out, and our own experience confirms, that the dreamer transforms the waking environment and events surrounding the dreamer just before sleep into symbols of one's inner concerns and emotions. Hence, in the first scene showing the four prisoners of war together in a church just before reveille, Fry assembles images and associations for the personal dreams that will follow when the prisoners go to sleep.

In attempting to dramatize mental states, expressionistic theater tends to reduce characters to personality types rather than to fully realized individuals. This move is clearly Fry's intention here. Each prisoner in his dream assumes the persona of the biblical figure whose temperament most closely resembles his own. Meadows dreams;[7] David dreams;[8] Peter dreams;[9] Adam also begins to dream,[10] and the others gradually join him in the final dream. Although one critic observes a progression in the dreams through the night until dawn as denoting the stages in each character's development,[11] it is still accurate to say that each prisoner represents a familiar personality trait rather than an individual person. Thus David, Peter, Adams, and Meadows represent, respectively, aggressiveness, passivity, conformity, and the moderation and wisdom that come with age. Together, all four represent humanity—but humanity at war with itself. Fry repeats this theme through the voices of more than one speaker: "But there's strange divisions in us, and in every man, one side or the other, " says Meadows.[12] And Adam, witnessing the first fratricide, embraces contradictions in the whole race: "Out of my body I made them both, the fury and the suffering."[13]

David shows the worst of aggressiveness when he almost strangles Peter. This compulsive activist sometimes resents the nature God has given him: "I loved life with a good rage you gave me. . . . How was I expected to guess that what I am you didn't want?"[14] However, the world is moved to good as well as ill by people who feel as David does: "Let me have some part in what goes on or I shall go mad!"[15] To David, Peter's imperturbable serenity feels like a "crime against humanity." "What's a little evil here and there among friends? Shake hands on it," he snarls sarcastically.[16] Peter himself eventually acknowledges: "I never remember I ought to be fighting until I'm practically dead. Sort of absent-fisted. Very worrying for Dave."[17] Men and women in every age who go to war to defend their homeland would agree with David when he says, "Why don't you do some slaughtering yourself sometimes? Why always leave it to me?"[18] Corporal Adam, on the other hand, finds his security in simply executing rules he feels no need to analyze or justify. The playwright seems to be arguing that an orderly world needs all these kinds of people, or at least is pointing to declaring all wars immoral.

Besides exemplifying basic personality types to the audience, the dream structure serves another psychological function. Fry takes poetic license by having each dream show the dreamer three visions of himself: as at heart he really is, as he sees himself, and as his comrades see him. In the first dream, for example, where God's dream of Eden turns into a nightmare, even God gets to see how he looks to others when Cain and Abel shoot dice for divine favor. In this visual metaphor, God gets to see how unfair his preference for Abel seems to Cain—and to people like him. In the final dream, all men begin to come together, a situation that is the playwright's dream for humanity. Fry wants the prisoners to progress from division to unity. In this movement, we recognize Fry's adaptation of the "tragic rhythm of action": purpose, passion, perception.[19]

Another feature of dreams that Fry exploits here is the way that a figure will suddenly become someone else: the dreamer's husband suddenly becomes a father, teacher, or employer. In *A Sleep of Prisoners*, each character takes four different roles: Joe dissolves to Adam, then Joab, then an angel; Peter dissolves to Abel, Absalom, and Isaac; David dissolves to Cain, King David, and Abraham; Meadows segues from the voice of God to that of human history.

Reflecting on Literary Style

Several aspects of Fry's style deserve comment in relation to literary history. First, we have already pointed out that Fry was one in a group of theater artists who went against a popular trend when they tried to restore dialogue in verse. As a matter of fact, drama began as poetry. Not until the age of Shakespeare did dramatists write dialogue in prose, and even then conversation on the stage was expected to be of a "higher order" than that on Main Street. Gradually, during the eighteenth century, poets produced comedies in prose, but still in elevated diction, while tragedies in verse were typically read, not staged. Not until the nineteenth century did actors routinely speak in the vernacular, and when Brecht introduced slang and profanity, he was considered a tasteless innovator. "Degenerate" speech was not fully accepted by theatergoers until one hundred years later, and even in the United States, plays by dramatists like Eugene O'Neill elicited comments like: "We don't go to the theatre to hear people talk like they do in any saloon!" Fry welcomed such a discriminating audience, for whom his style was eminently suited. By the 1940s and 1950s, however, pedestrian speech was so standard in the theater that the attempted revival of verse drama polarized professional critics and audiences. No matter how successful individual productions were, the movement never enjoyed widespread support.

A second feature of Fry's style also has some historic significance: his representation of the deity. Fry's occasional caricature of God as somewhat befuddled and helpless would be no surprise to an audience familiar with medieval drama. Fry is actually following an ancient tradition popular in dramas performed in church. In the Mystery Plays of medieval times, for example, humor often toyed with blasphemy. Since, as Fry observed, laughter is the surest touch of genius in creation, he believed in combining serious subject matter with wit and comic irony. What has been said of his most popular play, *The Lady's Not for Burning*, applies equally to all his works: "The humor, the irony, the wit, and the angst that each character exudes captures us and holds us throughout."[20] In *A*

Sleep of Prisoners, the clever puns with which the prisoners taunt each other are one form of linguistic humor that provides comic relief from Fry's grim subject matter, that is, "Police on earth. Aggression is the better part of Allah."[21]

Fry uses his most exquisite language to elicit not local laughter, but universal grief. Adam, in the presence of the world's first death, seizes a metaphor from God's blighted garden and utters humanity's first poem: "My heart breaks, quiet as petals falling one by one, but this is the drift of agony forever."[22]

The fact that the audience always knows the biblical stories better than the figures enacting them onstage affords Fry a continuing opportunity to exploit his strongest stylistic device, dramatic irony. One of the playwright's most eloquent and ironic statements can be appreciated only in performance. In the dream where Joab returns to report to King David, we read this exchange:

> David: What are you bringing back?
> Joab: The victory.

(Then the theater audience sees Joab silently present David with the dead body of his son.)

> David: Are you sure it's the victory?
> Are we ever sure it's the victory?[23]

Fry has stated that he wrote his plays in verse because "poetry is the language in which man expresses his own amazement."[24] Hence, the poet brings this religious play to a powerful culminating vision in Fry's frequently quoted poetry. First he expresses amazement—coupled with faith—that good survives all forms of evil:

> Good is itself, whatever comes.
> It grows, and makes, and bravely
> Persuades, beyond all tilt of wrong;
> Stronger than anger, wiser than strategy,
> Enough to subdue cities and men
> If we believe it with a long courage of truth.[25]

Then, on a stage where lighting envelops the prisoners in flames that do not consume them, first Peter and then Meadows articulate the play's final vision of hope and love.

> The blaze of this fire
> Is wider than any man's imagination.
> It goes beyond any stretch of the heart.

The human heart can go to the lengths of God.
Dark and cold we may be, but this
Is no winter now. The frozen misery
Of centuries breaks, cracks, begins to move;
The thunder is the thunder of the floes,
The thaw, the flood, the upstart Spring.
Thank God our time is now when wrong
Comes up to face us everywhere,
Never to leave us till we take
The longest stride of soul men ever took.
Affairs are now soul size.
The enterprise
Is exploration into God.[26]

Drawing from the Well
Theological Themes

The stories of Cain and Abel, ones of family conflict and strife, together with David's national, international, and family wars show us that conflict, violence, and war have always been part of the human condition. Murder, rooted in contempt and flowing from jealousy; the need to amass more and more power and control; and inordinate sexual desires that are acted upon which then violate persons and primary relationships are all situations that show us show the dismal side of the human condition that is still in need of redemption, still in need of transformation. Ancient struggles and crimes that we see in the biblical text we still continue to see in our world today, a situation that contemporary writers continue to shed light on through their creative works. These works cause us to pause and wonder if history and its course of violence will ever stop repeating itself, and whatever happened to the divine biblical vision of the new heavens and the new earth, a vision that offers hope for peace in the land, peace in the world.[27]

Today, a pedestrian definition of theology might read "the study of what humankind thinks about God." In *A Sleep of Prisoners*, Christopher Fry returns the favor by attempting to suggest what God thinks about humankind. The soldier to whom Fry assigns God's lines is, understandably, the oldest prisoner, Meadows. Meadows' attitude toward the younger men is that of a benign grandfather. Even when David attacks Peter, the elder soldier's reaction is shockingly gentle: "I see the world in you very well. T'isn't your meaning, but you're a clumsy, wall-eyed bulldozer. You don't know what you're hitting."[28] When we move into the first dream from the Book of Genesis, Meadows identifies himself as the voice of God. More importantly, he articulates the Creator's compromise of omnipotence by reason of the gift of free will. "No, no, no. I didn't ask to be God."[29] Consistently, Meadows gives the audience a merciful creator's view of humanity: never harsh, and less judgmental than our own judgment of each other, no matter how wrong objectively our words or behavior.

Fry renders the biblical account of the first transgression, with its dialogue between the first human and his creator, as a conversation between a private and his commanding officer:

Meadows: As you were, Adam.
Adams: No chance of that, sir.
Meadows: As you were, as you were.
Adams: Lost all track of it now, sir.
Meadows: How far back was it, Adam?
Adams: Too dark to see.
Meadows: Were you alone?
Adams: A woman with me, sir.
Meadows: I said, 'Let there be love.'
And there wasn't enough light, you say?
(Adams explains how unprepared the first couple were.)
Meadows: Be at peace.[30]

In the next dream of Cain and Abel, one can detect a prophetic voice in Fry's anticipation of contemporary eco-theology, which protests the pollution of the earth by modern weaponry. After the first murder, God calls out to Cain: "I hear your brother's blood crying to me from the ground."[31]

In the ensuing dreams, the play proceeds to lay out an argument that conflict and violence are endemic to human nature and, therefore, inevitable in human history. Softened by the vision of an understanding God, the play as a whole supports a theology of hope. Even David King, the least spiritual of the prisoners, is given lines suggesting that war can have some redemptive value: "God dips His hand in death to wash the wound, takes evil to inoculate our lives against infectious evil."[32]

In the lines Fry gives to the prisoner David King, he sometimes renders a simplistic adumbration of the mid-century European intellectual's atheistic form of existentialism. At the same time that Fry was staging his optimistic comedies, existentialism's most pessimistic and anarchic expression took the form of startling dramas in the Theatre of the Absurd.[33] Absurdist dramatists challenged—among every other religious belief—the notion of free will: "O God, are we to be shut up here in what other men do and watch ourselves be ground and battered into their sins?"[34]

Because Fry uses biblical heroes to present a vivid encapsulation of humanity's addiction to warfare, one is able to interpret easily the drama's overall sentiment as anti-war. The playwright's vision, however, is much more nuanced than that. Fry chooses to explore the morality of war and of its opposite, pacifism. He accomplishes this through the dramatic conflict of different human temperaments, none of which is purely evil or purely virtuous. Through a succession of four dreams, the dramatist's cleverly re-imagined biblical episodes expose these temperaments at their best and worst. In these scenes, modern audiences, separated by decades, have recognized themselves onstage re-enacting painful parallels to their own day. This happens because, as the dreams proceed, Fry's exploration of war becomes more psychological than theological.

David King, the aggressive, hot-tempered soldier, segues naturally first into the dream figure of Cain the proto-murderer and then into the figure of King David ordering the death of his rebellious son, Absalom. Predictably, the pacifist Peter Abel becomes the victim in each dream; but as a rebel, he is scarcely innocent. In the second dream, the warrior King David is transformed into the nonviolent Abraham, the father who must be willing to sacrifice his beloved son. This dream manages to be both a condemnation of war as human sacrifice and a sympathetic glimpse into the heart of every father of a nation whose anguish it is to save his people by sending their sons to death. Corporal Adam as King David's officer Joab slays the insurgent in this dream, and in the next, intervenes as an angel to save the innocent. In each case, Peter, like Abraham, is executing the will of "higher authority."

When Adam's own dream begins, having no orders to follow, he gropes around onstage, completely "at sea." Here Fry intends a visual pun for the state of humankind after the first transgression has occurred: adrift, unmoored, and confused spiritually. The fourth and final dream that begins with this weak and difficult-to-stage metaphor, however, does come to an effective theatrical climax when it becomes the corporate dream of the three youths in the fiery furnace. Now Meadows identifies himself as "under God's command." Fry stipulates that Meadows represents "human nature with hope." Then, each prisoner in turn articulates what he has learned in his dream.[35] David has discovered that a noble strength exists "beyond all action," and in the midst of flames, Peter acknowledges the purifying power of suffering.[36] Adam has learned to reject "the powers that ruin and not the powers that bless."[37] Together, the four prisoners achieve the perception that comes from purification in the furnace. Here, when circumstances tie both hands and feet,[38] the responsible person must find, not a way out, but a way to stay and change: "That leaves me without a word of command to cover the situation, except fall on your knees."[39] Like the people of biblical times living under the vision of peril and promise, and like the prisoners in Fry's drama, we too stay the course of life as we work for personal transformation and the transformation of our world, so that one day the dream, the vision of peace among ourselves and peace in the land, will become a lived reality and no longer something for which we hope.

Wading Deeper on Your Own

Questions for Reflection and Discussion

1. What do the authors of Genesis 4:1–16 and 2 Samuel 8–18 assume about their readers?
2. What questions do these biblical episodes provoke in you?
3. What are Christopher Fry's assumptions about his audience?
4. What does Christopher Fry do that the authors of the biblical stories do not do? To what effect?
5. Discuss the "just war theory" in relation to 2 Samuel 8–18 and *A Sleep of Prisoners.*
6. How does the character of Meadows either resemble or contradict your own concept of God the Creator?
7. In the argument between prisoners David and Peter, which side would you prefer to take? Which man would you prefer to be the president of your country? The head of your family?
8. Which dream did you find most memorable?
9. Which of the playwright's inventions, in your judgment, helps most with understanding the issue of war and peace?
10. What questions does the play provoke in you?'

Suggestions for Writing and Journaling

1. Rewrite Genesis 4:1–16 from the perspective of Abel. How is Abel, a person of peace, the counterpart to Cain, a person of violence?
2. Describe the role that God plays in Genesis 4:1–16 and 2 Samuel 8–15.
3. Write an essay that compares and contrasts the two biblical stories with *A Sleep of Prisoners.* What wisdom can be gleaned from these three texts?
4. Comment on one of the following quotations as poetry or prayer or both.

> "Show me an ending great enough
> To hold the passion of this beginning
> And raise me to it."[40]
>
> "God dips his hand in death
> To wash the wound,
> Takes evil to inoculate our lives
> Against infectious evil."[41]
>
> "They say I'm in a prison. Morning comes
> To prison like a nurse:
> A rustling presence, as though a small breeze came,
> And presently a voice. I think
> We're going to live."[42]

5. Choose one dreamer and write an essay profiling the dreamer in three visions of himself: as at heart he really is, as he sees himself, and as his comrades see him. Comment on which vision might be the most helpful to the world—or to your family—at this time in history.

Irrigating Other Fields

"Thank God our time is now when wrong comes up to face us everywhere, never to leave us till we take the longest stride of soul men ever took."[43] As you view the wrongs recorded in today's news media, observe how this statement applies. Then reflect on what "stride of soul" you might be willing to take to address these wrongs.

9
THE THEME OF LIBERATION

The Prophet of Justice
Amos 1:3–2:16; 4:1–5; 5:10–13; 8:4–14

The Weight of All Things
Sandra Benitez

Introduction

The socioeconomic situation in El Salvador during the decades covered in the fiction of the Latina novelist Sandra Benitez mirrors the situation condemned by the prophet Amos in Israel in the eighth century BCE. Biblical scholars Norman K. Gottwald and William J. Doorly have tried to reconstruct the historical situation and social climate of the eighth century BCE that prompted prophets like Amos to preach bold messages. Gottwald asserts:

> The greedy upper class, with governmental and judicial connivance, were systematically appropriating the land of the commoners so that they could heap up wealth and display it gaudily in a lavish "conspicuous consumption" economy. Hatred of other nations, military swaggering, and religious rhetoric were generously employed to persuade people to accept their miserable lot because it was, after all, "the best of all possible societies."[1]

Doorly adds that the people being oppressed in Amos's time were the poor, the needy, and even the righteous. Farmers were forced to grow cash crops such as wine and oil, which they did not need for survival. The powerful in Samaria needed the crops for the sake of cultivating and sustaining international trade. Laws that governed the passing on of land through the male line were ignored, and thus families were losing their land, becoming tenant farmers charged with excessive rents by wealthy landlords. Even the justice system became controlled by the urban rich who did not allow for "justice at the gate" (the city gate was the common area where legal disputes were often settled in biblical Israel) on behalf of the commoners.[2] The prophet Amos looked at this situation and addressed it accordingly from a prophetic stance that put those guilty of injustices "on notice."

In Latin America, a theological movement took root in the 1950s to respond to the dire situation in El Salvador. It blossomed in the 1960s and 1970s following the Second Vatican Council. During this time, Roman Catholic priests in Latin America began preaching that

Catholics should not be content to anticipate material happiness in the afterlife; they should work for economic justice now. Many active Catholics formed small groups called "base Christian communities," so named because they represented the crowd at the base of the pyramid of wealth and power dominated by the few at the top. At one time, there were 100,000 base Christian communities in South and Central America, each of which included twelve to fifteen people who met regularly to discuss Scripture in the light of their existential situation. For them, the Gospels provided a foundation for their struggle for social justice. This movement became known as liberation theology and has been variously defined by advocates and its critics alike.

On the one hand, as a liberal Catholic theology that attempts to interpret scripture from the perspective of the economically poor, liberation theology publicly criticized the Roman Catholic hierarchy for its association with military dictators and with people who became wealthy by exploiting those at the base of the pyramid. Its advocates taught that authentic Christians are called to solidarity with the poor through actively fighting for social justice. For its critics, however, the movement, in its dangerous attempt to synthesize Christianity with Marxism, corrupted theology into politics. In the 1980s, the Vatican issued two major documents commending liberation theologians for their commitment to end poverty and injustice but at the same time warning them of some unintended consequences from their efforts, including class warfare and atheistic communism. Pope John Paul II eventually censured a number of Latin American theologians, including Leonardo Boff and Jon Sobrino. Dom Helder Camara is often quoted as saying of himself as a politically active priest: "When I give food to the poor, they call me a saint. When I ask why they are poor, they call me a communist." In September 2013, very early in his papacy, the Argentine Pope Francis invited the Peruvian Dominican Gustavo Gutiérrez to Rome for a conversation, raising hopes for reconciliation. The same year, Gutiérrez widely considered the founder of liberation theology, had been publicly praised by Gerhard Mueller, prefect of the Congregation for the Doctrine of the Faith, in a book they had co-authored.[3]

Latina writer Sandra Benitez deliberately structures her novels to support the work of liberation theologians, making it vividly accessible to people unlikely to read theology. In her earlier, longer novel, *Bitter Grounds*,[4] Benitez spells out the chief tenets of liberation theology through both real and fictional characters who study Vatican II spirituality together in "base Christian communities." Benitez, while supportive of the movement, does not deny or conceal the controversial issues associated with it. By creating fictional surrogates for decades of innocent suffering, she draws attention to the plight of the poor and balances that account with vivid descriptions of some unintended damage caused by liberation's most zealous advocates. *The Weight of All Things*[5] acts out the worst of this paradox, the victimization of the poor by the violence intended to liberate them. This chapter explores the theme of liberation as it comes to the fore in selected texts from Amos and in *The Weight of All Things*.

Drinking from the Spring
The Biblical Text

Resplendent with rhetorical forms and expressive of a polished, impassioned, dynamic, and didactic style, the Book of Amos is a work that captures the imagination of its readers with its straightforward, "in your face" message. The book portrays a dynamic poet, a prophet, who preaches message after message that cuts to the chase in order to draw attention to the horrific injustices of his day (Amos 1:1–5:3; 5:7–13; 5:16–9:10). Such messages are not the only prophetic words of the poet; the book also contains words of encouragement (5:4–6, 14–15) and a vision of future restoration (9:11–15), one that speaks of hope and not of despair, life and not death.

As a literary work, the Book of Amos is a historical reflection of what life may have been like in eighth-century BCE Israel as seen through the eyes and experience of one of the book's central characters, Amos, a herder and sycamore dresser (7:14) from Tekoa (1:1) who becomes a prophet by God's choice (7:15). The texts selected for discussion on the theme of liberation include Amos 1:3–2:16; 4:1–5; 5:10–13; and 8:4–14.

Proclamations Concerning the Nations
Amos 1:3–2:16

This block of material is a collection of poems—proclamations—concerning eight centers of Syria and Palestine: Damascus (1:3–5); Gaza (1:6–8); Tyre (1:9–10); Edom (1:11–12); Ammon (1:13–15); Moab (2:1–3); Judah (2:4–5); and Israel (2:6–16). Each poem consists of three parts: a messenger formula, "thus says the Lord," an indictment (1:3, 6, 9, 11, 13; 2:1, 4, 6), and an announcement of chastisement (1:4, 7, 10, 12, 14; 2:3, 5, 13–16). In some instances, there is a concluding messenger formula, "says the Lord (God)" (1:5, 8, 15; 2:3, 16). Each poem presents examples of heinous, violent deeds.

"Because They Have Threshed Gilead"
Amos 1:3–5

The first proclamation concerns Aram and Damascus, the capital of Syria. The passage opens with the standard prophetic messenger formula that sets the stage for the words of divine wrath and also lends "authority" to both the prophetic message and the text. What is being spoken about here is a violent military campaign launched against Gilead, one of Israel's richest territories, near Damascus, the capital of Syria. Metaphorical language captures the brutality of the campaign: "They [the people of Damascus] have threshed [the people of] Gilead with threshing sledges of iron." (Amos 1:3). H. W. Wolff notes:

> The technique by which grain was cut up and crushed gives this metaphor its brutal cogency. Grain was threshed by drawing over it a heavy sledge, the boards of which were curved upward at the front and the underside of which was studded with prongs; the use of iron knives, rather than flintstones, for these prongs in the iron age sufficiently increased the efficiency of the sledge.[6]

This metaphor emerges from the context of an agrarian society. Both Israel and the surrounding nations were agricultural people. Thus, the metaphor speaks directly to the original audience's life experience. Amos makes it clear that such brutality will not go unchecked. The biblical writer has the prophet delivering a severe word from God, who promises a four-fold chastisement: (1) to torch the house of Hazael[7] and the strongholds of Ben-hadad;[8] (2) to break Damascus' gate bars; (3) to cut off the inhabitants from the Valley of Aven,[9] along with the one who holds the scepter from Beth-eden;[10] and (4) to exile Aram's people to Kir.[11] The poetry of Amos makes the point that injustice will not be tolerated. Israel's God deals with the perpetrators of injustice, and does so on behalf of those who have suffered injustices, all of which is good news. How the perpetrators are dealt with, however, raises questions for further consideration.

Amos' proclamation concerning Damascus portrays an extraordinary power play. Because Damascus oppressed Gilead violently, Damascus is to reap the same violence that it has sown. Damascus will be made to suffer just as Gilead was made to suffer. Damascus had "power over" Gilead; so, God will now assert "power over" Damascus. Thus, Israel's God will be seen as "all powerful," a "sovereign" who acts on behalf of those who have been oppressed.[12] In the ancient world, particularly during monarchical times, God was understood to be the one who had "power over" Israel and over the other nations. Perhaps the political agenda on the part of the poet was to present an image of God who is greater and more powerful than any one or any group of leaders.

In Amos 1:3–5, the poet portrays God as a "warrior god" who has "power over" injustice and over other peoples. This warrior god promises to deal with injustice by destroying the enemy, the perpetrator of injustice. This image of a warrior god and its association with the notion of having "power over," is due, in large part, to a gender-specific portrayal of and metaphor for God. In the ancient world, and in many circles today, God was and is imagined as a male deity. Furthermore, the historical and cultural times of the prophets were marked by nations in conflict with each other, with Israel being no exception. Consequently, experiences and ideologies of war shaped and informed Israel's self-understanding and self-expression. Also, in ancient times, warriors were, for the most part, male. Therefore, the understanding that the "warrior of warriors" would be a male God whose might would make right by avenging the enemy is not surprising.[13] Lastly, this image of God having power over a non-Israelite nation also comes from Israel's self-understanding that its God is the true God who is "ruler over all."

The text as it stands legitimizes violence as a way to deal with violence, which does raise ethical questions: "Is violence legitimate, and if so, when?" Furthermore, God is the perpetrator of the violence. Is this an accurate picture of God, or is it a portrait that results from Israel's historical and cultural experience that is projected onto God as Israel tried to make sense of its history and record its story?[14] Despite the text's marvelous statement on the unacceptability of perpetrating unjustified violence against others, the text implies an acceptance of violence that should not go unnoticed or unaddressed.

Finally, were all the people of Damascus guilty of committing injustice? According to the text, God's stinging chastisement will be all-encompassing. Imminent disaster is to come upon the Arameans. Corporate responsibility and corporate punishment were common motifs in Israel and in the ancient Near East.[15] A further injustice is to hold responsible those within a group who are innocent of wrongdoing and who, perhaps, may be victims themselves of power and oppression within the group. And yet in the ancient biblical world, liberation was often achieved through such large-scale violence; this, unfortunately, is still the case today in many global conflicts past and present.

"Because They Carried into Exile Entire Communities"

Amos 1:6–8

The poet's second proclamation concerns Gaza, one of the territories of the Philistines. Through the use of metonymy, Gaza represents the entire Philistine empire, just as Damascus in Amos 1:3–5 represented all of the Aramean empire. Speaking through the prophet Amos, God accuses Gaza of slave trade, a crime committed against defenseless people. In order to serve the interests of the powerful, entire communities were carried into exile and handed over to Edom (1:6).[16] In Amos 1:7–8 the poet describes the divine chastisement that will befall Gaza because of its crime. Here the poet brings to the fore a horrible injustice that existed in the ancient world and continues today: people using other people for their own gain, also known as the commodification of human beings. Once again the poet depicts God as a "warrior god" who will strike the oppressors with violent punishment to avenge the innocent victims. Fire is the central image of chastisement (1:7).[17] Once again, the poet communicates the message that injustice is not divinely sanctioned; the powerful will be crushed. The means, however, will be violent.

While Amos 1:6–8 may offer hope to those who suffer oppression, this text does not present a model for dealing with the violation of human rights and dignity that we can follow today. Clearly, the text reveals that during the eighth through fifth centuries BCE, when the experience was being lived and the text being shaped, many human beings were the prey of other powerful humans who used violence to settle disputes, just as is often true today. But an important question comes to the fore: Is this the way of God? The text, as it stands, could have us think so if we take the text on face value and read it literally without understanding its cultural, political, and ideological influences.

"They Did Not Remember the Covenant of Kinship"

Amos 1:9, 10

Tyre, the chief city of the Phoenicians during the mid-eighth century BCE, is the focus of the third proclamation. The poet depicts God accusing Tyre of the same crime as Gaza had committed, but Tyre took the crime one step further: Tyre "did not remember the covenant of kinship" (1:9b). Tyre disregarded and violated treaties, with "the covenant of kinship" being a "paradigm of all treaties."[18] Divine anger and the promise of divine chastisement is the response to such blatant disregard and disrespect for communal legislation.

"Because He Pursued His Brother with the Sword"

Amos 1:11, 12

Edom is declared guilty of pursuing his brother with the sword without pity in the fourth proclamation. Edom is also in violation of "the customary ethos of kinship obligations."[19] In other words, Edom is guilty of harboring anger and wrath relentlessly. The divine chastisement to be meted out is the same for Edom as it will be for Damascus: fire. Once again the poet drives home the message that injustice will not be tolerated, and justice will be restored through the use of violence.

"Because They Have Ripped Open Pregnant Women in Gilead"

Amos 1:13–15

This proclamation that the poet delivers against the Ammonites is perhaps one of the most gruesome and violent images in the entire collection of proclamations concerning the nations. The poet accuses the Ammonites of ripping open "pregnant women" of Gilead as part of a campaign to enlarge their own territory. Here the poet portrays the abuse of power and war at its worst because it involved women, children, and the poor, the most vulnerable members of their society. Once again, the punishment promised is as violent as the crime itself. Divine power puts in check the unbridled, selfish, human power, but according to the text, the assertion of divine power will be just as violent and destructive as the Ammonites' use of power. Once again, power is portrayed as a violent oppressive force that can be exercised in the name of justice and injustice alike.

"Because He Burned to Lime the Bones of the King of Edom"

Amos 2:1–3

Moab, the topic of the sixth proclamation, burned the royal bones of Edom's king. Burning the bones of a human being was a severe desecration and an act usually reserved for the bones of the most despicable of criminals.[20] Such a deed was unacceptable, especially to God, who in this proclamation intends to send fire upon Moab, cut off the ruler from its midst, and kill all its officials with him.

This text presents a devastating and confusing picture indeed. First, it shows the lack of reverence on the part of some people for the remains of another. Second, it highlights a deed that differentiates between human beings at the point of death, namely, that it is acceptable to treat the bodies of criminals but not other human beings in certain ways. Third, the punishment that God promises is similar to that of the other texts—fire—and yet, the chastisement is even more lethal. God promises to cut off Moab's ruler from its midst and to kill all Moab's officials with him. Such a desire is in complete contrast to God's own law that forbids killing (e.g., Exod. 20:13).

"Because They Have Rejected the Law of the Lord"
Amos 2:4, 5

The proclamation that the poet delivers concerning Judah is different from the other proclamations concerning the nations. Unlike the crimes of other countries, Judah's crime involves neither explicit use of power nor any violence. Judah's crime is that the people have rejected God's law and have gone astray. Such a crime is a serious offense for Judah, because the nation's ethical conduct is linked to the commandments expressed in the Torah. Forgetfulness of God leads to forgetfulness of God's ways. This forgetfulness then leads to political, social, economic, and religious disorder and dysfunction. Such is precisely Judah's state before the nation completely collapses in 587 BCE. In Amos 2:5, as in former judgment oracles, God promises to send fire on Judah "to devour" the strongholds of Jerusalem.

The violence of warfare common to Judah is aptly captured by the familiar imagery of fire. When the image of fire is used in association with God, the poet presents an image of a wrathful God who seeks vengeance upon the nations even when that nation has not been indicted for any explicit violent crime. The poet shows us that God makes no distinctions between the expressions of indictment and their respective punishments. All receive the same—fire (1:4, 7, 10, 12, 14; 2:2; 2:4–5) Is this justice? Or is it a projection of what justice is and who God is as conditioned by one's particular culture, theology, and social location? Or is the poet establishing Israel's God as the Sovereign One who is Lord of Creation and Lord of History, one more powerful than all the leaders on the earth?

"Because They Sell the Righteous for Silver"
Amos 2:6–16

The proclamation concerning Israel presents God listing all the transgressions of the nation. Each transgression is a violation of right relationship. The transgressions include: the economic exploitation of the righteous and needy on the part of some Israelites (2:6); the abuse of the poor (2:7a); and the pushing of the afflicted "out of the way," which means that the victims of injustice are denied access to and deprived of fair treatment by the court systems.[21] Other transgressions include the sexual exploitation of a maiden by a father and his son (2:7b); the exploitation of debtors, especially poor men and widows (2:8a); purchasing wine from fines imposed upon the poor and then drinking the wine in holy places (2:8b);[22] and making the Nazirites drink wine. Drinking wine was forbidden by their vows of consecration (see Num. 6:3ff; Judges 13:14ff), and thus the Nazirites were being forced to break their vows. Others were guilty of silencing the prophets (Amos 2:12). From the text, one can see that the threads of power, domination, and control were part of the fabric of Israelite society and were contributing factors in the breakdown of right relationship.

Finally, the poet describes God's response in Amos 2:3–16. God will come as a foe against those guilty of injustices. God will side with the vulnerable and will press down the perpetrators of injustice. While this is an accurate picture, it must not be forgotten that the text legitimates the assertion of violent power in order to eliminate injustice.

"You Cows of Bashan . . . Who Oppress the Needy and Crush the Poor"
Amos 4:1–5

Perhaps one of the most famous proclamations in the Book of Amos is the one directed against the well-kept women of Samaria, who are referred to in the text as the "cows of Bashan."[23] Bashan was a plain in the Transjordan that was famous for its "plush pastures and robust cows."[24] Bashan connoted quality of lifestyle and quality of life. When the poet compares Samaria's pampered women to the well-fed and pleasantly plump bovines, he introduces the element of imagination and surprise into his poem. With this metaphor, the poet stresses the point that these women are focused on their own self-indulgence, irrespective of the cost to others. Thus, the poet uncovers the role of Samaria's women in the social dynamics of the state's economic aristocracy. These women have grown fat on the plunder of the poor. They are never satisfied, and because they always want more, they nag their husbands, whom Amos ironically calls "lords," for "fresh drinks"—new acts of injustice. Here, the men are featured as servants of the women. Thus, with metaphorical language drawn from the culture of his day that appeals to the culture of his day, the biblical poet launches his attack. For audiences of the text then and now, the poet's point is clear: injustice will not be the final word; innocent people will be liberated from their pain and suffering.

"They Hate the One Who Reproves in the Gate"
Amos 5:10–13

Amos 5:10–13 is part of the first of three woe proclamations (see Amos 5:7, 10–17; 5:18–27; 6:1–14). In verses 10–13 the central issue is Israel's neglect of justice, righteousness, and truth. With a spirit of passion and vehemence, the poet exposes the people's transgressions: they hate the one who reproves in the gate (v. 10a); they abhor the one who speaks the truth (v. 10b); they trample on the poor and take grain levies from them (v. 11a); and they afflict the righteous, take bribes, and push aside the needy in the gate (v. 12b). Thus, certain members within the community fall prey to the unjust power of others, but those who exert such power will receive from God their just deserts: even though they have built houses with hewn stone, they will not inhabit them; even though they planted pleasant vineyards, they will not enjoy the fruit of the vine, namely, fine wine, because God will deliver justice for the oppressed to liberate them from their heavy burdens.

"Hear This, You That Trample on the Needy"
Amos 8:4–14

Amos 8:4–14 is a judgment speech. In verses 4–14, the poet continues to expose the transgressions and injustices borne by some members within the Israelite community. In this passage, Amos boldly and passionately addresses a group of Israelites who have acted unethically on several counts. First, they are guilty of exploiting the poor economically (v. 5; cf. 2:6ff.; 4:1; 5:10–13). Second, the poor are made into bartered goods in human trade (v. 6). Third, those persons doing the exploiting also are selling the sweepings of wheat from their harvests (v. 6). Torah insists that the gleanings of the harvest are to be left for the poor (Lev. 19:9–10; 23:22).

In Amos 8:7–14 and specifically in verses 9–14, the poet next depicts God's wrath as an earthquake. The injustices committed and the suffering of the people do not go unnoticed. Israel's God will act on behalf of the oppressed and will liberate them from their miserable conditions. Retributive measures include the sun going down, feasts turning into mourning and songs into lamentations (vv. 9–10), sackcloth covering loins and shaved heads (v. 10b, c), people deprived of hearing God's words, with a resultant aimlessness in their lives (vv. 11, 12), and famine adversely affecting the people (v. 13).

Similar to Amos 4:6–13, the poet shows us that injustice affected all creation, both human and nonhuman forms of life. For Israel, sin and suffering were linked. According to their worldview, infidelity to God, breaking of the covenant, and forgetfulness and transgression of Torah led to punitive divine chastisement in the name of justice. In Amos 8:7–8 the poet portrays God taking an oath, swearing never to forget any of the unethical deeds (v. 7) and promising to chastise the mercenaries and barterers (v. 8; see also vv. 9–14). Because unethical behavior is unacceptable, injustice will not go without divine reprimand.

Playing in the Fountain
The Literary Text
The Weight of All Things

About the Author
Sandra Benitez

Sandra Benitez was born in 1941 in Washington, D.C., the child of Puerto Rican parents who raised her in El Salvador. She was educated in Missouri and Minnesota, where she resides today. Her first novel, *A Place Where the Sea Remembers*,[25] is set in Mexico. *Bitter Grounds*, a novel with a theme similar to that of *The Weight of All Things*, combines a factual account of the historic struggle for economic and political justice in El Salvador with a fictional dramatization of the teachings of Vatican II as embodied in the lives of earnest Latin American Catholics. In 2004, for these and other works of fiction, Benitez was awarded the National Hispanic Heritage Award for Literature.

Benitez' work has been seen by American critics as part of an attempt by some Latino/a writers in the United States "to reconstruct the memory and history of El Salvador, to transform the Salvadoran body into a representation of the 'disappeared' Salvadoran collective memory, in an act of cultural restoration that illuminates the political meaning of the body in contemporary Latino/a literature."[26] Benitez differs from the other writers in this group to the extent that she focuses on the theological function of the body as the locus of forgiveness.[27] Benitez' fiction also differs from the other polemical novels of her contemporaries by its gentle tone and consistent representation of both active and passive involvement in the struggle.

Reflecting on Genre and Style

The Weight of All Things is historical fiction based on factual accounts of two civilian massacres by government forces in El Salvador: one at the funeral of Archbishop Oscar Romero, who had been murdered during Mass on March 24, 1980; the other, six weeks later, the slaughter of six hundred campesinos at the Sumpul River.[28] Participants in this struggle were descendants of the "mantanza," or massacre, the first peasant rebellion backed by the communists that occurred in 1932. The entire novel takes place on numerous battlegrounds of the Salvadoran government's war on the peasantry who were scattered throughout the hills and villages from 1980 to 1992. One can hear strains of the text of Amos in Benitez' description of the social and political climate of El Salvador.

Casualties in the bloody years of 1980–1992 included 75,000 dead and 500,000 homeless and displaced persons. This struggle for economic justice in Central America is important, not only for those interested in history and political science, but also for those interested in the Bible and pastoral theology, because out of the existential experience of Central American Catholics emerged the movement known as liberation theology.

Contemporary historical fiction frequently heightens awareness of the spiritual significance of a social, political, or economic situation by an implied comparison. Benitez makes this comparison very specific in *Bitter Grounds*, which shows the battle within the Catholic Church in parallel with the bloody political conflict in Latin America. In *Bitter Grounds,* she refers directly to the fact that, whereas liberation theology was officially endorsed in 1968 by the Latin American Bishops Conference in Medellin, Columbia, the Vatican Congregation for the Doctrine of the Faith did not support this endorsement. In fact, the Vatican authorities later issued a "theological notification" admonishing the Peruvian Dominican, Gustavo Gutiérrez. As head of the Vatican Congregation for the Doctrine of the Faith, Joseph Ratzinger—later Benedict XVI—reprimanded liberation theologians for what he perceived as their endorsement of political divisiveness, class warfare, and anarchy, which seemed to cause great suffering among the very people they wished to rescue. Ratzinger also blamed liberation theologians for contributing to the politicization of the faith, which caused some Latin American Catholics to migrate to ultra-conservative Protestant congregations.

Benitez creates fictional characters to voice the peasants' reaction when the bishops "urged the poor to take the lead in achieving their own temporal as well as spiritual freedom."[29] "Watch what you say, girl. 'The people saving themselves,' that's the language of insurrection." 'Oh yes, I forgot,' Berta said, 'It's the church that saves the people' . . . True your life is full of hardships, but oh! The rewards awaiting you in heaven.'"[30]

While all of the characters in *The Weight of All Things* are fictional, *Bitter Grounds* incorporates real people like the populist Salvadoran priest Rutilio Grande, S.J. (1928–1977).[31] A close friend of Archbishop Oscar Romero, Rutilio Grande, was gunned down with two companions on March 12, 1977. Benitez expresses the contrast between liberationist priests like Rutilio and traditionalist clerics by inventing a conversation with an imaginary Padre Hortensio, Rutilio's stereotypically ignorant and stubborn antithesis: "For years el padre Rutilio has assured us that the church is in the world and for the world, and not unearthly or out of touch. Now that the council's work is ended, el padre's message is confirmed. The council charges us to address the worldly needs of the people and not just the condition of their souls."[32]

Benitez' method of teaching the gospel of liberation theology imitates the pedagogical method of Jesus, who dramatized his message in stories of ordinary people. Benitez' fiction dramatizes not only the physical conflict between the powerful and the powerless, but also the perennial crisis in conscience for those committed Christians who reject violence as an acceptable solution to injustice. In *The Weight of All Things*, she presents a brief summary of the dilemma of peace-loving peasants who don't want to be involved with the "Popular Liberation Forces" in El Salvador.[33] Both sides, those opposed to the government and those opposed to communism, are identified by what they are *against*. Neither side seems to be *for* anything. The militants on both sides consider themselves martyrs willing to die for their cause, but "most of the dying was done by the people."[34]

In *The Weight of All Things*, the theological message and literary style are inextricably interwoven. All of Benitez' literary decisions are designed to dramatize how simple men and women, living 2,000 years after Jesus Christ, relive his identification with the poor and his suffering and death for them. Among the author's decisions are the choice of narrative point of view, incorporation of fact with fiction, accessible symbolism, and micro-stylistic details of magic realism.

Although she tells her story in the third person, Benitez' narrative point of view is just as focused as a first-person account. Each scene is limited to what is seen and experienced by Nicolas, a child who has witnessed the massacre in the cathedral and survived the attacks on the campesinos. The author's decision to tell the story of these two violent historical events through the eyes and the voice of a nine-year-old boy renders these realities both more shocking and more poignant, more brutal and more gentle.

The author takes many incidents directly from the Salvadoran local newspapers. There were, in fact, 80,000 people in and near the cathedral for the funeral of Oscar Romero, and massive explosions and shooting did kill 35 of them and wound 450 more. These cold facts become more intimately painful in the novel when a single bullet to the body of one mother leaves her child an orphan. Representatives of impersonal categories like "communists" and "Sandinistas" can be mourned by the reader as if they were blood relatives and innocent school children.[35] By this simple, nonpolitical technique, Benitez has argued against war, portraying every victim of war as someone's mother or father, brother or sister, companion or child. Benitez' simple device transforms political episodes into personal tragedy.[36]

Although Benitez is reporting on actual historical events, her style is more poetic than journalistic. Moreover, the author chooses to adopt the style, popular among twentieth-century Latin American novelists, that came to be known as "magic realism." As the label suggests, this style combines ordinary pedestrian reality with extraordinary, unrealistic events. Magic realism combines descriptions that spare no raw detail with dream-like supernatural or preternatural episodes. These latter often dissolve the wall separating the living from the dead, the human from other species.[37] Benitez provides plenty of realism in long, periodic sentences that heap up multiple sense impressions, both lurid and lyric. She gives special emphasis to smell, for example, by contrasting sweat and rose petals, rotting flesh and incense.[38] The author's predilection for contrast creates situational irony as well, as she presents scenes without commentary, painfully picturing ironic contrasts between intention and reality. For example, the peasants build bombs in a kitchen where meals are prepared, and both soldiers and their victims decorate a cross with flowers.[39]

In *The Weight of All Things*, the apparitions of the Virgin Mary to the protagonist provide the only element of "magic."[40] Modern psychology would explain Nicolas' "visions" as natural phenomena, products of a child's faith-based imagination. The author makes no attempt to argue for or against their validity. Benitez simply records the interaction of Nicolas with the Virgin, whose presence is as real and as natural to him as any phenomenon in the physical landscape.

Some critics interpret this device as a metaphor that dramatizes the naïve trust in God that contributes to the exploitation of the peasantry by those with spiritual and ecclesiastical power. Among other literary devices Benitez employs throughout the novel are symbolism and metonymy, often in combination. Just as Amos used metonymy to make Gaza stand for all Philistines (see Amos 1:6–8), Benitez uses one divided family to represent the divisions within the nation and within the church. In general, in the historical struggle from which liberation theology emerged, the Catholic hierarchy, fearing the atheistic element in communism, sided with the government. While preventing the spread of communism, the government also protected the wealthy. This separated the hierarchy from the liberation theologians who sided with the poor. There were good people on both sides of this divide, and for both, violence corrupted good intentions: "It was either the army or the guerrillas. In the end, they're both the same."[41]

Both the communists and their enemies translated the word killing as "liberation."[42] When government forces, attempting to stamp out the peasant rebellion, destroy village churches, the novelist symbolically implies the destruction of the church itself by the divisions within it. "They got the church too . . . The sons of bitches ruined half of it. . . . The ground alongside the church and sloping down toward him was a series of wounds. The exposed rocky earth showed how thin the topsoil truly was. Most of the church's roof was gone, and the sunlight pointed out the damage."[43]

From beginning to end, Benitez' symbolism expresses ironic contradiction. A whole paragraph describing Nicolas lying in the fetal position under his mother's wounded body can be interpreted as a symbol of the new Latin American church waiting to be born. But Nicolas' musing on a cave in which he felt safe is clearly Benitez' symbol for the old church, which kept the peasantry confined and infantilized and their exploiters protected.

> He imagined himself back home inside the cave he had found carved into one of the hills behind his rancho. In his secret place he was confined like this, en-caved, but it was a condition that brought him comfort. His cave was shadowy, but the shadows did not frighten him. On the contrary; shadows and even the deep dark were an advantage over the light of broad day, the light that could expose you and point you out accusingly as a finger.[44]

Drawing from the Well
Theological Themes

In the book of Amos, we see that Amos' eight proclamations concerning the nations are a mind-shattering, heart-wrenching, and soul-splitting picture of how power and control, when used violently, result in oppression and destruction—even when the intent is to bring about goodness, restoration, or liberation. In each proclamation, the poet describes a series of unacceptable injustices done to men and women. These men and women, who are treated so poorly and unjustly, are victims of people who have exercised power and control over them. In some instances, the victims are the most vulnerable, the most powerless of a society. The oppression done is not explicitly gender or class specific.

The fact that each proclamation comes from a "prophet through whom God speaks" offers a sense of hope to those who are victims of injustice. The people's plight has not gone unnoticed; something will be done to the perpetrators of injustice. The God of liberation who once liberated the Israelites from the grip of the Egyptian Pharaoh (see the

Exodus story) will once again act of behalf of Israel, even if this means upbraiding the Israelites themselves for their own transgressions.

These texts show us that in the biblical world, a hierarchy of power existed, with God being the most powerful of the gods, who could win out against even the most powerful of human beings.

Looking at the texts as whole, we see that the poet portrays God as one whose anger at injustice is so great that the impending action against the unjust is as violent as the injustices themselves. Here, the principle of *lex talionis* seems to be in full operation: "an eye for an eye, and a tooth for a tooth." Although anger provokes passion and calls for justice, the response, ultimately, is destructive. Thus, through the texts that detail the proclamations to the nations, we encounter an aggressive and destructive God. Justice will be meted out, liberation from injustice will be secured, but at what expense to others?

In Amos 4:1–5; 5:10–13; 8:4–14, the poet exposes the graft that some of the Israelites are mired in. It causes them to commit a whole host of injustices that make others suffer when Torah is violated and right relationship is breached. In all of these passages, the poet makes clear that justice will once again be established in the land, and that innocent victims of injustice will be liberated from the suffering and loss they have had to endure at the hands of others. The method, however, is punitive and oftentimes riddled with violence. These episodes invite further conversation and additional critical theological reflection, since history has borne out that violence begets violence; that violence is not the way to establish enduring peace; and that after countless battles have been waged and fought, conflicts continue to arise in the quest for power. On the other hand, liberation from injustice is a divine mandate proclaimed by poets and prophets down through the ages, whose message is as potent today as on the day when it was first proclaimed or the day it was composed on parchment for future generations.

Like the selected texts from the Book of Amos, *The Weight of All Things* also embodies several theological themes related to the biblical concept of justice. One of the most important themes heard in both Amos and *The Weight of All Things* is the theme of liberation. In part, liberation theology arose in response to the use of the Bible as a tool of oppression, to appease the poor and the abused and distract them from injustice. The basic conviction of Latin American liberationists, that God sides with the oppressed, is evident throughout the Bible. But because the same Bible has been used as an instrument of oppression in so many cultures, a primary principle of liberation theology is a *hermeneutics of suspicion*, which makes clear that any theology that does not challenge oppression is suspect.[45] A hermeneutics of suspicion questions any biblical interpretation that does not challenge societal values that accommodate domination and exploitation of the poor, of women, of the marginalized.

Liberation theology often focuses on the way in which both prophets of the Old Testament and evangelists of the New Testament reverse conventional concepts of power and urge a shift from what can be called "a paradigm of power over to a paradigm of power with."[46] Moreover, contemporary biblical theology often rejects hierarchical models that place humanity at the peak of a pyramid. Recent theology favors an interdependent cosmological model that embraces all the nonhuman inhabitants of creation. With this point in mind, it is not hard to see that "power can be used to dominate, to liberate, to engender harmonious relations."[47]

Throughout Central and South America, many priests and lay leaders took seriously the Second Vatican Council's definition of the church as "the people of God." This definition was not new; rather, the phrase drew attention to the traditional doctrine of the communion of saints in a way that deemphasized the importance of the clergy. Defining the church as the people of God included the notion that the faithful should be liberated from domination by "top-down" dogma and from biblical interpretations controlled by the hierarchy.

In *The Weight of All Things*, the author's theological message is inseparable from her poetic style. Only after we have read the whole novel do we recognize how Benitez has communicated liberation theology's teachings symbolically from the story's opening pages. In the very first episode, Benitez combines an act of faith in liberation theology with a symbolic act of faith in the unity of clergy and laity, the living and the dead. Gunned down by the government forces which had murdered Archbishop Romero, the dying mother whispers into her son's ear: "Do not fear. La Virgen is with us. Monseñor is with us too."[48] With this simple assertion, Benitez launches her entire novel as a cumulative metaphor, dramatizing liberation theology not as a revolutionary new doctrine, but as the continuing evolution of the tradition of the communion of saints.

Once we become aware of the novelist's method, we recognize frequent symbolic embodiments of liberation theology. References to the Earth, for example, are an expression of liberation theology's insistence that religion is properly concerned with life on Earth, not in some distant pneumatic future. We have already pointed out how Benitez uses the child narrator Nicolas symbolically to express both hope and condemnation.

Throughout the opening scene, Benitez uses physical details as a symbolic commentary on the relationship of the institutional church to the faithful: "They stood against the iron-railed barricade separating the general crowd from the cathedral doors and from Archbishop Romero's casket."[49] No religious entity seems free of ambiguity. Nicolas carries the statue of the Virgin with him physically wherever he goes. Symbolically, she is both his protector and his burden, and the author uses the statue of the Virgin to imply symbolically how religion both aids and obstructs "liberation" of the poor. Nicolas' mother reminds him that the church is his mother.[50] Benitez uses the damaged statue of the Virgin to symbolize how violent political conflict has damaged the church itself.

Thus, both the texts from Amos and Sandra Benitez's novel *The Weight of All Things* offer us both a sense of hope and a challenge. Oppression does not have to exist in our world today, but systemic change, as well as a change in attitudes and a change of heart, has to happen if we are to engage in the noble work of transformation that turns swords into plowshares and spears into pruning hooks. Prophets like Amos and novelists like Benitez are heralds and standard bearers of justice, but as inspiring as their texts may be, one cannot avoid taking into account and assessing how violence has been used in the task of liberation, as seen in the Amos texts. Both a collection of poems and a contemporary gripping novel call us readers today to engage in the pursuit of justice and the work of liberation so that all creation may enjoy the gift of a full and flourishing life lived peacefully under divine promise.

Wading Deeper on Your Own

Questions for Reflection and Discussion

1. In what ways is *The Weight of All Things* prophetic?
2. How is Sandra Benitez like the prophet Amos?
3. What are the salient points of liberation embedded in the Amos texts and in *The Weight of All Things?*
4. With what assumptions about English-speaking readers do you think Sandra Benitez writes her novels? Did reading her novel challenge your assumptions about anything?
5. One of the novel's comments on political life is that there are good people on both sides of many issues and that both good and bad people can do damage. Identify some situations during your lifetime that exemplify this problem.
6. Psychologists tell us that symbols act upon our emotions through our unconscious minds even before we apprehend symbols

intellectually. Discuss your emotional response to this novel before and after you became aware of its symbolism.

7. How does the novel demonstrate the insight of contemporary science about the interdependence of everything with everything else?
8. How does *The Weight of All Things* communicate a feminist aspect of liberation theology?
9. What do you think Sandra Benitez is saying to the Catholic Church through the damaged statue of the Virgin?

Suggestions for Writing and Journaling

Scan this week's newspapers and select a situation involving violence or injustice.

1. Rewrite the article as a first-person report by yourself as a nine-year-old child.
2. Write a prayer expressing your emotional response to the situation. Dare to question God and dare to include anger, confusion, and frustration.

Irrigating Other Fields

One of the perennial debates among creative people—poets, artists, architects, and more—is whether art should serve as political argument. Imagine a cathedral in which the architectural design, windows, and other artifacts preach liberation theology as clearly as Sandra Benitez' fiction. Consider how this might enhance or interfere with your experience of "sacred space."

EPILOGUE

The famous poet and playwright T. S. Eliot once wrote:

> We shall not cease from exploration
> And the end of all our exploring
> Will be to arrive where we started
> And know the place for the first time.
> —Excerpt from *Four Quartets*

All great literature, whether from the Bible or from works by contemporary authors, has the ability to draw its readers into the action of a storyline, the drama of characters' lives, and the experiences and worldviews that shaped both text and character. What readers discover as they enter into worlds and lives not their own is that from the beginning of time, the human community has been grappling with enduring questions about life, sin, suffering, natural disasters, love, war, hate, oppression, the search for the sacred presence called God, and the silence of this God in the midst of suffering, among others. Great literature has the ability to take readers on a journey where they encounter the beauty and shame of the human condition. At the end of the journey—at the end of a story or a poem—readers are brought back home to their familiar surroundings, only to realize that they have discovered a deeper understanding of self and others. The journey may have even transformed them as they turned page after page or moved from verse to verse.

This book, a collaborative process that has engaged two different disciplines, has attempted to show how one of the oldest works of literature—the Bible—continues to have an impact on the shaping of great literature today. The volume explored forms, genres, and themes of just a few biblical texts that have influenced the many authors in the twentieth and twenty-first centuries—authors who keep the Bible alive in countries around the world. As mentioned in the Introduction, the dialogue that occurs between the biblical stories and poems, and in the contemporary multicultural literature included in this text, is one of commonality and difference. At times the biblical text became a source of inspiration for a contemporary writer; at other times a contemporary writer used the biblical text as a backdrop or springboard for the creation of new stories, plays, and poems. Sometimes genres and themes between biblical texts and contemporary works of literature intersected and complemented each other; other times they stood juxtaposed to each other and offered readers different perspectives, new understandings, and new insights into both the human condition and life in general. Whatever the case may be, one point remains constant: the stories and poems of both biblical and contemporary literature continue to inspire audiences around the world, drawing them deeper into the heart of life and into their own hearts wherein lies the perennial search for truth, the search for self, and even for some, the search for the Sacred Presence that is both revelatory and illusive.

Our hope in writing this book is that readers of all ages will drink from the spring, play in the fountain, and draw from the well of reflection, imagination, and creativity to discover the transformative effects that ancient and contemporary literature can have on a person's life, and, in discovering this gift, come in contact with that which is Divine whose Spirit remains alive in the texts, alive in those who have composed the texts, and alive in those who will receive the texts as word and Word.

NOTES

Introduction

1.This material is gleaned from "Speaking of Faith," National Public Radio, September 25, 2008.

2. See *New York Times Magazine*, November 30, 2008, 18; see also Joshua 1–27.

3. See Walter Wink, "Evangelization in a Culture of Pluralism: Challenges and Opportunities," *Australian Journal of Theology* (March 2007): 16.

4. See, e.g., Ezek 21:1–17; Amos 2–3:15.

5. Two texts, among others, that focus on the Bible *and* literature are Alison Jack, *The Bible and Literature*; SCM Core Text (London: SCM Press, 2012) and David Jasper and Stephen Prickett, eds. *The Bible and Literature: A Reader* (Malden, MA: Blackwell Publishers, 1999). Two texts, also among others, that focus on the Bible *as* literature are Jeanie C. Crain, *Reading the Bible as Literature: An Introduction* (Cambridge, England: 2010) and John B. Gabel, Charles B. Wheeler, and Anthony D. York, *The Bible as Literature: An Introduction* (New York: Oxford University Press, 2000).

Chapter 1: Myth

1. For further concise discussions on myth, see Michael L. Humphries, "Myth" in *Eerdmans Dictionary of the Bible*; ed. David Noel Freedman, Allen C. Myers, and Astrid B. Beck (Grand Rapids, MI: Eerdmans, 2000), 934–35; see also Joyce A. Zimmerman, C.PP.S., "Myth, Mythology," in *The Collegeville Pastoral Dictionary of Biblical Theology*, ed. Carroll Stulmueller et al. (Collegeville, MN: Liturgical Press, 1996), 661–64; John L. McKenzie, "Aspects of Old Testament Thought," in *The New Jerome Biblical Commentary*, ed. Raymond E. Brown, S.S., Joseph A. Fitzmyer, S.J., and Roland E. Murphy, O. Carm. (Englewood Cliffs, NJ: Prentice Hall), 1289–90. For a more detailed discussion on biblical myth, creation, and the ancient Near Eastern world and its texts, see the classic commentary by Claus Westermann, *Genesis 1–11,* trans. John J. Scullion, S.J. (Minneapolis: Augsburg Publishing House, 1984), 1–47.

2. See the work by Elizabeth Michael Boyle, *Science as Sacred Metaphor: An Evolving Revelation* (Collegeville, MN: Liturgical Press, 2006), especially pp. 1–14, "Reflections on a Quantum Universe" and pp. 80–96, "Reflections on String Theory." Also see Barbara Brown Taylor, *The Luminous Web: Essays on Science and Religion* (Cambridge, MA: Cowley Publications, 2000) and Brian Greene, *The Elegant Universe: Superstrings, Hidden Dimensions, and the Quest for the Ultimate Theory* (New York: W. W. Norton, 1999).

3. For further discussion on creation and evolution, see Jerry A. Coyne, *Why Evolution Is True* (New York: Penguin); Keith B. Miller, ed., *Perspectives on an Evolving Creation* (Grand Rapids, MI: Eerdmans, 2003); John F. Haught, *God after Darwin: A Theology of Evolution* (Boulder, CO: Westview Press, 2000); Ian

G. Barbour, *Religion and Science: Historical and Contemporary Issues* (New York: HarperCollins, 1997); Thomas Berry, (San Francisco: Sierra Club Books, 1990).

4. Derived from the Greek, etiology is the investigation or attribution of the cause or reason for something, often expressed in historical or mythical terms. In the ancient world, the biblical writers tried to explain why there was sin in the world, why disease and death occurred. Thus, the writers created stories to explain why certain things existed—things that they did not understand or fully comprehend. Genesis 3 tries to explain how sin entered into the world, why people do not live in an idyllic state, why pain in childbirth and manual labor exists, why sexual desire is a passion that sometimes cannot be satisfied, how a male human being came to have a prominent hierarchical place over the female in gender exchanges, and why some animals do not have legs.

5. For an excellent discussion on myth in relation to Genesis 1–2, see Karl Loning and Erich Zenger, *To Begin with, God Created . . .* (Collegeville, MN: Liturgical Press, 2000), 18–30.

6. Bruce C. Birch, Walter Brueggemann, Terence E. Fretheim, and David L. Petersen, *A Theological Introduction to the Old Testament* (Nashville: Abingdon Press, 1999), 46.

7. We are aware of the many interpretations of the creation account, particularly with respect to the creation of man and woman. While we agree that the story is androcentric, anthropocentric, and hierarchical when read through a feminist lens, we are reading the text through a cosmological and mythical lens.

8. Birch, Brueggemann, Fretheim, and Peterson, *A Theological Introduction to the Old Testament*, 49.

9. Ibid., 50.

10. Ibid.

11."Restoring Creation for Ecology and Justice: A Report Adapted by the 202nd General Assembly (1990)," Presbyterian Church (USA), 7. For further discussion on "to till" and "to keep," see the classic work by Phyllis Trible, *God and the Rhetoric of Sexuality,* Overtures to Biblical Theology (Philadelphia: Fortress Press, 1978), 85. Here Trible argues that the exercise of power over the garden is to have reverence for it. Neither "tilling" nor "keeping" imply, according to Trible, exploitation. Both words suggest that humankind is to be in service to the garden.

12. Birch, Brueggemann, Fretheim, and Petersen, *A Theological Introduction to the Old Testament,* 46.

13. Langdon Gilkey, *Blue Twilight: Nature, Creationism, and American Religion* (Minneapolis: Fortress Press, 2001), 66.

14. Throughout the ancient Near East serpents functioned as objects of worship or charms against evil. They were sometimes associated with evil, danger, and punishment. Serpents also represented life and served as a millennial signpost of when the proper balance of nature has been restored.

15. Cf. Gen. 3:7.

16. To be noted is that, according to the biblical text, only the man is cast out of the garden; see v. 24.

17. Par Lagerkvist,"Father and I," *The Marriage Feast*, trans. Alan Blair (New York: Hill and Wang, 1954), 34.

18. Par Lagerkvist, *Barabbas*, trans. Alan Blair (New York: Random House, 1951).

19. Par Lagerkvist, *The Death of Ahasuerus*, trans. Naomi Walford (New York: Random House, 1962), 114.

20. Everett M. Ellested, *Par Lagerkvist and Cubism: A Study of His Theory and Practice: A Critical Essay* (Cork, Ireland: Rainbow Press, 1971), 37–52.

21. Par Lagerkvist, Lagerkvist, "Literary Art and Visual Art" (Cork, Ireland: Rainbow Press, 1996).

22. Nobel Committee Presentation Speech.

23. Par Lagerkvist, *The Holy Land*, trans. Naomi Walford (New York: Random House, 1966), 34–35.

24. Par Lagerkvist, *The Sybil*, trans. Naomi Walford (New York: Viking Vintage, 1963), 11–12. All references to the novel are to this paperback edition.

Chapter 2: Archetypal and Historical Myth

1. Carl Jung, "The Structure and Dynamics of the Psyche," in *Collected Works, v*ol. 8, trans. Gerhard Adler (Princeton, NJ: Princeton University Press, 1969), 342.

2. Isaiah 50:4–9 is considered by scholars to be one of the servant songs even though it makes no specific reference to a servant.

3. R. Norman Whybray, "Isaiah 40–66," *New Century Bible Commentary* (Grand Rapids, MI: Eerdmans, 1981), 170; cf. Job 29:8–9.

4. For a detailed study of Isaiah 52:13–53:12, see Carol J. Dempsey with Anthony J. Tambasco, "Isaiah 52:13–53:12: Unmasking the Mystery of the Suffering Servant" in *The Bible on Suffering*, ed. Anthony J. Tambasco (Mahwah, NJ: Paulist Press, 2001), 34–50. This article not only analyzes the Isaian passage but also connects many of the images to the text of Jeremiah.

5. Only in the Gospel of Luke do the following passages appear: Lk. 2:24–30, the Dispute about Greatness; Lk. 22:35–38, the Purse, Bag, and Sword; Lk. 23:6–12, the Appearance of Jesus before Herod. Luke omits both the stories about the Anointing at Bethany and Peter's Denial. Only Matthew contains the stories about Judas' Suicide (Matt. 27:3–10) and the Tomb Secured (Matt. 27:62–66). The Interrogation of Jesus (Matt. 27:11–14) is somewhat different from Mark's and Luke's rendition of the story.

6. Shusaku Endo quoted by Philip Yancey in "Japan's Faithful Judas," www. the ethe-real world.com, November 29, 2007.

7. Accounts appear in the *New York Times,* April 3, 2003; April 19, 2003; and December 25, 2003, November 24, 2008.

8. William T. Cavanagh, "The God of Silence: Shusaku Endo's Reading of the Passion," *Commonweal*, March 3, 1998.

9. T. S. Eliot, "Murder in the Cathedral," *The Complete Poems and Plays* (New York: Harcourt Brace, 1952), 196.

10. Shusaku Endo, *Silence* (New York: Taplinger, 1980), 13.

11. Ibid., 227-29.

12. Ibid., 35.
13. Ibid., 58, 67, 243, 258.
14. Ibid., 210.
15. Ibid., 84, 85, 204, 210, 254.

Chapter 3: Parable

1. For a fuller discussion on the ancient background to and influences on the biblical story of the great flood, see Victor Hamilton, *The Book of Genesis: Chapters 1–17* (Grand Rapids, MI: Eerdmans, 1990), 252–54. See also Claus Westermann, *Genesis 1–11,* trans. John J. Scullion (Minneapolis: Fortress Press, 1984), 398–404.

2. Here the use of the term "wind," also translated as "spirit" can be connected to Genesis 1:2 where before creation begins, God's "wind," God's "spirit" hovers over the earth, and then creation begins. In the Flood Story God sends forth a wind, the waters begin to recede, and creation is about to begin anew once again.

3. For further discussion on Genesis 6:5–8:22, see David W. Cotter, O.S.B., *Genesis,* Berit Olam, *Studies in Hebrew Narrative & Poetry* (Collegeville, MN: Liturgical Press, 2003), 49–63; Hamilton, *The Book of Genesis: Chapters 1–17*, 272–311; Westermann, *Genesis 1–11*, 384–458.

4. For further discussion on the Parable of the Two Sons in Luke's Gospel, see Luke Timothy Johnson, *The Gospel of Luke; Sacra Pagina*, vol. 3; ed. Daniel J. Harrington, S. J. (Collegeville, MN: Liturgical Press, 1991). See also Joel B. Green, *The Gospel of Luke* (Grand Rapids: Eerdmans, 1997).

5. Robert Coover online interview, *Thoughtsifting*, September 9, 2008.

6. Robert Coover, online interview, *Bookslut*, March 1, 2010.

7. The literary term "alienation device" was introduced in Chapter 1: any means by which the author makes a familiar idea, character, or situation deliberately strange or "alien" to the audience.

8. Marie-Eloise Rosenblatt, "Parable," in *Collegeville Dictionary of Pastoral Theology,* ed. Carroll Stuhlmueller (Collegeville, MN: Liturgical Press, 1996), 689.

9. Barbara Reid, *Parables for Preachers: The Gospel of Matthew—Year A* (Collegeville, MN: Liturgical Press, 2001); see also *Parables for Preachers: The Gospel of Luke—Year C* (Collegeville, MN: Liturgical Press, 2000); *Parables for Preachers: The Gospel of Mark—Year B* (Collegeville, MN: Liturgical Press, 1999); Lk. 8:11–15; Mt. 13:36–43; Mk. 7:17–23.

10. Hundreds of midrash were composed by Hebrew commentators between 800 and 2,500 years ago. Hence, Hebrew commentators read Mark's story of Jesus' Temptation in the Desert (Mt. 4:1–11) as a midrash on Israel's forty-year sojourn in the desert (see Deut. 6–8).

11. Amos Wilder, *The Bible* and *the Literary Critic* (Minneapolis: Augsburg Fortress Press, 1991), 21.

12. Ibid., 22.

13. For further discussion on parables, see C. W. Hedrick, *Parables as Poetic Fictions: The Creative Voice of Jesus* (Peabody: Hendrickson Publishers, 1994); W. R. Herzog II, *Parables as Subversive Speech* (Louisville: Westminster John Knox,

1994); *Dictionary of Biblical Imagery*, s.v. "Parable" (Downers Grove, IL: InterVarsity Press, 1998), 623–24.

14. Edgar Allan Poe, Rev. of *Twice Told Tales in Edgar Allan Poe, Essays and Reviews* (Cambridge: University of Cambridge Press, 1984), 586.

15. Robert Coover, "Dying Fathers 'Stirring Still,' " *Kenyon Review* 23 (Spring 2001): 2.

16. For further discussion, see Reid, *Parables for Preachers: The Gospel of Matthew—Year A*; see also *Parables for Preachers: The Gospel of Luke—Year C*; *Parables for Preachers: The Gospel of Mark—Year B*.

Chapter 4: Dramatic Poetry

1. Matthew Fox, "Afterword: The Trial of God, The Trial of Us," *The Trial of God* (New York: Schocken Books, 1995), 164.

2. Archibald MacLeish interview, *New York Times,* December 7, 1958.

3. These words contain the element of irony, the main literary technique used throughout the Book of Job. The claim being made is that God puts no trust in God's servants. In Job 1:8, God calls Job "my servant" and, by allowing the wager to take place between God and the satan, God is placing divine trust in Job.

4. Only in Chapters 29–31 is the speech of Job comparably longer.

5. For further study on the Book of Job, see especially these two commentaries: Samuel E. Balentine, *Job,* Smyth & Helwys Commentary (Macon, GA: Smyth & Helwys, 2006) and James A. Wharton, *Job,* Westminster Bible Companion (Louisville: Westminster John Knox, 1999).

6. Archibald MacLeish, cited in Scott Donaldson, *Archibald MacLeish: An American Life* (New York: Houghton Mifflin Company, 1992), 225.

7. Elie Wiesel, *Night*, trans. Stella Rodway (New York: Hill and Wang, 1960), 43.

8. Elie Wiesel interview, *Speaking of Faith,* American Public Radio, July 15, 2006.

9. Ibid.

10. Nicholas Boyle, *Sacred and Secular Scriptures: A Catholic Approach to Literature* (Notre Dame, IN: University of Notre Dame Press, 2005), 149.

11. Archibald MacLeish, *J.B.* (Boston: Houghton Mifflin, 1956), 3.

12. Ibid., 111.

13. Elie Wiesel, *The Trial of God* (New York: Schocken Books, 1995), 15–16.

14. Ibid., 88.

15. MacLeish, cited in Scott Donaldson, *Archibald MacLeish,* 110.

16. Wiesel, *The Trial of God,* 114.

17. Works which raise the possibility that God is a God who suffers include among others: John Paul II, "Lord and Giver of Life" (Washington, D.C.: United States Catholic Conference, 1986), #39; Jurgen Moltmann, *The Crucified God: The Cross of Christ as the Foundation and Criticism of Christian Theology* (New York: Harper and Row, 1974); Abraham Heschel, *The Prophets: An Introduction* (New York: Harper Colophon Books, 1955); Jon Sobrino, S.J., *Christology at the Crossroads: A Latin American Approach.,* trans. John Drury (Maryknoll, NY: Orbis

Books, 1978); Elizabeth A. Johnson, *She Who Is: The Mystery of God in Feminist Theological Discourse* (New York: Crossroads, 1993).

18. Wiesel, *The Trial of God*, 115.
19. Ibid., 106–17.
20. See, e.g., Eliphaz's statements in Job 4:7–11.
21. Macleish, *J.B.*, 38.
22. Ibid.
23. Martin Buber, *The Prophetic Faith* (New York: MacMillan, 1949), 191ff.
24. Fox, "Afterword: The Trial of God, The Trial of Us," 166.
25. Wiesel, *The Trial of God,* 174.

Chapter 5: Lyric Poetry as Prayer

1. Examples of metaphorical descriptions of God include: God as shepherd (Pss. 23:1; 119:176), as a farmer caring for a vineyard (Ps. 80:8–12), as a father (Ps. 68: 5; 89:26; 103:13), as a warrior (Ps. 68:1–2, 11, 17, 21–23), among other images.
2. Gerard Manley Hopkins, *Hopkins: Poems and Prose* (New York: Alfred Knopf, Everyman's Library Pocket Poets, 1995), 15.
3. The website www.negrospirituals.com, containing lyrics, history, composers, and singers, is considered the official site of this art form.
4. Toni Craven, *The Book of the Psalms*; Message of Biblical Spirituality 6 (Collegeville, MN: Liturgical Press, 1992), 29.
5. See the Exodus story, especially Exodus 1–15, where the biblical writer describes vividly, imaginatively, and fantastically how God delivered Israel from oppression. See also the writings of the Prophets, e.g., Isa. 43:1–6; Ezek. 34:11–31, among others.
6. Recall Exodus 2:23–24 where the biblical writer features God hearing the groaning of the oppressed Israelites and then does something about their oppressive situation—God raises up Moses to set the people free (Exod. 3:1–12).
7. Walter Brueggemann and William H. Bellinger, Jr., *Psalms,* New Cambridge Bible Commentary (Cambridge: Cambridge University Press, 2014), 64.
8. See 1 Kings 22:38 for a similar image.
9. Artur Weiser, *The Psalms,* Old Testament Library (Philadelphia: Westminster, 1962), 255.
10. Carroll Stuhlmueller, *The Spirituality of the Psalms,* ed. Carol J. Dempsey (Collegeville, IN: Liturgical Press, 2002), 109.
11. For further discussion on parallelism, see Konrad Schaefer, OSB, *Psalms*; Berit Olam, *Studies in Hebrew Narrative & Poetry* (Collegeville, MN: Liturgical Press, 2001), xiv–xix; Wilfred G. E. Watson, *Classical Hebrew Poetry: A Guide to Its Techniques* (Sheffield: Sheffield Academic Press, 1995), 114–59.
12. See also Psalm 44:4 where the psalmist's use of the personal pronoun "my" implies a close relationship with the Holy One of Israel.
13. Krista Tippett, "Joe Carter and the Legacy of African-American Spirituality," Interview on Speaking of Faith (National Public Radio, December 2003).
14. Richard Newman, *Go Down Moses: Celebrating the African-American Spiritual* (New York: Clarkson Potter, 1998), 214.

15. Cf. John 5:7.

16. Cf. Exod. 14.

17. Newman, *Go Down Moses*, 82.

18. Craven, *The Book of Psalms*, 107.

19. Cited by Newman, *Go Down Moses,* 174.

20. See Tippett, the interview "Joe Carter and the Legacy of African-American Spirituality."

21. Ibid.

22. Ibid.

Chapter 6: The Theme of the Spiritual Quest

1. Nineveh was an ancient city on the left bank of the Tigris River. The city was occupied from the fourth millennium BCE to around 612 BCE when it was invaded and fell to the Babylonians and Medes.

2. Israel's legal codes, as well as its wisdom tradition, warned against killing innocent people (see, e.g., Deut. 19:10, 13; 27:25; Prov. 6:17). A procedure for purging a community's guilt when an unknown person takes another innocent person's life is prescribed in Deuteronomy 21:1–9.

3. J. Limburg (*Jonah* [Louisville: Westminster John Knox, 1993], 83) remarks that "this [Jonah 3:7–8] is one of many biblical illustrations of the solidarity between humans and animals," and "since both humans and animals are creatures of the sixth day (Gen. 1:24–25 . . .), the relationship between them is close."

4. For further study on the Book of Jonah, see Barbara Green, *Jonah's Journeys*; Interfaces (Collegeville, MN: Liturgical Press, 2005); Tara Soughers, *Fleeing God: Fear, Call and the Book of Jonah* (New York: Cowley Publications, 2007); James Limburg, *Jonah,* Old Testament Library (Louisville: Westminster/John Knox, 1993); and Hans Walter Wolff, *Obadiah and Jonah,* trans. Margaret Kohl (Minneapolis: Augsburg, 1986).

5. Sabine Sielke, "The Empathic Imagination: An Interview with Yann Martel." *Canadian Literature* 177 (2003): 15.

6. Ibid., 14.

7. Alfred Margulies, *The Empathic Imagination* (New York: W. W. Norton, 1989).

8. Sielke, "The Empathetic Imagination," 25.

9. Ibid., 24–25.

10. Ibid., 14–15.

11. Yann Martel, *Life of Pi* (New York: Harcourt, 2001), x.

12. Sielke, "The Empathetic Imagination," 14.

13. Ibid.

14. Martel, *Life of Pie*, 208–9.

15. Ibid.

16. Ibid., 303.

17. Allistair Brown, "Life of Pi," *The Pequod Essays,* http:://www.thepequod.org.uk.

18. Ray Suarez, "Conversation: *Life of Pi*," *PBS Online Newshour* (November 11, 2002). http://pbs.org/.

19. Martel, *Life of Pi*, 66.

20. Ibid., "Interview with Tasha Robinson," *The A. V. Club* (November 6, 2007).

21. Martel, *Life of Pi*, 24.

22. Ibid., 28.

23. Ibid., 294.

24. Ibid., 298.

25. Sielke, "The Empathetic Imagination," 25.

26. Andrew Steinmetz, "Pi: Summing up Meaning from the Irrational: An Interview with Yann Martel," *Books in Canada* 31.6 (December 6, 2004), http://proquest.umi.com.

27. Martel, *Life of Pi*, 119.

28. Ibid., 179.

29. Ibid., 248–49

30. Ibid., 248.

31. Ibid., 298–99.

32. Ibid., 306.

33. Ibid., 57.

Chapter 7: The Theme of Love

1. For a discussion of the Song of Solomon in relation to the Church Fathers and medieval allegory, see E. Ann Matter, *The Voice of My Beloved: The Song of Songs in Western Medieval Christianity* (Philadelphia: University of Pennsylvania Press, 1990) among other texts that treat the Song of Solomon allegorically and then see the work as a mystical or spiritual love song.

2. See J. Cheryl Exum, *Song of Songs: A Commentary* (Louisville: Westminster John Knox, 2005), 1.

3. Othmar Keel, *The Song of Songs: A Continental Commentary*, trans. Frederick J. Gaiser (Minneapolis: Fortress Press, 1994), 75.

4. For additional comments on the Song of Solomon, see Dianne Bergant, C.S.A., *The Song of Songs*, Berit Olam, *Studies in Hebrew Narrative & Poetry* (Collegeville, MN: Liturgical Press, 2001); Tremper Longman III, *Song of Songs* (Grand Rapids: Eerdmans, 2001); and Carey Ellen Walsh, *Exquisite Desire: Religion, the Erotic, and the Song of Songs* (Minneapolis: Fortress, 2000).

5. Graham Greene, quoted in Norman Sherry, *The Life of Graham Greene I: 1904–1939* (New York: Viking, 1989), xxii.

6. Graham Greene, *A Sort of Life* (New York: Penguin, 1974), 121.

7. Ibid., cited in *The Other Man: Conversations with Graham Greene* (New York: Simon and Shuster, 1983), 37.

8. Graham Greene, *The End of the Affair* (New York: Viking, 1951), 20.

9. Ibid., 206.

10. Ibid., 39ff.

11. Ibid., 206.

12. Ibid., 18.

13. Ibid., 16.

14. C. C. Martindale, S.J., cited by Norman Sherry, *The Life of Graham Greene, II: 1939–55* (New York: Viking, 1992), 298.

15. Graham Greene, quoted by Norman Sherry, *The Life of Graham Greene, III: 1955–91* (New York: Viking, 2004), 257.

16. Greene, *The End of the Affair*, 4.

17. Ibid., 82.

18. Such writers include George Bernanos, Leon Bloy, Francois Mauriac, and Charles Peguy, among others.

19. Graham Greene, *The Heart of the Matter* (New York: Viking Penguin, 1946).

20. Raven Shutterworth, "The Art of Fiction: Interview with Graham Greene," *The Paris Review* 3 (Autumn, 1953): 24–41.

21. Greene, *The End of the Affair,* 133.

22. Ibid., 107.

23. Ibid., 226.

24. Ibid., 238–39.

25. Ibid., 149–50.

26. Ibid., 147.

27. See Mark Bosco, S.J., *Graham Greene's Catholic Imagination* (New York: Oxford University Press, 2005), 41–42.

28. Graham Greene, *Ways of Escape* (New York: Viking Penguin, 1981), 114–15.

Chapter 8: The Theme of War

1. Joab was the son of King David's sister Zeruiah. He was the commander-in-chief of David's army, beginning when David captured Jerusalem from the Jebusites (1 Chr. 11:4–9). He became a dominant figure in David's regime. He often appears in command of David's professional troops (cf. 2 Sam. 10:9–14). During the course of time, Joab became more and more powerful, and David tried unsuccessfully to curb his power because Joab was a field commander par excellence. Even though David was a strong leader, Joab appears at times to be more forceful and shrewder than David. When Joab slays Absalom, David's third son, a permanent rift seems to have developed between David and his nephew. David's bitterness toward Joab reaches its depths when David instructs Solomon to use his wisdom—his treachery—to have Joab put to death (1 Kgs. 2:5–9). Solomon seizes this opportunity especially when Joab supports the bid of his older brother Adonijah for the throne. The rightful heir to the throne was Solomon, David's son, and not Adonijah, who was David's nephew. Thus Solomon has Benaiah, the commander over Solomon's army and the son of Jehoiada the priest, execute Joab. Even though Joab's life came to a bitter end, Joab represented the strength and virtue of David's earliest loyalists. Though loyal to David, he had a mind of his own, did what needed to be done, and took responsibility for his actions. In his time, Joab was seen as a man of great integrity.

2. Uriah was one of David's elite thirty warriors (1 Chr. 11:41).

3. Rabbah was a city on the Transjordan plateau. This city was the center of surrounding cities and villages (cf. Ezek. 25:1–11). It is mostly directly related to the Ammonites, and consisted of two parts: the upper city or acropolis, known as the "royal city" (2 Sam. 12:26), and the lower city, the "city of waters" (2 Sam. 12:27), which ran along two wadis at the base of the plateau in the valley. The two parts of the city were connected via an underground passageway.

4. For further study on the stories of David, see Craig E. Morrison, *2 Samuel*; Berit Olam, *Studies in Hebrew Narrative & Poetry*, ed. Jerome T. Murphy (Collegeville, MN: Liturgical Press, 2013). See also A. Graeme, *I & II Samuel*; Old Testament Library (Louisville: Westminster John Knox, 2011).

5. Stanley Wiersma, *Christopher Fry: A Critical Essay* (Grand Rapids: Eerdmans, 1970), 6.

6. Cited by Benedict Nightingale in "Christopher Fry Obituary," *New York Times*, July 5, 2005.

7. See Christopher Fry, *Three Plays* (New York: Oxford University Press, 1968), 170–79.

8. Ibid., 180–85.

9. Ibid., 188–95.

10. Ibid., 100.

11. Emil Roy, *Christopher Fry (*Carbondale, IL: Southern University of Illinois Press, 1968) 100.

12. See Fry, *Three Plays,* 169.

13. Ibid., 177.

14. Ibid., 179.

15. Ibid., 201.

16. Ibid., 164.

17. Ibid. 166.

18. Ibid., 167.

19. Roy, *Christopher Fry*, 100.

20. Review of "Prisoner Produced on NET Playhouse," *Chicago Critic* (December 9, 1966).

21. See Fry, *Three Plays,* 169.

22. Ibid., 177.

23. Ibid., 186.

24. Christopher Fry, cited in Nightingale, "Obituary."

25. Fry, *Three Plays,* 208.

26. Ibid., 209.

27. See Isa. 65:17–25

28. See Fry, *Three Plays,* 165.

29. Ibid., 170.

30. Ibid.

31. Ibid., 178.

32. Ibid., 191.

33. Samuel Beckett, Albert Camus, Eugene Ionesco, Jean Genet, Harold Pinter.

34. Fry, *Three Plays*, 201
35. Emil Roy, *Christopher Fry*, 105.
36. Ibid., 207.
37. Ibid., 208.
38. Ibid., 203.
39. Ibid.
40. Ibid., 172.
41. Ibid., 191.
42. Ibid., 188.
43. Ibid., 209.

Chapter 9: The Theme of Liberation

1. N. K. Gottwald, *The Hebrew Bible: A Socio-Literary Introduction* (Philadelphia: Fortress Press, 1985), 356.

2. W. J. Doorly, *Prophet and Justice: Understanding the Book of Amos* (Mahwah, NJ: Paulist, 1989), 24–25.

3. Gustavo Gutiérrez and Gerhard Muller, *Taking the Part of the Poor: Liberation Theology, Theology of the Church* (Germany, 2004).

4. Sandra Benitez, *Bitter Grounds* (New York: Picador, 1998).

5. Sandra Benitez, *The Weight of All Things* (New York: Hyperion, 2000).

6. H. W. Wolff, *Joel and Amos*, Hermeneia (Philadelphia: Fortress, 1977), 154.

7. It is assumed that Hazael was the name of an Aramean ruler, but here the reference is to the kingdom of Aram and not to the specific ruler. For further discussion, see Shalom M. Paul, *Amos*, Hermeneia (Minneapolis: Fortress, 1991), 50.

8. Ben-hadad is also the name of an Aramean ruler. Here it seems that the reference is to a dynasty or a ruler. For further discussion, see Paul, *Amos*, 50; F. I. Andersen and D. N. Freedman, *Amos* (AB 24A; New York: Doubleday, 1989) 245–50.

9. The exact identity and site of the Valley of Aven (lit., "the valley of sin") is unknown. One suggestion by Andersen and Freedman is that it is probably "the Biq'ah Valley in present-day Lebanon" (*Amos*, 255).

10. Beth-eden, lit., "house of pleasure," seems to be Bit-Adini, an Aramaean state situated between two rivers: the upper Euphrates and the Balih (see Andersen and Freedman, *Amos*, 255).

11. The exact location of Kir is unknown. One suggestion is that it may be in Mesopotamia (M. L. Barre "Amos," in *NJBC*, ed. R. F. Brown, J. A. Fitzmyer, and R. E. Murphy [Englewood Cliffs: Prentice Hall, 1990], 211); cf. H. McKeating, *The Books of Amos, Hosea, and Micah* (Cambridge: Cambridge University, 1971), 16; Andersen and Freedman, *Amos*, 257.

12. For a comprehensive view of God in the ancient biblical world and texts, see E. S. Gerstenberger, *Yahweh the Patriarch: Ancient Images of God and Feminist Theology* (Minneapolis: Fortress, 1996). See also, e.g., Exod. 1–15.

13. For a detailed study on conflict in Israel and the Ancient Near East, see S. Niditch's work, *War in the Hebrew Bible: A Study in the Ethics of Violence* (New York: Oxford University, 1993). Wolff (*Amos*, 154–55) adds that "the imagery of

devouring fire in our text carries with it the further connotation of Yahweh as a military leader and conqueror. The use of fire in conquering enemy cities, and especially in destroying residential palaces, was an accepted military practice in the ancient Near Eastern world."

14. On the suggestion of divine violence as a human projection, see R. Girard, *Violence and the Sacred*, trans. P. Gregory (Baltimore: Johns Hopkins University, 1977); R. Schwager, *Must There Be Scapegoats? Violence and Redemption in the Bible* (San Francisco: Harper and Row, 1987).

15. For further study on corporate punishment and corporate responsibility, see J. Kaminsky, *Corporate Responsibility in the Hebrew Bible* (JSOT Supp. 196; Sheffield: Sheffield Academic Press, 1995).

16. Paul (*Amos*, 56) notes that "the wholesale deportation of the population was for the economic gain that occurred through slave traffic (compare Ezek. 27:13; Joel 4:6–7). The sale of human booty on the slave market was a well-known practice that became a profitable by-product for the victors in war." See also Wolff, *Amos*, 157–58.

17. Ibid., 48–49. See also Deut. 9:3. The use of fire to destroy an enemy city first occurs in Numbers 21:27–30. Paul notes that the motif of divine fire is common in ancient Near Eastern mythology and is usually associated with military assaults (*Amos*, 49).

18. Wolff, *Joel and Amos*, 159.

19. Paul, *Amos*, 63. See also J. L. Mays, *Amos* (OTL; Philadelphia: Westminster, 1969), 35.

20. See, e.g., Gen. 38:24; Lev. 20:14; 21:9.

21. B. Birch, *Hosea, Joel, and Amos,* Westminster Bible Companion (Louisville: Westminster John Knox, 1997), 186. See also Isaiah 3:15 and Proverbs 22:22 for the abuse of the poor and deprivation of their rights.

22. Law codes restricted the taking of certain items for collateral, and also set limits on how long something could be kept. For example, a widow's garment could not be taken from her (Deut. 24:17) nor could a poor person's cloak be kept overnight (Exod. 22:25–27; Deut. 24:12–13).

23. The majority held scholarly view is that the "cows of Bashan" is a reference to the upper-class women of Samaria. See, e.g., Paul, *Amos,* 128–29; Mays, *Amos,* 71. Other scholars, i.e., Wolff (*Joel and Amos*, 204–205) and Andersen and Freedman (*Amos,* 421), are not as definitive. Andersen and Freedman suggest that the metaphor refers to men and serves as a parody.

24. Paul, *Amos*, 129. See also Deut. 32:14; Ezek. 39:18; Ps. 22:12–13; Jer. 50:19; Mic. 7:14.

25. Sandra Benitez, *A Place Where the Sea Remembers* (New York: Hyperion, 1993).

26. Kelli Lyon-Johnson, "Acts of War, Acts of Memory: Dead Body Politics in U.S. Latina Novels of the Salvadoran War," *Latino Studies* 3 no. 2 (2005): 20–25.

27. Ibid., 215.

28. Benitez, *The Weight of All Things*, 92ff.

29. Benitez, *Bitter Grounds*, 397.

30. Ibid., 364.
31. Ibid., 323.
32. Ibid., 348–49.
33. Benitez, *The Weight of All Things*, 51–52.
34. Ibid., 18.
35. Ibid., 21–22.
36. Ibid., 52.
37. Ibid., 199.
38. Ibid., 121.
39. Ibid., 91, 160ff.
40. Ibid., 42–43, 66, 95, 99, 179.
41. Ibid., 192.
42. Ibid., 74.
43. Ibid., 30–31.
44. Ibid., 3.
45. See John R. Levison, "Liberation Hermeneutics," *Dictionary of Jesus and the Gospels: A Compendium of Contemporary Biblical Scholarship,* ed. Joel Green, Scott McKnight, and I. Howard Marshall (Downers Grove, IL: InterVarsity Press, 1992) 464–69.
46. See Carol J. Dempsey, *The Prophets: A Liberation Critical Reading* (Minneapolis: Fortress, 2000), 1.
47. Ibid.
48. Benitez, *The Weight of All Things*, 2–3.
49. Ibid., 1–2.
50. Ibid., 16.

SCRIPTURE INDEX

INDEX